ANTHROPOLOGICAL PAPERS OF
THE UNIVERSITY OF ARIZONA
NUMBER 10

AN APPRAISAL OF TREE-RING DATED POTTERY IN THE SOUTHWEST

DAVID A. BRETERNITZ

THE UNIVERSITY OF ARIZONA PRESS
TUCSON, ARIZONA

Printed in the U.S.A.

LC Card Catalog Number 66-64118

PREFACE

This monograph is a slightly revised and shortened version of a doctoral dissertation (Breternitz 1963) prepared under the supervision of a dissertation committee consisting of Emil W. Haury, Raymond H. Thompson, and Edward P. Dozier, all of the Department of Anthropology, University of Arizona, Tucson.

The dissertation resulted primarily from data recovered and problems recognized during a project conceived by Bryant Bannister to correlate the dendrochronological records and specimens currently housed at the Laboratory of Tree-Ring Research, University of Arizona. The tree-ring materials include the collections of the Laboratory of Anthropology, Santa Fe; the Museum of Northern Arizona, Flagstaff; Gila Pueblo, Globe; and the Laboratory of Tree-Ring Research, Tucson.

Many references in the original document indicating my indebtedness to numerous individuals and institutions have been deleted in the present volume because of format changes; thus, I wish to again acknowledge the assistance of everyone involved in the various facets of research, writing, and necessary revision.

The initial processing of materials was done while serving as a graduate research assistant in the Laboratory of Tree-Ring Research, under the supervision of Bryant Bannister. William G. McGinnies, then Laboratory Director, assisted at all stages of the work, provided me with study and working space, and offered timely encouragement, all of which are sincerely appreciated.

The final phase of my graduate work at the University of Arizona was greatly accelerated through the award of a National Science Foundation Graduate Fellowship.

The Society of the Sigma Xi supported the necessary research at the Museum of Northern Arizona, the Southwest Archeological Center, and the Museum of New Mexico through a Scientific Research Society of America (RESA) Grant-in-aid award.

Gordon R. Vivian was particularly helpful during my stay at the Southwest Archeological Center.

Alexander J. Lindsay, Jr. and Alan P. Olson, as representatives of the Museum of Northern Arizona, gave generously of their time, talents, and materials.

The resources of the Museum of New Mexico were made available to me mainly through the courtesy and efforts of Alfred E. Dittert, Jr., Bertha P. Dutton, Frank W. Eddy, Marjorie F. Lambert, and Stewart L. Peckham.

The University of Colorado Museum, through Roy L. Carlson, made the unpublished materials of the late Earl H. Morris available for study.

In addition, I am indebted for specific guidance, information, and assistance to Rex E. Gerald, Thomas P. Harlan, Jane Holden Kelley, John B. Rinaldo, Arthur H. Rohn, Jr., Albert H. Schroeder, Watson Smith, and William W. Wasley.

Raymond H. Thompson and Emil W. Haury not only encouraged me to undertake revision of the original dissertation, but provided me with invaluable counsel during the ensuing involved processes which eventually resulted in the present document.

Finally, and most important, I sincerely appreciate the continued help, understanding, and encouragement of my wife and children and my parents. This extended project has been a real sacrifice for all of them and their patience has been the outstanding contribution toward final completion.

David A. Breternitz
University of Colorado

CONTENTS

ILLUSTRATIONS

TABLES

ABSTRACT

The interpretation of approximately 5715 dated tree-ring specimens from about 342 archaeological sites in the American Southwest is the basis for "dating" the associated pottery types. The time involved spans the period from the introduction of fired ceramics to the Spanish Entrada, approximately A.D. 1550.

Provenience and site information for both the dated tree-ring specimens and the associated pottery is summarized from the more complete data available in Breternitz (1963) for each site and site-area which have tree-ring dates.

Criteria for establishing the validity of the association and provenience of the tree-ring specimens and the pottery are presented. The interpretation and evaluation of the validity of these dates and associations is the basis for "dating" the various pottery types. The occurrence of pottery in "indigenous" and "trade" situations is presented separately; the pottery types in these categories are dated separately, insofar as possible, and then evaluated in terms of total distribution and context.

Approximately 325 pottery types, varieties, and ceramic categories are dated on the basis of archaeological associations with tree-ring specimens. The data presented do not change the gross time placement of previous workers, but they do (1) refine some pottery dates, (2) reject others, and (3) give differing validity to additional ceramic dates.

The concept of "pottery type" is used as the analytical unit for dating Southwestern ceramics. Tree-ring material is not as useful for dating "ceramic style" because time periods are not as well defined and the "style" concept represents synthesis at a level of abstraction above that of "pottery type."

A progressive increase in the amount and range of traded pottery is noted through time. The increase in the distribution of various pottery types after about A.D. 1250 is also accompanied by an increase in attempts to make local copies of certain traded pottery types.

Southwestern pottery was distributed in prehistoric times on the basis of hand-to-hand or person-to-person contact. Although the amount of trade and the spatial dispersal increased in time, particularly after 1250, this trade never reached the same degree of institutionalization seen in Mesoamerica. An associated feature was an emphasis on the trading of small decorated vessels, as opposed to large utility or undecorated ceramic containers.

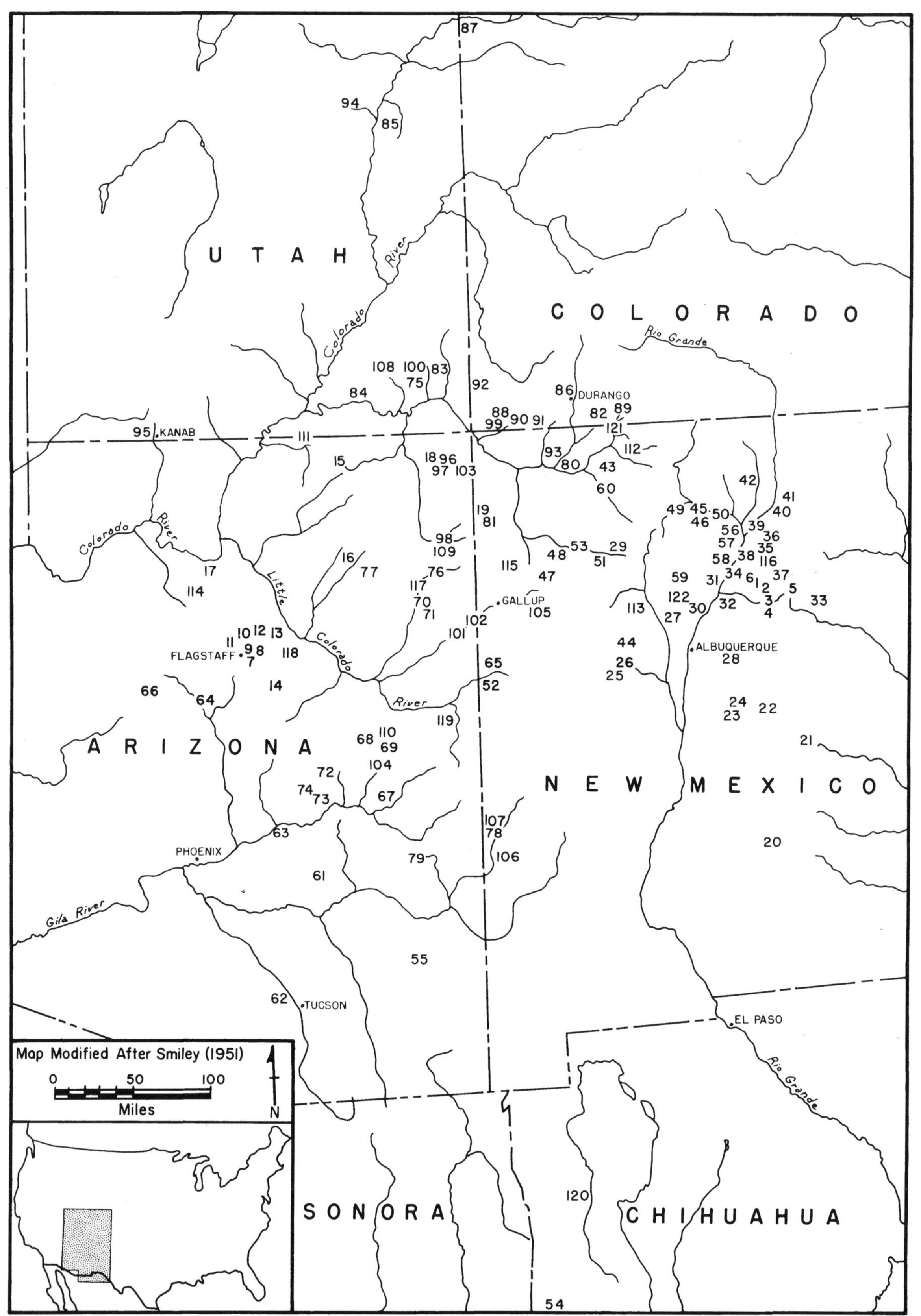

Map of the Southwestern United States showing location of archaeological sites and site-areas with dated tree-ring specimens.

1. INTRODUCTION

DENDROCHRONOLOGY, the science of tree-ring dating, provides Southwestern archaeology with a chronological technique that is both unique and absolute. It is small wonder that archaeological applications and interpretations of tree-ring dates have been developed and most intensively used for the "dating" of various aspects of prehistory in the southwestern United States. The absoluteness of a tree-ring date applies only to the tree-ring specimen itself. Through the interpretation of the archaeological context and association, we are able to use tree-ring specimens to "date" certain prehistoric events and to state, with some degree of validity, that certain archaeological manifestations, whether they be sites, cultural stages, or pottery types, occur within a certain bracket or period of time.

The problem to be dealt with in this paper – or more correctly, the body of material to be treated – concerns the dating of prehistoric Southwestern ceramics through the interpretation of dated tree-ring specimens which are found in an archaeological context. Emphasis will be on the dating of particular "pottery types," both within the areas where they were originally made and in those areas where they appear as exotic trade items. This interest in prehistoric Southwestern trade items is clearly stated by Colton (1960: 88, 91):

> As you cast your eye over the Southwest, it becomes evident that pottery, particularly attractive small bowls and small jars, furnished an important medium of exchange.
>
> Commerce has always been an activity among the Indians of the Southwest, past and present. The finding of foreign objects by an archaeologist is among the most exciting incidents of his work. The archaeologist cannot help but speculate on where the objects came from and how they got there.

For the archaeologist who is establishing regional chronologies and determining cultural (archaeological) similarities and relationships, it is more important to know *when* the items of material culture – the pottery in this case – were made and traded than it is to know *who* was responsible for the actual hand-to-hand transfer of the objects themselves. The ceramic remains do not tell us about the socio-cultural factors involved in this commercial or personal exchange. These factors can be inferred only through ethnological comparisons and from analysis of the *total* archaeological picture of a prehistoric culture, which may be known from the excavation of one or more sites.

Given the availability of archaeological tree-ring dates in Southwestern prehistory, the problem remaining is the correlation of these tree-ring dates with the associated pottery. Pottery is used because it is *the* material culture item that has proved to be the most widespread and useful for archaeological interpretation in the Southwest. The concept of "pottery type" – a group of pottery vessels which are alike in every important characteristic, including techniques of manufacture, methods of decoration, and kinds of decoration – is the best analytical tool available for the dating of Southwestern ceramics. The standard published archaeological reports, unpublished manuscripts, and laboratory analysis records customarily present and quantify the ceramics recovered during excavation in terms of pottery types. Analysis is frequently carried down to the level of the "variety" (Wheat, Gifford, and Wasley 1958; as modified by Phillips 1958), but we can combine the varieties of any given pottery type and make reference to the "parent type."

The concept of "style of design" will be shown to lack the preciseness necessary for accurate overall dating using the interpretive tool of associated tree-ring specimens. "Style of design" (Wasley 1959:289) is "a device for lumping pottery types on the basis of design." Consequently, a higher level of abstraction and analysis is involved – a level that is not as specific as that represented by the pottery type and one that, generally, involves larger periods of time.

Pottery types are considered to be potentially datable if they occur in association with dated tree-ring specimens. Dating becomes more valid when this association can be shown to be (1) repetitive, during the same time period and in a variety of archaeological sites, and (2) in a definite and specific archaeological context, which concerns both the pottery and the tree-ring specimens.

Bannister (1953: 35) notes the classes of information necessary for the interpretation of tree-ring dates:

> In summary, there are three classes of basic information necessary for the interpretation of tree-ring dates. The first class concerns the way in which a dated specimen was originally used; the second category deals with the relationship between a dated specimen and the context in which it was found; and the final factor involves the degree of similarity between the tree-ring date of a specimen and the year in which the original tree died.

Four types of chronological error are also noted by Bannister (1962: 508):

> Type 1. The association between the dated tree-ring specimen and the archaeological manifestation being dated is direct, but the specimen itself came from a tree that died or was cut prior to its use in the situation in question.
>
> Type 2. The association between the dated tree-ring specimen and the archaeological manifestation being dated is not direct, the specimen having been used prior to the feature being dated.
>
> Type 3. The association between the dated tree-ring specimen and the archaeological manifestation being dated is direct, but the specimen itself represents a later incorporation into an already existing feature.
>
> Type 4. The association between the dated tree-ring specimen and the archaeological manifestation being dated is not direct, the specimen having been used later than the feature being dated.

The validity of the so-called dating of the pottery type in question is increased when there is specific, detailed information available concerning the tree-ring specimen and the associated pottery. For example, much more validity can be placed on the interpretation of a pottery type found on the floor of a pit house whose main roof-support posts produce a series of cutting dates than on a pottery type identified from a collection of surface sherds from a site yielding a single non-cutting date that lacks provenience data. This means that the classes of information and the types of chronological error noted previously are considered in interpreting all instances of tree-ring dates in an archaeological situation.

The term cutting date is applied to specimens that show some evidence of having the last ring put down by the tree before it died. If some of the outer rings are missing, or there is no evidence to indicate otherwise, a non-cutting date is applied.

Smiley (1951) has assembled a list of all the published tree-ring dates in the Southwest; however, interpretation of the majority of these tree-ring dates is left up to the archaeologist. Interpretation can be made only through individual effort to determine the archaeological context and associations of these dates. The nonspecific nature of Smiley's list perhaps accounts for the fact that many archaeologists have, unfortunately, ignored the large body of information contained therein. Nonetheless, Smiley (1951) provides the overall background for this paper.

METHODS OF ANALYSIS AND PRESENTATION

Since 1951, approximately 2750 individual tree-ring dates from about 200 Southwestern archaeological sites have been obtained by the Laboratory of Tree-Ring Research, exclusive of dates derived as an adjunct of the various Indian Land Claims Cases. Two recent, major works that utilize the medium of tree-ring dates to correlate prehistoric archaeological material are Smiley, Stubbs, and Bannister (1953) treating the Rio Grande area, and Bannister (1965) dealing with Chaco Canyon. Harlan's (1962) reanalysis of tree-ring specimens from the Flagstaff area constitutes another new body of material available for archaeological interpretation.

Several statements which define, clarify, and interpret the methods of dendrochronology have appeared within the past decade. Among the more important publications are Bannister (1953, 1962, 1965), Bannister and Smiley (1955), and Smiley, Stubbs, and Bannister (1953). These publications outline many of the field and laboratory problems of tree-ring dating and establish a theoretical framework for the interpretation of tree-ring dates derived from an archaeological context.

The present analysis is carried out within the framework of the procedures, cautions, and controls outlined in the publications just listed. It involves an effort to quantify and qualify the provenience and context of each individual tree-ring date or group of tree-ring dates recorded in an archaeological situation. The validity of each tree-ring date or group of dates depends upon the amount of detailed information concerning the dated specimen itself, its context in relation to the archaeology, and finally, the strict archaeological interpretation of the pottery types which we are attempting to date.

The "raw data" summarized in Chapter 2 are used in Chapter 3 as the basis for presenting and discussing examples of the application of tree-ring dates to the dating of prehistoric Southwestern pottery in a variety of situations. The use of differing amounts of information produces varying degrees of interpretive validity. Fundamental to interpretation is the recognition of the classes of information and the types of chronological errors involved in dealing with tree-ring data.

Chapter 3 serves as the framework for an evaluation; Chapter 4, for the dating of all Southwestern pottery types found at sites with tree-ring dates.

In 1966 the Laboratory of Tree-Ring Research began issuing "Quadrangle Reports" which include many additional tree-ring dates. Neither these new dates nor the ceramic material associated with the dates were available at the time this report was compiled.

This paper is not concerned with the preceramic Southwestern cultures, specifically Basketmaker II, nor does it consider sites assignable to the period following Spanish contact. The latter sites are mentioned only when previously reported upon in Smiley (1951) or Smiley, Stubbs, and Bannister (1953). Further information on the dating of post-Spanish contact sites may be found in Bannister (1965), Hall (1944, 1951), Hester (1961), Indian Land Claims Cases (as they become available), Peterson (1935), Smiley (1951), Smiley, Stubbs, and Bannister (1953), Stallings (1937), and Vivian (1960).

The method of presentation for the dendrochronological and ceramic data is explained individually in the introductory remarks of each pertinent chapter.

The two classes of abbreviations and symbols used in presenting the tree-ring data and associated material are listed in Tables 1 and 2.

TABLE 1
INSTITUTIONAL ABBREVIATIONS

AF	Amerind Foundation, Inc., Dragoon, Arizona.
ASM	Arizona State Museum, Tucson, Arizona.
CM*	Chacra Mesa area. Southwest Archeological Center, Globe, Arizona.
GP	Gila Pueblo, Globe, Arizona.
LA*	Laboratory of Anthropology. Museum of New Mexico, Santa Fe, New Mexico.
NA*	Museum of Northern Arizona, Flagstaff, Arizona.

*Site number prefix.

TABLE 2
SYMBOLS USED IN CONJUNCTION WITH TREE-RING DATES
(Modified after Bannister 1965: 127)

+	Outer rings crowded, probably some absent in series.
++	Outer rings very crowded, ring count made, probably many absent in series.
v	Last ring variable around circumference, probably several rings lost.
vv	Last ring very variable around circumference, probably many rings lost.
inc	Final ring incomplete.
year	Last ring on specimen.
+x & x	Last ring on specimen, unknown number of rings lost.
year ±10	Estimated cutting date. (The number 10 is an example only.)
year	Last year on specimen, cutting date. (Used by Gila Pueblo and the Laboratory of Tree-Ring Research for some of its early dates.)
r	Outer ring constant over significant portion of the circumference, probable cutting date.
c & C	Last ring constant around circumference, probable cutting date.
b & B	Bark present, definite cutting date.
G	Beetle galleries present on surface, probably very near cutting date.
L	Probable cutting date, presence of distinctive surface color condition with Chaco Canyon specimens.
(OS)	Outside, implies cutting date. (Used by Mc.Gregor and as it appears in the Laboratory of Tree-Ring Research Files.)
(end)	No rings estimated lost from outside, implies cutting date. (Used by Hawley for Chaco Canyon dates.)

2. SOUTHWESTERN ARCHAEOLOGICAL SITES WITH TREE-RING DATES

PRESENTATION OF DATA

THE VARIOUS CATEGORIES of information for the archaeological sites considered in this chapter are explained individually. Pertinent data for each site or site-area are presented in the same order. The reader is reminded that this paper merely summarizes certain categories of information presented in detail in the original source (Breternitz 1963).

Site number. All sites and localities shown on Figure 1 and in the text are numbered after Smiley (1951). The numbers were assigned at random by Smiley without regard to geographical location. The system of numbering has been continued here to avoid confusion. New numbers (117–122) have been added to accommodate localities that have produced tree-ring dates since 1951. Newly dated sites in previously numbered localities are indicated by the addition of lowercase letters. This numbering and lettering system has been followed even in site-areas with only one listing so that new sites may be added.

Site name, institutional number or site-area. If a site is named in the literature, this designation is given first; if also known by a specific institutional number it, too, is given (Table 1). Unless necessary, general and specific notations of the site-area, location, and description have been deleted from the present paper (see Breternitz 1963).

Dates. The references listed contain specific information on individual tree-ring specimens by date and provenience. All the tree-ring dates given are in the Christian era; consequently, the abbreviation A.D. is not used.

Summary of dates. Summaries of the lists of tree-ring dates include such information as ranges and clusters of dates, and cutting dates. Certain provenience information for individual specimens or groups of specimens is frequently included.

Pottery types. Reference is made to the published source for the site under discussion if it is readily available and specific; otherwise, the source usually cited is Breternitz (1963), which contains not only unpublished details on pottery from many sites, but also revisions of or pertinent comments on the published sources.

Pottery from sites with tree-ring dates is designated either indigenous or trade. These categories are explained in the introductory paragraphs of Chapter 4.

Comments. Included under this heading are interpretive remarks, miscellaneous and summary information, cautionary notes, cross-references, and other comments.

The relative interpretive validity of tree-ring specimens and associated ceramics is discussed through the use of various examples in Chapter 3 and summarized in Chapter 4 for each pottery type.

In the Rio Grande area which contains many sites for which no additional tree-ring dates or archaeological information has been made available since 1953, reference is made to Smiley, Stubbs, and Bannister (1953). The tree-ring information for these Rio Grande area sites is summarized in the Master Tree-Ring Date Chart (Table 3) and discussed in Chapter 4.

1. ARROYO HONDO AREA

1a. Chamisa Locita, LA 4

Comments. Mera 1940: 2; Smiley, Stubbs, and Bannister 1953: 15.

1b. Los Alamos, LA 8

Comments. Smiley, Stubbs, and Bannister 1953: 17.

1c. Arroyo Hondo, LA 76

Comments. Smiley, Stubbs, and Bannister 1953: 19–20.

1d. Mocho, LA 191

Comments. Smiley, Stubbs, and Bannister 1953: 25–6.

1e. Peña Negra, LA 235

Comments. Smiley, Stubbs, and Bannister 1953: 27.

2. GALISTEO CREEK AREA

2a. Lamy, LA 10

Comments. Smiley, Stubbs, and Bannister 1953: 17.

2b. Lamy, LA 27

Comments. Mera 1940: 2; Smiley, Stubbs, and Bannister 1953: 18.

2c. Galisteo, LA 309

Comments. Mera 1940: 2; Smiley, Stubbs, and Bannister 1953: 30–1.

2d. Manzanares, LA 1104

Comments. Mera 1940: 2; Smiley, Stubbs, and Bannister 1953: 37.

3. SAN CRISTOBAL

3a. San Cristobal, LA 80

Comments. Smiley, Stubbs, and Bannister 1953: 20–1.

4. PUEBLO LARGO

4a. Pueblo Largo, LA 183

Dates. Breternitz 1963: 19–20; Smiley, Stubbs, and Bannister 1953: 25.

Summary of dates. A total of 52 dates range from 1219vv to 1457, with 15 between 1292+v to 1299C. Plaza V rooms were probably built during the last quarter of the 13th century. Nelson's (1914) Building IV is later, dating in the early 1400's.

Pottery types. Breternitz 1963: 20–1.

Comments. The rooms in Plaza V are not trash filled. The ceramic material of the fill is the same from top to bottom. According to Dutton, Plaza V is mostly Glaze I period with Galisteo Black-on-white in the minority.

5. PECOS AREA

5a. Pecos Pueblo, LA 625

Dates. Breternitz 1963: 21; Smiley, Stubbs, and Bannister 1953: 33.

Pottery types. Smiley, Stubbs, and Bannister 1953: 33–4.

5b. Pecos Mission (Nuestra Señora de Los Angeles de Porcinucula)

Comments. Smiley, Stubbs, and Bannister 1953: 42–3; Stubbs, Ellis, and Dittert 1957.

5c. Rowe (Guthe's Ruin), LA 108

Comments. Kidder and Shepard 1936: 343; Smiley, Stubbs, and Bannister 1953: 22.

5d. Arrowhead Ruin, LA 251

Dates. Smiley, Stubbs, and Bannister 1953: 27–8.

Pottery types. Holden 1955; Pearce 1937.

Comments. Neither Pearce (1937) nor Holden (1955) mention Poge Black-on-white or Heshotauthla Polychrome. They do, however, list an occasional sherd of Biscuit B (Bandelier Black-on-gray), Glaze II, Glaze III, and Chihuahua Polychrome.

The "2nd room from kiva" has been identified as Room 18.

The kiva was built during Glaze I, probably toward its end (Kidder 1958: 51).

Kidder (1958: 43) dates the abandonment of Arrowhead ruin about 1400.

5e. Forked Lightning, LA 672

Comments. Smiley, Stubbs, and Bannister 1953: 35.

Kidder (1958: 42–3) adds a few pertinent details on the associated pottery noting the presence of an incipient, glaze-decorated redware, perhaps a proto-Pinedale Polychrome, and the absence of Heshotauthla Polychrome. The main occupation of the site is from about 1225 to 1300. The tree-ring dates close to 1115, associated with the Chaco II (Kwahe'e Black-on-white) sherds, probably represent an earlier occupation of some part of the site.

6. SANTA FE RIVER AREA

6a. Pindi Pueblo, LA 1

Summary of dates. Smiley, Stubbs, and Bannister (1953: 12–4) list 149 dates ranging from 1051 to 1349, with 49 between 1151 and 1260, and 56 between 1300 and 1338.

Pottery types. Stubbs and Stallings 1953: 17, 22–3, 156–62, Fig. 70.

Comments. The correlation of tree-ring dates and stratigraphic techniques for Pindi Pueblo is exemplary for archaeological interpretations of this kind.

6b. Agua Fria, LA 2

Comments. Smiley, Stubbs, and Bannister 1953: 14–5.

6c. Arroyo Negro, LA 114

Comments. Smiley, Stubbs, and Bannister 1953: 22–3.

7. WALNUT CANYON AREA

7a. Walnut Canyon, NA 310

Dates. Breternitz 1963: 25, as modified from Harlan 1962: 34.

7b. Walnut Canyon, NA 323

Dates. Breternitz 1963: 25.

7c. Walnut Canyon, NA 333

Dates. Breternitz 1963: 25, as modified from Harlan 1962: 35; Douglass 1947: 11.

7d. Walnut Canyon, NA 739

Dates. Breternitz 1963: 25–6, as modified from Harlan 1962: 43; Colton 1946: 76; Rixey 1949: 87; Schulman 1950b: 21.

Pottery types. Breternitz 1963: 26; Colton 1946: 76; Rixey 1948: 31–4, 42; Rixey and Voll 1962: 89–90.

8. WINONA VILLAGE AND RIDGE RUIN AREAS

8a. Piper's Crater Fort, NA 534

Dates. Breternitz 1963: 27, as modified from Harlan 1962: 41.

Pottery types. Breternitz 1963: 27.

8b. Winona Village, NA 2133A

Dates. Breternitz 1963: 27–8, as modified from Harlan 1962: 85–6; Colton 1946: 185; Mc.Gregor 1941: 18.

Summary of dates. There is obviously some duplication of original timbers among the 52 individual dates, which range from 1071 to 1090. The latest date for each "group" of material is 1084, 1085, 1085, 1087, and 1090.

Specimen F-4676 (Harlan 1962: 85) dated 1078 and listed as being from NA 2133A has been mislabeled (see Winona Village, NA 2133G).

Pottery types. Colton 1946: 185–6.

Comments. The construction of NA 2133A is convincingly dated about 1090. The ceramic associations are important for interpretative purposes.

8c. Winona Village, NA 2133B

Dates. Breternitz 1963: 29, as modified from Harlan 1962: 86; Mc.Gregor 1941: 18.

Summary of dates. The three roof timber dates are possibly from the same original timber. Construction is postulated in the 1080's, with occupation and repair until at least 1101.

Pottery types. Colton 1946: 187.

Comments. Both the ceramics and the tree-ring dates substantiate the contemporaneity of NA 2133A and NA 2133B.

8d. Winona Village, NA 2133C

Dates. Breternitz 1963: 29.

Pottery types. Colton 1946: 189.

Comments. The pottery indicates that NA 2133C is definitely post-Sunset Crater in date and that the single tree-ring date is either a reused timber or a fragmentary specimen.

8e. Winona Village, NA 2133D

Dates. Breternitz 1963: 30, as modified from Harlan 1962: 86; Colton 1946: 190; Mc.Gregor 1941: 18.

Summary of dates. The seven dates may be from the same original beam.

Pottery types. Colton 1946: 190.

Comments. Both the ceramics and the tree-ring dates indicate occupation about 1100.

8f. Winona Village, NA 2133G

Dates. Breternitz 1963: 31, as modified from Harlan 1962: 85; Colton 1946: 190; Mc.Gregor 1941: 18.

Summary of dates. Only a single date, 1085, is published. Specimen F-4676 (Harlan 1962: 85) dated 1078 from NA 2133A is mislabeled; it is from NA 2133G. Construction of NA 2133G at 1085 is suggested.

Pottery types. Colton 1946: 190.

Comments. Colton (1946: 190) notes the absence of some pottery types normally associated with the late 1000's from sites in the Flagstaff region.

8g. Winona Village, NA 2134A

Dates. Breternitz 1962: 31–2, as modified from Harlan 1962: 88; Colton 1946: 192; Mc.Gregor 1941: 18.

Summary of dates. The 20 individual dates do not represent more than 17 original timbers, ranging from 1089 to 1131. Thirteen of the dates are between 1110 and 1131.
Pottery types. Colton 1946: 194.
Comments. Both the tree-ring dates and the associated ceramics indicate construction and occupation within the 1100 to 1131 period.

8h. Winona Village, NA 2134E or E1

Dates. Breternitz 1963: 33, as modified from Harlan 1962: 88; Colton 1946: 194; Mc.Gregor 1941: 18.

Summary of dates. All four dates are post-Sunset Crater. The pit houses were inhabited around 1100. Both Colton and Mc.Gregor state that the dated tree-ring specimens are from NA 2134E, but it is doubtful whether these specimens can be definitely assigned to one or the other structures.
Pottery types. Breternitz 1963: 33, as modified from Colton 1946: 194, 196.
Comments. NA 2134E is cut through NA 2134E1 with some obvious mixture of the refuse and ceramic material from the two pit houses, as well as the possibility of reused – salvaged? – timbers.

8i. Winona Village, NA 2135C

Dates. Breternitz 1963: 34, as modified from Harlan 1962: 90.

Summary of dates. The seven dates range from 1051 to 1098, with five falling after 1087.
Pottery types. Colton 1946: 199.
Comments. The pit house, definitely post-Sunset Crater, was probably constructed in the 1090's.

8j. Winona Village, NA 3644C

Dates. Breternitz 1963: 35; Colton 1946: 226; Mc.Gregor 1941: 18.
Summary of dates. The one, outside (bark?) date suggests construction about 1115.
Pottery types. Colton 1946: 226.
Comments. The high percentage of Black Mesa Black-on-white in this pit house seems to indicate that the pottery type continued to be made during the first quarter of the 12th century.

8k. Winona Village, NA 3644J

Dates. Breternitz 1963: 35; Colton 1946: 227; Mc.Gregor 1941: 18.
Pottery types. Colton 1946: 228.
Comments. The tree-ring dates indicate occupation around 1100. The associated ceramics are similar to those of other nearby contemporaneous sites.

8l. Winona Village, NA 3644K

Dates. Breternitz 1963: 36; Colton 1946: 230; Mc.Gregor 1941: 18.

Summary of dates. The three dates in the 1070's may be from the same specimen.

Pottery types. Colton 1946: 230.

Comments. NA 3644K is actually two superimposed pit houses. The 1060 date is either a reused timber or a fragmentary specimen; the 1115 date may belong to the latest of the two houses(?).

8m. Winona Village, NA 3644P

Dates. Colton 1946: 232; Mc.Gregor 1941: 18.

Pottery types. Colton 1946: 233.

Comments. The single tree-ring date is 1100. The associated ceramics are similar to other nearby pit houses dating around 1100.

8n. Ridge Ruin, NA 1785

Dates. Breternitz 1963: 37–8, as modified from Harlan 1962: 65–7; Colton 1946: 138; Mc.Gregor 1941: 18.

Summary of dates. The 39 dates for Room 6 range from 1085 to 1207, roughly the same as the range of dates from Wupatki, 13d. The room was probably built by, or in, the early 1130's. The dates in the 1200's could represent repair wood or, since the room is trash-filled, they may not be associated with the actual occupation of the room.

Perhaps the bark date of 1127 from the test of Room 8 represents construction.

The test of Room 11 indicates that construction just before 1120 seems probable.
Pottery types. Breternitz 1963: 38–9; Colton 1946: 142, 144.

Comments. Generally speaking, the tree-ring dates indicate that construction activity was heaviest during the 20 years preceding 1130. The ceramics show a close similarity to nearby sites dated in the late 1000's and the early 1100's.

Ridge Ruin is assigned to the Elden phase.

8o. NA 3673R

Dates. Breternitz 1963: 39, as modified from Harlan 1962: 98; Colton 1946: 237; Mc.Gregor 1941: 18.

Summary of dates. Harlan (1962: 99) shows Specimen F-4874 as being from NA 3674, but it is part of the "T" post specimen from NA 3673R.

Pottery types. Breternitz 1963: 39–40; Colton 1946: 237.

Comments. Both the pottery and the tree-ring dates are post-Sunset Crater. Construction soon after 1081 is postulated.

8p. Winona Village, NA 2134T

Dates. Breternitz 1963: 40, as modified from Harlan 1962: 88.

Pottery types. Colton 1946: 196–7.

Comments. The ceramics from Layer C of this trash mound are post-Sunset Crater. The tree-ring dates are not from construction timbers; consequently, they are of doubtful value for interpretive purposes.

9. ELDEN AREA

9a. Elden Pueblo, NA 142

Dates. Breternitz 1963: 41, as modified from Harlan 1962: 31.

Pottery types. Breternitz 1963: 41; Colton 1946: 45.

Comments. The single tree-ring date from a timber found on the backdirt is of little interpretive value.

9b. Elden Pit House, NA 1531

Dates. Breternitz 1963: 42, as modified from Harlan 1962: 55.

Summary of dates. The 17 individual dates, ranging from 687 to 965, represent only nine original timbers. The pit house was built possibly about 850 with occupation and repair until 965.

Pottery types. Breternitz 1963: 43; Colton 1946: 110.

Comments. NA 1531 is a Pueblo I pit house whose late date of 965 is significant because there are no Pueblo II pottery types present.

9c. Turkey Hill Pueblo, NA 660

Dates. Breternitz 1963: 43, as modified from Harlan 1962: 42.

Summary of dates. The six dates, all lacking provenience data, indicate building activity for over 100 years.

Pottery types. Breternitz 1963: 43–4; Colton 1946: 73.

Comments. Colton (1946: 74) says the site was occupied before 1100 until almost 1300 with the main occupation between 1150 and 1225. The range of pottery types represents a longer time span than the range of tree-ring dates for which there is no provenience or associational information.

10. DEADMANS DRAINAGE AREA

10a. Baker Ranch, NA 2551

Dates. Breternitz 1963: 44, as modified from Harlan 1962: 92.

Summary of dates. Five dates range from 687 to 888, with three between 884 and 888. Construction or at least occupation and repair until 888 is indicated.

Pottery types. Breternitz 1963: 45; Colton 1946: 204.

Comments. The ceramic material of this unit is pure Pueblo I.

10b. Baker Ranch, NA 2798

Dates. Breternitz 1963: 45, as modified from Harlan 1962: 93.

Summary of dates. Twenty-three dates range from 710 to 937, with probably some duplication of specimens. The post, dated 937, is significant because it indicates that the pit house was occupied and repaired until at least 937.

Pottery types. Breternitz 1963: 46; Colton 1946: 209.

Comments. This structure is also pure Pueblo I.

10c. Baker Ranch, NA 2800

Dates. Breternitz 1963: 46, as modified from Harlan 1962: 95.

Summary of dates. There is probably some duplication of original specimens among the 22 individual dates, which range from 678 to 883. The seven dates from 877b to 883 indicate building or repair until the 880's.

Pottery types. Breternitz 1963: 46; Colton 1946: 211.

Comments. The ceramic material of this pit house is also pure Pueblo I.

10d. Jack Smith Alcove House, NA 408A

Dates. Breternitz 1963: 47, as modified from Harlan 1962: 39–40; Colton 1946: 64.

Summary of dates. The 28 individual dates range from 911+ to 1021+ and represent 5(?) original timbers.

Pottery types. Colton 1946: 64.

Comments. Architecturally, alcove houses are a post-Sunset Crater manifestation in the Flagstaff region (Colton 1946: 270). Because the pottery from NA 408A is predominantly post-Sunset Crater in time, an explanation is needed for the earlier tree-ring dates, which are all from small posts and boards with no cutting dates.

10e. NA 192B

Dates. Breternitz 1963: 48, as modified from Harlan 1962: 32; Colton 1946: 48.

Summary of dates. The 18 dates probably include some duplicates. There are perhaps seven beams with dates of 910, 925, 1085, 1089, 1093, 1104, and 1106.

Pottery types. Colton 1946: 48.

Comments. The former dates of 924 and 925 (Colton 1946: 48) are from the same original log. Harlan could verify neither the 910 nor the 925 date.

Although the ceramics and the tree-ring dates both indicate occupation soon after the eruption of Sunset Crater, I agree with Colton (1946: 49) that there may be an earlier occupation indicated by the dates in the 900's and the presence of Rio de Flag Brown and Deadmans Black-on-red.

10f. NA 1570A

Dates. Breternitz 1963: 49; Mc.Gregor 1938b: 6.

Pottery types. Colton 1946: 113.

Comments. There are two sets of dates from NA 1570A, one obtained by Douglass and the other by Mc.Gregor. Colton (1945, 1946), on the basis of Mc.Gregor's dating – particularly the 1046 date, uses NA 1570A as a key site for dating the eruption of Sunset Crater.

Strict interpretation of the archaeological and ceramic data, indicating occupation in the 1000's, supports Mc.Gregor's tree-ring dates rather than Douglass' which are in the 800's.

See Breternitz (1963: 49–50) for further details on individual dated specimens.

10g. NA 1920B

Dates. Breternitz 1963: 50, as modified from Harlan 1962: 69–70; Colton 1946: 158.

Summary of dates. There is obviously some duplication of specimens in the 24 individual dates, which range from 745 to 907.

Pottery types. Colton 1946: 159.

Comments. Mc.Gregor's (1936a: 17) building date of 875 is given added validity by the clustering of six newly derived board(?) dates of 873 to 875. Occupation and repair continued into the 900's.

There are no bark or cutting dates, but the upper range of dates agrees with the ceramic dates of 850–950 as the probable period of occupation.

10h. NA 1925B

Dates. Breternitz 1963: 51, as modified from Harlan 1962: 72; Colton 1946: 160.

Summary of dates. None of the four dates, which range from 703 to 855, are outside or cutting dates, but the 834 and 855 specimens are probably from construction beams.

Pottery types. Colton 1946: 161.

Comments. Even though all the tree-ring dates fall within the ceramic dates of 700 to 900, construction is probably closer to 860, as estimated by Mc.Gregor (1936c: 5).

The published date of 859 for Specimen F-2450 (Douglass 1936: 29) is apparently a misprint, for both Mc.Gregor (1936c: 5) and the Tree-Ring Laboratory files show this timber to have been dated by Douglass at 855±1.

10i. Medicine Fort, NA 862

Dates. Breternitz 1963: 52, as modified from Harlan 1962: 44; Colton 1946: 84.

Summary of dates. The 27 individual dates are possibly from only four separate beams, three dating between 1059 and 1061, and one, an artificially squared plank, dated at 904. Although Mc.Gregor (1936a: 17) estimated the building date at 1060, the present analysis suggests a building date of 1061.

Pottery types. Colton 1946: 84.

Comments. Medicine Fort is definitely a pre-Sunset Crater site. Colton (1946: 81–4) summarizes the discussions that have centered around the cultural affiliations of Medicine Fort.

10j. Medicine Cave, NA 863

Dates. Breternitz 1963: 53, as modified from Harlan 1962: 46; Colton 1946: 85.

Comments. Neither dated specimen can be correlated with any associated archaeological material; consequently, no interpretation of the two dates has been attempted. Colton (1946: 86) notes that the ceramics from Medicine Cave range in time from 700 to later than 1600.

10k. NA 1238

Dates. Breternitz 1963: 53–4, as modified from Harlan 1962: 49–51; Colton 1946: 96.

Summary of dates. The 50 individual dates probably represent 12 original timbers, ranging in time from 851 to 1066B. The construction date of the pit house is thought to be A.D. 1066, based on the strength of 19 individual dates of 1066 from four original timbers.

Pottery types. Colton 1946: 97.

Comments. NA 1238 is a pre-Sunset Crater pit house whose associated pottery types are important for interpretive purposes. Breternitz (1962) uses NA 1238 as the key site for postulating that the eruption of Sunset Crater took place after the trees which grew in 1066 were incorporated into the pit house and before the growing season of 1067.

10l. NA 1244B

Dates. Breternitz 1963: 55, as modified from Harlan 1962: 52; Colton 1946: 98.

Summary of dates. The 15 individual dates, which range from 817 to 1094, are from four beams and three miscellaneous specimens.

Pottery types. Colton 1946: 98.

Comments. Archaeologically, this pit house is pre-Sunset Crater, which makes it difficult to reconcile the two dates in the 1090's. We can only assume that these dates, plus the few Winona Brown sherds, represent a later occupation in the locality. The four dates from 977 to 1011 fit best with the associated pottery, based on corroborative evidence from similar Flagstaff sites.

The specimen dated 821 by Mc.Gregor (1938b: 6) was later dated as 1094 by both Douglass and Harlan.

10m. NA 1625B

Dates. Breternitz 1963: 56; Colton 1946: 122.

Pottery types. Breternitz 1963: 56.

Comments. Colton (1946: 122) cites two dates published by Mc.Gregor (1938b: 6) as also coming from NA 1625B. Smiley (1951), however, does not list these dates. The original catalog and laboratory records show that these two specimens are obviously from NA 1625*C*. See the comments for NA 1625C, 10n.

The single date of 1045 and the small sherd sample from the excavation indicate that NA 1625B is a pre-Sunset Crater pit house. Further interpretation is unjustified.

10n. NA 1625C

Dates. Breternitz 1963: 57, as modified from Harlan 1962: 57; Colton 1946: 122.

Summary of dates. Twenty individual dates represent only eight original timbers, ranging from 799 to 1093.

Pottery types. Breternitz 1963: 57; Colton 1946: 122.

Comments. Because this site, archaeologically, is definitely pre-Sunset Crater, we are at odds to explain the three late tree-ring dates, especially since there is no pottery that can be ascribed to the 1090's.

The date for the SW post and a duplicate date for the SE post are the specimens cited by Colton (1946: 122) and Mc.Gregor (1938b: 6) as coming from NA 1625B. As noted under NA 1625B, 10m, the original records indicate that both specimens are from NA 1625*C*.

Further interpretation based on the evidence from either "dated" pit house at NA 1625 is unwarranted.

10o. Medicine Pit House, NA 1680

Dates. Breternitz 1963: 58, as modified from Harlan 1962: 62; Colton 1946: 127.

Summary of dates. The 18 individual dates, which range from 840 to 1031, probably represent eight specimens. Mc.Gregor (1936a: 17) estimated the construction date of the pit house at 910 with occupation and repair until at least 1031.
Pottery types. Colton 1946: 127.
Comments. The pottery from Medicine Pit House and Medicine Fort is very similar, not only in the types represented but also in percentage distribution. The large size of Medicine Pit House suggests that it might be ceremonial or intercommunity in nature. Perhaps Medicine Fort was built as a replacement for Medicine Pit House, succeeding it in both time and purpose.

10p. NA 2001

Dates. Breternitz 1963: 59–60, as modified from Harlan 1962: 74; Colton 1946: 169; Douglass 1947: 11.
Summary of dates. All the dated tree-ring specimens are probably from NA 2001A, a pit house. The 16 individual dates, which range from 826 to 1003, may represent only seven or eight specimens. Mc.Gregor (1936a: 17) estimated the building date at 970 with occupation and repair apparently lasting until at least 1003.
Pottery types. Breternitz 1963: 60; Colton 1946: 170.
Comments. No record of the specimen dated 1008 (Douglass 1938: 11) could be found.

10q. NA 2002A

Dates. Breternitz 1963: 60–1, as modified from Harlan 1962: 76–83; Colton 1946: 170; Douglass 1947: 11.
Summary of dates. There are 110 individual dates; many are obviously duplicates of the same original timber. The 24(?) specimens range in date from 918 to 1127, with six between 1115 and 1127. Mc.Gregor (1936a: 17) estimated three building dates of 950, 1050, and 1120. The site was occupied and repaired until at least 1127.
Pottery types. Colton 1946: 170.
Comments. All the pottery is indicative of post-Sunset Crater occupation although there is no type present with cinder temper.

To account for the earlier tree-ring dates, we must again rely on the hypothesis of reused timbers (see Colton 1946: 171).

10r. NA 2004B

Dates. Colton 1946: 173.
Summary of dates. Mc.Gregor (1936a: 17) cites two dates, giving an estimated number of missing rings, and suggests that this granary was constructed in 950.
Pottery types. Colton 1946: 173.
Comments. NA 2004A, 10t and NA 2004B are contemporaneous, as shown by the ceramic similarity; therefore, reused beams must be hypothesized to account for the earlier tree-ring dates.

10s. NA 1121

Dates. Harlan 1962: 47.
Summary of dates. The five individual non-cutting dates, which range from 872 to 898, are possibly from the same original timber.
Pottery types. Colton 1946: 88.
Comments. Although this pit house was only tested, the ceramics indicate that it is definitely pre-Sunset Crater and should probably date soon after 900.

10t. Whistle House, NA 2004A

Dates. Breternitz 1963: 64, as modified from Harlan 1962: 84.
Pottery types. Colton 1946: 173.
Comments. The ceramics show that this pit house is definitely post-Sunset Crater. The two non-cutting dates in the late 900's must be interpreted as reused beams or fragmentary specimens.

10u. NA 2218

Dates. Breternitz 1963: 64, as modified from Harlan 1962: 91.
Summary of dates. The three non-cutting dates are without definite context, but they do cluster well around 1090.
Pottery types. Breternitz 1963: 65.
Comments. The ceramics indicate occupation after 1100.

10v. McCormack Spring, NA 5866

Summary of dates. A single date of 813 comes from a timber pulled out during modern development of the walled-up spring (Harlan 1962: 101).
Pottery types. Breternitz 1963: 65.
Comments. The ceramics indicate a long use of the spring. The single non-cutting date is of little value for archaeological interpretation.

10w. NA 3056

Summary of dates. Harlan (1962: 97) obtained a single non-cutting date of 812.
Pottery types. Colton 1946: 217.
Comments. Colton (1946: 217) gives 800 to 1000 as the ceramic dates for this pit house.

10x. Jack Smith Alcove House, NA 1295A

Dates. Harlan 1962: 54.
Pottery types. Breternitz 1963: 66–7; Colton 1946: 103.
Comments. Not much emphasis can be placed on this site which has two pre-Sunset Crater tree-ring dates in the 800's, a mixture of pre- and post-Sunset Crater ceramics, and a posteruptive architectural manifestation.

10y. NA 1571A

Dates. Harlan 1962: 56.
Pottery types. Colton 1946: 115.
Comments. Neither tree-ring specimen gives an outside or a cutting date, but both fall at the beginning of the 900 to 1050 ceramic dates.

10z. NA 1922A

Dates. Harlan 1962: 71.
Pottery types. Breternitz 1963: 68; Colton 1946: 160.
Comments. Both tree-ring dates, 701 and 787, are too early for the ceramic dates of 850 to 950. Since neither is an outside or a cutting date, little emphasis can be placed on them for interpretative purposes.

10aa. NA 1927A

Dates. Harlan 1962: 73.
Pottery types. Colton 1946: 163.
Comments. The single non-cutting date of 811 falls within the 700 to 900 range of the ceramic dates.

11. UPPER RIO DE FLAG DRAINAGE AREA

11a. Coyote Range Pit House, NA 1959

Dates. Douglass 1938: 11.
Pottery types. Breternitz 1963: 69; Colton 1946: 166.
Comments. The Wingfield Plain bowl is listed as "unidentified" by Colton (1946: 166).

NA 1959 is a Pueblo I pit house with an intrusive Pueblo II burial in the fill, which probably accounts for the two sherds of Black Mesa Black-on-white listed by Colton.

11b. NA 5903

Dates. Harlan 1962: 102.
Pottery types. Breternitz 1957: 27–8.
Comments. The single tree-ring date of 820+ does not have much interpretative value because it is not an outside date, and it is also too early for the associated ceramics.

12. JUNIPER TERRACE

12a. NA 1814C

Dates. Harlan 1962: 68.
Summary of dates. None of the four specimens, ranging from 914 to 942, has a cutting date.
Pottery types. Colton 1946: 150.
Comments. Harlan (1962: 68) hedges on identifying the dated specimens as being from NA 1814C; however, information in Colton (1946: 147) and the Museum of Northern Arizona files indicates that all the above dates are from NA 1814C.

All the tree-ring dates are too early to be in archaeological association with the ceramics, which leads me to agree with Colton's (1946: 154) suggestion of reused beams.

12b. NA 1814E

Dates. Schulman 1950b: 21.
Pottery types. Colton 1946: 152.
Comments. The 1135+vv date fits the associated ceramics very well. Reexamination of NA 1814E has shown that it was originally a kiva, which was later remodeled into a masonry pit house (Smith 1952a: 77–80).

12c. NA 1814, Burial 1

Dates. Harlan 1962: 68.
Pottery types. Breternitz 1963: 72.
Comments. Both the burial offerings and the pottery from NA 1814E indicate that the burial should date sometime after 1100. The single non-cutting date of 903, from a nonconstruction timber, should be disregarded for interpretative pur-

poses. Burial 1 is under the floor of NA 1814E; thus the date of 1135+, from the roofing material of NA 1814E, 12b, leads one to believe the earlier date for the burial specimen comes from either deadwood or a reused pole.

13. WUPATKI AREA

13a. Citadel, NA 355

Dates. Colton 1946: 52; Douglass 1947: 11.
Pottery types. Colton 1946: 52.
Comments. Although the single non-cutting date of 1192v and the surface pottery are in agreement, the Citadel material should not be weighted too heavily.

I can find no record of the specimen supposedly dated by Douglass at 1260.

13b. Nalakihu, NA 358

Dates. Breternitz 1963: 73, as modified from Harlan 1962: 36; Colton 1946: 54; King 1949: 132.
Pottery types. Breternitz 1963: 73–4; King 1949: 111–3.
Comments. All the ceramics fit Ceramic Group 7, dated 1130–1210 (King 1949: 132); hence they are in basic agreement with the tree-ring date of 1187. Mc.Gregor's latest date of 1183 for the tree-ring specimen does not alter the basic time period involved.

13c. Lomaki, NA 379

Dates. Colton 1946: 54; Douglass 1935: 52.
Pottery types. Breternitz (1963: 74) combines the ceramic information in Colton (1946: 55) and King (1949: 168).
Comments. "The tree-ring date of 1192 A.D. agrees well with the pottery" (Colton 1946: 55).

Lomaki is Fewkes' (1904: 44) Ruin J.

13d. Wupatki, NA 405

Dates. Breternitz 1963: 75–7, as modified from Harlan 1962: 37–8; Colton 1946: 58; Mc.Gregor 1942a: 21; Stanislawski 1963.
Summary of dates. One hundred and fifty-four individual dates range from 1028+ to 1205?. There is probably some duplication of specimens, but nonetheless most of the dates fall between 1127 and 1194. There are 28 dates between 1120 and 1130, 25 between 1135 and 1150, and 63 between 1160 and 1194.
Pottery types. Breternitz 1963: 77–9; Carlson 1961, P1. 24 *i;* Colton 1946: 59; Hargrave 1933: 22.
Comments. The bulk of the tree-ring dates and the associated material culture from Wupatki Pueblo can be attributed to habitation of the site during the last three-quarters of the 12th century.

13e. Heiser Spring, NA 1754A

Dates. Harlan 1962: 63.
Summary of dates. There is some duplication of specimens in the 15 individual dates; however, all the dates except one are after 1092. The date of construction appears to be 1096.
Pottery types. Breternitz 1963: 79–80; Colton 1946: 129.
Comments. Colton (1946: 131) assigns this slab-lined pit house to the Medicine Valley phase, but it is almost certainly Klethla phase. NA 1754A is a Pueblo III pit house (see Bliss 1960) whose tree-ring dates are important for the interpretation of the associated pottery types.

14. ANDERSON MESA AREA

14a. Kinnikinnick Pueblo, NA 1629

Dates. Breternitz 1963: 80–1; Colton 1946: 123; Harlan 1962: 59–61; Mc.Gregor 1942b: 21–3.
Summary of dates. The 88 individual dates range from 1031 to 1320, with 41 dates after 1300. There is some duplication of specimens. It is postulated that Room 3 was constructed about 1309.
Pottery types. Breternitz 1963: 81–2; Colton 1946: 123; Mc.Gregor 1942b: 21–3.
Comments. The tree-ring dates from Room 3 (the only room excavated at Kinnikinnick Pueblo) and the pottery from the site cannot be correlated on a one-to-one basis, but the late dates and the "late" pottery types are probably coeval. The site shows occupation from about 1200 until the first quarter of the 14th century.

14b. Pollock Site, NA 4317

Dates. Harlan 1962: 100.
Pottery types. Breternitz 1963: 82–3.
Comments. Room 11 is a relatively early room which was abandoned and partly filled with trash

during the later occupation (Mc.Gregor 1956: 50). The early tree-ring date of 1078 for this room and the "late" pottery types in the fill support this interpretation.

The dates in the late 1200's and the "late" pottery types indicate that the latest occupation of the Pollock site is contemporaneous with that of Kinnikinnick Pueblo. Further interpretation would be speculative.

14c. Pershing Site, NA 7207

Dates. Breternitz 1963: 84, as modified from Harlan 1962: 103.

Pottery types. Breternitz 1963: 84; Mc.Gregor 1958: 35.

Comments. A tentative house chronology for NA 7207, supplied by Mc.Gregor, shows Pit House Q, with non-cutting dates of 760 and 771, to be the earliest at the site. Pit House A, with a single non-cutting date of 1083, was one of the first structures built and occupied after the eruption of Sunset Crater. Final analysis of the site has not yet been completed.

15. TSEGI CANYON AREA

15a. Swallows Nest, NA 2507

Summary of dates. No provenience is given for either the 1249 or the 1250 date (Douglass 1938: 11; Mc.Gregor 1934: 10).

Pottery types. Breternitz 1963: 85.

Comments. Hargrave (1935: 28) places Swallows Nest in the Pueblo III period; Colton (1939a: 59) assigns it to the Tsegi phase.

15b. Betatakin, NA 2515

Dates. Breternitz 1963: 85–6; Mc.Gregor 1938b: 6; Schulman 1948a: 19.

Summary of dates. The 14 dates range from 1242+ to 1277c, with ten from 1266 to 1277.

Pottery types. Breternitz 1963: 86.

Comments. Betatakin is a Late Pueblo III ruin of the Tsegi phase (Colton 1939a: 58).

The preceding information and the dates indicated in Table 5 do not include the results of recent work by Dean, who has obtained a total of 154 dates for Betatakin. The earliest cutting date at Betatakin is 1248 and the latest, 1286. At least two peaks of building activity are indicated by the 19 dates at 1269 and the 18 at 1276 (Dean 1964a: 25–6).

15c. Kiet Siel, NA 2519

Dates. Breternitz 1963: 87–8; Mc.Gregor 1934: 8; Schulman 1948a: 19.

Summary of dates. Thirty dates range from 1109vv to 1285, with 25 dates between 1269 and 1285.

Pottery types. Breternitz 1963: 88.

Comments. Kiet Siel is primarily a Late Pueblo III site assigned to the Tsegi phase (Colton 1939a: 58), but a few earlier tree-ring dates and pottery types indicate an earlier occupation also.

The reexamination of all available tree-ring specimens from Kiet Siel by Dean is not considered in the preceding statements or shown in Table 5. There are now 133 tree-ring dates for Kiet Siel, ranging from 945vv to 1286; sixty dates are between 1272 and 1275 and 11 are between 1283 and 1286 (Dean 1964b).

15d. Lolomaki, NA 2530

Dates. Mc.Gregor 1936b: 37.

Pottery types. Breternitz 1963: 89.

Comments. According to Hargrave (1935: 30), the potsherds show that Lolomaki was occupied in Middle Pueblo III. Colton (1939a: 59) assigns it to the Tsegi phase.

15e. Bat Woman House, NA 2531

Dates. Mc.Gregor 1936b: 37.

Summary of dates. One of the two 1275 dates is a construction beam.

Pottery types. Breternitz 1963: 89.

Comments. Bat Woman House, a Late Pueblo III site contemporaneous with Kiet Siel and Betatakin (Hargrave 1935: 32), is assigned to the Tsegi phase (Colton 1939a: 59).

15f. Twin Caves, NA 2536

Dates. Breternitz 1963: 90; Mc.Gregor 1934: 10; 1936d: 15.

Summary of dates. Eighteen dates range from 1104+ to 1289+, with 14 between 1272 and 1278+, and five with outside (bark?) dates of 1272.

Pottery types. Breternitz 1963: 90–1.

Comments. Hargrave (1935: 34) says Twin Caves is a Pueblo III site with some Pueblo I and II evidence. Colton (1939a: 59) assigns it to the Tsegi phase.

15g. NA 2542

Summary of dates. The single date of 1018(OS) (Mc.Gregor 1934: 10) is from a timber found in the nearby sandbank.

Comments. All the published references to the tree-ring specimen dated 1018(OS) state that it is from NA 2542, except the Museum of Northern Arizona files, which identify the site as NA 2544. The tree-ring date is not valid for interpretive purposes because the specimen was not found *in situ,* nor was any cultural material found with the pit house (Hargrave 1935: 42).

15h. Ladder House, NA 2543

Dates. Mc.Gregor 1934: 10.

Summary of dates. The literature repeatedly cites 1065 as the date for this site.

Pottery types. Breternitz 1963: 92.

Comments. Hargrave's (1935: 22, 37) map and description indicate that NA 2543 is Ladder House. Both Smiley (1951) and Colton (1939a: 56) refer to NA 2543 by this name; however, neither Beals, Brainerd, and Smith (1945: 22) nor the Museum of Northern Arizona files refer to NA 2543 as Ladder House.

15i. NA 2606

Summary of dates. The single date of 1275(OS) (Mc.Gregor 1936b: 37) is from an unknown provenience.

Pottery types. Breternitz 1963: 92–3.

Comments. Hargrave (1935: 32) says the site is Late Pueblo III; Colton (1939a: 59) assigns it to the Tsegi phase.

15j. Lenaki, NA 2630

Dates. Mc.Gregor 1934: 10; Schulman 1948a: 19.

Summary of dates. The three dates cluster around 1130.

Pottery types. Breternitz 1963: 93.

Comments. Hargrave (1935: 37) places great emphasis on Lenaki as a site on the dividing line between Pueblo II and Pueblo III. Colton (1939a: 58) assigns Lenaki to the Klethla phase.

15k. RB 551, NA 3338

Summary of dates. Beals, Brainerd, and Smith (1945: 50, Pl. 10 *a*) mention only the one date of 1078+, but the Tree-Ring Laboratory files indicate that 11 specimens, all with the same field catalog number, were dated as follows: one at 1067, two at 1076, six at 1077, and two at 1078. The specimens are roofing material found on the kiva floor.

Pottery types. Beals, Brainerd, and Smith 1945: 62, Tables 4, 5.

Comments. Whether there are 11 dates or only one does not alter the interpretation that "the kiva was apparently constructed in 1078 or very shortly thereafter, according to the wood dating" (Beals, Brainerd, and Smith 1945: 62). The lower levels of the stratigraphic test in the trash mound produced some Pueblo I pottery, but these types are not in association with the "dated" kiva or the surface pueblo. The excavators estimate that the site was occupied for a century or more.

15l. Calamity Cave, NA 2637

Dates. Mc.Gregor 1936b: 37; 1938b: 6.

Pottery types. Breternitz 1963: 95.

Comments. Hargrave (1935: 38) says Calamity Cave is definitely Pueblo III; Colton (1939a: 59) assigns it to the Tsegi phase.

15m. Turkey House, NA 2521

Dates. Mc.Gregor 1934: 6, 8.

Pottery types. Breternitz 1963: 95.

Comments. It is not possible to determine the pottery associated with the single tree-ring date of 977+. Hargrave (1935: 30) says the site is mainly Pueblo II, although used to some extent in Pueblo III.

Turkey House is not listed in Smiley (1951) because he notes (in the Laboratory of Tree-Ring Research files) that the tree-ring specimen catalog number is duplicated by a specimen from Kiet Siel. It is now clear that the duplication is confined to the catalog number and not the actual specimens.

16. HOPI VILLAGES

16a. Oraibi

16b. Shungopovi

16c. Shipaulovi

16d. Walpi (including Sichomovi)

Comments. Tree-ring dates for these villages are given in Douglass (1935: 51) and Peterson

(1935: 24; 1937: 24; 1939: 6–8). Smiley (1951: 10) discusses these dates as an example of the correlation between history and archaeology.

17. TUSAYAN RUIN

17a. Tusayan Ruin, Echo Cliffs 13:1 (GP)

Dates. Haury 1931: 13–4.

Summary of dates. The six dates range from 1170 to 1205, with four between 1183 and 1189.

Pottery types. Breternitz 1963: 97.

Comments. Haury (Gila Pueblo Files at the Arizona State Museum) notes that the Tusayan ruin is ". . . comparatively late in the scale of proto-Kayenta chronology, say about 1200 A.D., or contemporaneous with Wupatki and the Citadel group . . ." This statement still holds true.

18. VANDAL CAVE

18a. Vandal Cave

Dates. Breternitz 1963: 98; Haury 1938: 3.

Pottery types. Breternitz 1963: 98; Haury 1939: 40–1, Pl. 19.

Comments. The Gila Pueblo catalog cards imply that "all" the tree-ring specimens, which range from 607+ to 683, are from the Basketmaker III horizon in Vandal Cave. Without specific provenience information, it is only suggested that the tree-ring dates in the 600's are associated with the Basketmaker III material; there is a possibility that they are associated with Basketmaker II material. Vandal Cave was dug in 1927 and the tree-ring specimens were collected in 1936!

The only readily accessible published report on Vandal Cave is that of Haury (1936b), which is nonspecific.

Not much weight can be placed on Vandal Cave for interpretive purposes.

19. TOCITO AREA

19a. Site at South End of Tocito

Dates. Douglass 1938: 12.

Comments. E. H. Morris (1932 Field Notes on file at the University of Colorado Museum) states that the ruin which burned and produced the tree-ring specimen dated 1126 is Pueblo III in age.

J. P. Wilson reports that a recent resurvey of LA 7611 shows only ceramics belonging to the 900 to 1050 or 1075 period; consequently, the Tocito date should be used with caution.

20. THREE RIVERS AREA

20a. Three Rivers Ruin, LA 1231

Summary of dates. Smiley, Stubbs, and Bannister (1953: 38) list 27 dates from 1310 to 1347, with 17 between 1345 and 1347C. The Cosgroves (1925: 8–9, 12, 30, 33) indicate that Rooms 5A and 7 burned, and although no provenience is given, perhaps some of the tree-ring dates are from these rooms.

Pottery types. Breternitz 1963: 99–100; Cosgrove and Cosgrove 1925: 34; Smiley, Stubbs, and Bannister 1953: 38.

Comments. The site was apparently built in the 1340's and occupied afterward for an unknown number of years.

21. ARMSTRONG RUIN

21a. Armstrong Ruin, LA 1225

Comments. Smiley, Stubbs, and Bannister 1953: 37.

22. TABIRA MISSION

22a. Tabira Mission (Humanas, San Buenaventura)

Comments. This is a post-Spanish contact site. Smiley, Stubbs, and Bannister 1953: 46.

23. ABO MISSION

23a. Abo Mission (San Gregorio)

Comments. This is a post-Spanish contact site. Smiley, Stubbs, and Bannister 1953: 40.

24. QUARAI MISSION

24a. Quarai Mission, LA 95

Comments. This is a post-Spanish contact site. Smiley, Stubbs, and Bannister 1953: 43–4.

25. ACOMA MISSION

25a. Acoma Mission (San Estevan)

Comments. This is a post-Spanish contact site. See Stallings (1937: 5) and Kubler (1940: 92–5) for tree-ring dates.

26. LAGUNA MISSION

26a. Laguna Mission (San José)

Comments. This is a post-Spanish contact site. Smiley, Stubbs, and Bannister 1953: 42.

27. RIO PUERCO AREA

27a. Rio Puerco Ruin, LA 875

Comments. Smiley, Stubbs, and Bannister 1953: 36.

28. CEDRO RANGER STATION AREA

28a. Cedro Ranger Station Ruin, LA 581

Comments. Smiley, Stubbs, and Bannister 1953: 32.

29. STAR LAKE AREA

29a. Star Lake, LA 1063 and CM-139

Comments. This site consists of a forked-stick Navajo hogan.
Bannister 1965: 192–3.

30. SANTA ANA MISSION

30a. Santa Ana Mission

Comments. This is a post-Spanish contact site. Smiley, Stubbs, and Bannister 1953: 44–5.

31. COCHITI CHURCH

31a. Cochiti Church (San Buenaventura)

Comments. This is a post-Spanish contact site. Smiley, Stubbs, and Bannister 1953: 41.

32. TUNQUE PUEBLO

32a. Tunque Pueblo, LA 240

Comments. Smiley, Stubbs, and Bannister 1953: 27.

33. TECOLOTE

33a. Tecolote, LA 296

Comments. Smiley, Stubbs, and Bannister 1953: 29.

Marjorie F. Lambert emphasizes that there is *no* Rio Grande Glaze I at this site.

34. LOS AGUAJES

34a. Los Aguajes, LA 5

Comments. Smiley, Stubbs, and Bannister 1953: 15–7.

35. NAMBE MISSION

35a. Nambé Mission

Comments. This is a post-Spanish contact site. Smiley, Stubbs, and Bannister 1953: 42.

36. CUNDIYO

36a. Cundiyo, LA 31

Comments. Smiley, Stubbs, and Bannister 1953: 18.

37. SANTA FE, NEW MEXICO

37a. Guadalupe

37b. Cathedral

37c. Oldest House

37d. Palace of the Governors

37e. San Miguel

Comments. These are all post-Spanish contact sites. Smiley, Stubbs, and Bannister (1953: 45), and Stubbs and Ellis (1955: 3) give nine new dates for San Miguel.

38. SAN ILDEFONSO

38a. San Ildefonso

Comments. This is a post-Spanish contact site. Smiley, Stubbs, and Bannister 1953: 44.

39. SAN JUAN — SANTA CRUZ AREA

39a. San Juan Mission

Comments. This is a post-Spanish contact site. Smiley, Stubbs, and Bannister 1953: 44.

39b. Santa Cruz Church (Santa Cruz de la Cañada)

Comments. This is a post-Spanish contact site. Smiley, Stubbs, and Bannister 1953: 45.

39c. La Vita Church

Comments. This is a post-Spanish contact site. Smiley, Stubbs, and Bannister 1953: 42.

40. TRAMPAS CHURCH

40a. Trampas Church (Santo Tomás)

Comments. This is a post-Spanish contact site. Smiley, Stubbs, and Bannister 1953: 46.

41. TAOS AREA

41a. Talpa Chapel

Comments. This is a post-Spanish contact site. Smiley, Stubbs, and Bannister 1953: 46.

41b. Ranchos de Taos Church

Comments. This is a post-Spanish contact site. Smiley, Stubbs, and Bannister 1953: 44.

41c. Jeancon's Llano Site, LA 1892

Comments. Smiley, Stubbs, and Bannister 1953: 38.

41d. San Geronimo

Comments. This is a post-Spanish contact site. Smiley, Stubbs, and Bannister 1953: 44.

42. OJO CALIENTE AREA

42a. Howiri, LA 71

Comments. Smiley, Stubbs, and Bannister 1953: 19. Hewett (1953: 28) states that Howiri was occupied at the same time as Hupobi, 42b.

42b. Hupobi, LA 380

Comments. Smiley, Stubbs, and Bannister 1953: 31. Hewett (1953: 27) states that Hupobi was occupied mainly in the 15th century.

42c. Posi, LA 632

Comments. Smiley, Stubbs, and Bannister 1953: 34–5.

According to Hewett (1953: 27), the site was occupied from 1275 until the 1600's.

43. GOBERNADOR AREA

43a. Muñoz Canyon, LA 1687

Comments. This is a Navajo period site dated by Stallings (1937: 3).

43b. Dos Cerritos, LA 2136

Comments. This is a Navajo period site dated by Hall (1951: 27).

43c. Gobernador Canyon, LA 1868

Comments. This is a Navajo period site dated by Stallings (1937: 3).

43d. San Rafael, LA 1869

Comments. This is a Navajo period site dated by Stallings (1937: 3).

43e. San Rafael, LA 1872

Comments. This is a Navajo period site dated by Stallings (1937: 3).

43f. Pueblo Canyon, LA 1684

Comments. This Navajo period site, dated by Stallings (1937: 3), is listed as La Jara in Smiley (1951).

43g. La Jara, LA 2138

Comments. This is a Navajo period site dated by Hall (1951: 27).

43h. Morris' Sites – Gobernador

Comments. The four Navajo period dates, obtained by Stallings (1937: 3), are from more than one site.

43i. San Rafael, LA 1871

Comments. This is a Navajo period site dated by Stallings (1937: 3).

43j. Santo Niño, LA 2137

Comments. This is a Navajo period site dated by Hall (1951: 27).

43k. Frances (Francais) Canyon, LA 2135

Comments. This is a Navajo period site dated by Hall (1951: 27).

43l. LA 2298

Comments. This is a Navajo period site dated by Stallings (Laboratory of Tree-Ring Research Files).

43m. Gob-1, LA 2120

Comments. This is a Rosa phase site also designated Vaqueros Canyon, Site 1, by Smiley (1951). See Vaqueros Canyon, 112a–c.

43n. Gob-12

Comments. This is a Rosa phase site also designated Vaqueros Canyon, Site 12, by Smiley (1951). See Vaqueros Canyon, 112d–h.

43o. Gob-17

Summary of dates. The four dates (Hall 1951: 27) between 844 and 860 are from posts in the clay wall of Surface Structure 2.

Comments. There is no sherd collection for this Rosa phase site at the Museum of New Mexico.

43p. Gob-25

Comments. This is a Navajo hogan dated by Hall (1944: 6; 1951: 27).

43q. Gob-72

Comments. This Navajo hogan site, also having Pueblo IV material, was dated by Hall (1951: 27).

44. CEBOLLETA CHURCH

44a. Cebolleta Church (Sebogeta)

Comments. This is a post-Spanish contact structure. Smiley, Stubbs, and Bannister 1953: 40–1.

45. RIANA RUIN

45a. Riana Ruin, LA 920

Comments. Three of the four dates listed by Smiley, Stubbs, and Bannister (1953: 36) as provenience unknown are now known to come from Rooms 13, 18, and 19.

It is conclusive that the kiva and Rooms 13, 18, and 19 were constructed about 1335, since seven of the ten dates are either 1334 or 1335. This date pinpoints Wiyo Black-on-white, which Hibben (1937: 32) says is the only pottery type found at Riana ruin.

46. TSIPING

46a. Tsiping, LA 301

Comments. Smiley, Stubbs, and Bannister 1953: 30.

According to Hewett (1953: 26), the site was occupied from 1250 to 1400.

47. KIN YA-A

47a. Kin Ya-a

Summary of dates. Six dates, from 1097+ to 1106C, with four at 1106C, are from the tower kiva and one room (Bannister 1965: 172–3).

Comments. It is inferred from the data that the ceramic content is similar to contemporary Chaco Canyon pueblos (see Chetro Ketl, 53e, and Pueblo del Arroyo, 53k).

48. KIN BINEOLA

48a. Kin Bineola

Summary of dates. Nine dates range from 941 to 1124, with four between 941 and 943, and five between 1119 and 1124 (Bannister 1965: 169).

Pottery types. In the absence of excavated material, we can only make inferences about the ceramic associations for the latest cluster of dates by referring to other late Chaco Canyon sites such as Kin Kletso, 53s, and the Tri-Wall Unit at Pueblo del Arroyo, 53u.

Comments. "The Kin Bineola dates are significant in that they contain two well-defined clusters that represent the earliest and latest dated construction periods of the large Chaco Canyon pueblos" (Bannister 1965: 168).

49. GALLINA AREA

General Comments

The following information may be applied to the Gallina area sites that have tree-ring dates, but lack specific mention of the associated pottery.

There are no sherd counts for individual houses or specific information on the percentage occurrences of the pottery types at these Gallina sites or within the structures with tree-ring dates.

Hibben (1939: 89–109; 1949) describes the following Gallina pottery types:

Gallina Black-on-gray
Gallina Plain Undecorated
Gallina Plain Unfired
Gallina Plain Utility (some is neck-banded)
Gallina Coarse Utility

Gallina Punched Ware
Eastern Colorado Woodland Cord-marked (trade)
Eastern Colorado Maize-marked (Woodland?) – one sherd (trade)

"It must be emphasized that the absence of trade wares in the Gallina is an outstanding characteristic. Trade sherds are confined to . . . cord-marked specimens . . . " (Hibben 1939: 88).

49a. Capulin, LA 641

Dates. Breternitz 1963: 110.

Pottery types. Breternitz 1963: 110, 116–7; Mera 1938: 242.

Comments. Stallings (1937: 3) gives eight dates for this house, but the Tree-Ring Laboratory files indicate that there are only four original timbers, all dated 1106.

49b. Kiva House, LA 653

Dates. Breternitz 1963: 111.

Summary of dates. Nineteen dates range from 1164 to 1256, with nine between 1253 and 1256. The five dates for Beam C may be from a single beam. Construction at the site is indicated as being in the 1250's.

Pottery types. Breternitz 1963: 111, 116–7; Mera 1938: 242.

Comments. Stallings (1937: 3) lists 181 dates and Smiley (1951) lists 71 dates from LA 653. The Laboratory of Tree-Ring Research files indicate that these are duplicate dates from the specimens just discussed.

49c. Chupadero, LA 654

Dates. Breternitz 1963: 112.

Summary of dates. House A seems to have been constructed about 1260.

Pottery types. Breternitz 1963: 112, 116–7; Mera 1938: 242–3.

Comments. Stallings (1937: 3) lists 14 dates and Smiley (1951) lists 11 dates from this site; the Laboratory of Tree-Ring Research files show that these are duplicate dates from the four specimens shown in Breternitz (1963: 112).

49d. Cerrito Ruin

Dates. Hibben 1939: 248; 1948.

Pottery types. Breternitz 1963: 112, 116–7.

49e. Nogales Cliff House, Bg-3

Dates. Bannister 1951: 22; Breternitz 1963: 113; Hibben 1939: 248–9; 1948.

Summary of dates. The six dates suggest construction and occupation in the 1250's and 1260's.

Pottery types. Breternitz 1963: 113, 116–7.

49f. Cuchillo House, Bg-2

Dates. Bannister 1951: 22; Breternitz 1963: 113; Hibben 1948.

Summary of dates. The surface room was probably built in 1254 or shortly thereafter.

Pottery types. Breternitz 1963: 114, 116–7.

49g. Rattlesnake Point, Bg-21

Dates. Breternitz 1963: 114; Hibben 1948.

Pottery types. Breternitz 1963: 114, 116–7.

49h. Rattlesnake Point, Bg-22

Dates. Breternitz 1963: 114; Hibben 1948.

49i. Rattlesnake Point, Bg-23

Dates. Bannister 1951: 22; Breternitz 1963: 114; Hibben 1948.

Pottery types. Breternitz 1963: 114, 116–7.

49j. Llaves, Bg-30

Dates. Bannister 1951: 22; Hibben 1948.

Pottery types. Breternitz 1963: 115–7.

49k. La Jara, Bg-50

Dates. Breternitz 1963: 115; Hibben 1948.

Pottery types. Breternitz 1963: 115–7.

49l. Evans Site, Bg-7

Dates. Breternitz 1963: 115; Lange 1941: 36.

Summary of dates. Nine dates range from 1181+x to 1268+x, with four between 1258 and 1268+x. Both occupation and construction at the site are indicated in the 1250's and 1260's.

Pottery types. Breternitz 1963: 116–7; Lange 1941, Table C.

50. CHAMA RIVER AREA

50a. Abiquiu Mission (Santo Tomás)

Comments. This is a post-Spanish contact structure.

Smiley, Stubbs, and Bannister 1953: 40.

50b. Poshu, LA 274

Comments. Smiley, Stubbs, and Bannister 1953: 29.

50c. Santa Rosa de Lima

Comments. This is a post-Spanish contact site. Smiley, Stubbs, and Bannister 1953: 46.

51. CHACRA MESA AREA

51a. Pueblo Pintado

Summary of dates. Five of the six tree-ring dates are either 1060 or 1061 (Bannister 1965: 190–91).

Comments. There are no published excavation reports; however, Gordon Vivian says that Pueblo Pintado is a classic Chaco site. Consequently, we may look to the better known Chaco ruins to make inferences about its ceramic content (see Chetro Ketl, 53e, and Pueblo del Arroyo, 53k).

51b. Chacra Mesa, CM-100

Summary of dates. The single date of 1095+vv is from the fallen wall rubble of a kiva (Bannister 1965: 160).

Pottery types. Breternitz 1963: 118.

Comments. No excavation has been undertaken at this late Mesa Verde site. The dated specimen is not a cutting date and "the only inference that can be made . . . is that the pueblo was used or, more likely, built after 1095" (Bannister 1965: 161).

52. HAWIKUH

52a. Hawikuh

Summary of dates. Seven dates range from 1381 to 1480?, with five at 1381, and one each at 1391 and 1480?. R. B. Woodbury informs me that all the dates are from the post-Spanish contact mission at Hawikuh and represent reused(?) beams.

53. CHACO CANYON AREA

53a. Judd's Pit House No. 2

Summary of dates. Two specimens have estimated cutting dates of 720+x and 777±10 (Bannister 1965: 167).

Pottery types. Breternitz 1963: 119; Judd 1924, Pls. 4–7.

Comments. According to Bannister (1965: 168), "the dates suggest only that the pit house was constructed after 777." Gordon Vivian (in Bannister 1965: 168) suggests that the date appears to be too early for the archaeology.

53b. Peñasco Blanco

Summary of dates. Although none of the 47 dates, which range from 898 to *1088*, have adequate provenience information, Bannister discusses the correlation of two groups of dates, six between 898 and 943 and 31 between 1051 and *1088*, and Hawley's masonry periods (Bannister 1965: 176–9).

Pottery types. Breternitz 1963: 120; Roberts 1927; Vivian and Mathews 1965.

Comments. Peñasco Blanco was obviously undergoing construction activity at the same time as the other major Chaco Canyon pueblos. Information from Chetro Ketl, 53e, and Pueblo del Arroyo, 53k, permits inferences about the overall pottery associations.

53c. Pueblo Bonito

Summary of dates. There are 113 dates from Pueblo Bonito and the nearby area. Included are 98 dates from Pueblo Bonito proper; eight from the adjoining Braced-up Cliff (Judd 1959a); three from Ackerly House; two from Hyde Kitchen; and two from Wetherill's Block House, also known as Tanner's Garage (Bannister 1965: 180–2, 185–6). Dates from the last three named locations represent beams taken from Pueblo Bonito and incorporated into recent structures. Dates range from 828 to 1126vv. Bannister (1956: 183) summarizes a discussion of the date clusters by stating:

> . . . two main building periods stand out – the first in the early part of the 10th century and the second in the latter part of the 11th century. Minor construction seems to have gone on continuously, and repair work was carried out until 1130 at the least.

Pottery types. Breternitz 1963: 121–2; Judd 1954; Vivian and Mathews 1965.

Comments. Although the ceramics associated with the Pueblo Bonito tree-ring dates can be determined, it is not possible to quantify the information. (See Chetro Ketl, 53e, and Pueblo del Arroyo, 53k.)

53d. Una Vida

Dates. Bannister 1965: 196; Breternitz 1963: 123.

Summary of dates. A total of 15 dates range from 847+ to 1093+ with no important clusters.

Pottery types. Breternitz 1963: 123.

Comments. Una Vida remains inadequately excavated, although the most recent work consists of National Park Service stabilization operations.

Bannister (1965: 196–7) discusses the significance of the Una Vida dates, particularly the early dates and their correlation with Hawley's masonry classification.

53e. Chetro Ketl

Summary of dates. Bannister (1965: 139–45) lists 379 dates from 47 rooms, eight kivas, and four miscellaneous locations. The dates range from 911+ to 1116, with 62 between 989 and 1029 (Hawley's First Building Period), 294 between 1030 and 1090 (Hawley's Second Building Period), and 14 between 1099 and 1116 (Hawley's Third Building Period). Bannister (1965: 146–51) treats the significance of the Chetro Ketl dates in a lengthy discussion.

The 201 dates from construction timbers in Rooms 43–65 are also cited by Bannister (1960: 20):

> There are, for example, 89 dates in the 1036–40 interval and 48 dates in the 1043–47 interval. Minor clusters occur at 1020–21, 1028–29, and 1050–51. Only 12 dates precede 1020 and only one date falls after 1051. In the overwhelming majority of cases, the pre-1036 beams were found associated with greater numbers of pieces that dated later and, consequently, the earlier specimens probably represent reused timbers.

Pottery types. Breternitz 1963: 124–5; Vivian and Mathews 1965.

Comments. There are more tree-ring dates from Chetro Ketl than any other Southwestern ruin. It is indeed unfortunate that we do not have more data on the associated cultural material, specifically ceramic content, to make full use of the chronological information for archaeological interpretation.

53f. Hungo Pavi

Summary of dates. Twenty dates, representing 18 beams, which range from 942 to 1077, are probably from ten individual rooms and three miscellaneous locations (Bannister 1965: 166).

Comments. There has been no excavation at Hungo Pavi, but according to Gordon Vivian it is contemporaneous with other medium- and large-sized Chaco pueblos.

53g. Kin Klizhin

Summary of dates. The single date of 1084(end) is from the south wall of the room located immediately to the south of the tower (Bannister 1965: 173).

Comments. There has been no excavation at Kin Klizhin, but Bannister (1965: 172) says: "The date falls within the range of dated specimens from similar, and presumably contemporaneous Chaco Canyon pueblos." See Chetro Ketl, 53e, and Pueblo del Arroyo, 53k, for inferences about the probable associated ceramics.

53h. Tzin Kletzin

Summary of dates. There are two dates of 1111(end), one from the first floor and the other from an unknown provenience (Bannister 1965: 195).

Comments. No excavation has been reported. Bannister (1965: 195–6) says ". . . Tzin Kletzin contains rooms built in the latest dated period of construction among the Chaco Canyon pueblos, but there are not sufficient dates to definitely place the ruin as a whole in time."

53i. Wijiji

Summary of dates. The single date of 1027v lacks provenience information (Bannister 1965: 198).

Comments. Since there has been no excavation at Wijiji, we can only assume that it is roughly contemporaneous with similar Chaco sites, such as Chetro Ketl, 53e, and Pueblo del Arroyo, 53k.

53j. Bc-50, Tseh Tso

Summary of dates. The single date of 922+ is from a beam found on the floor of Room 15 (Bannister 1965: 132; Brand and others 1937: 81, Pl. 1 *c*).

Pottery types. Breternitz 1963: 128; Brand and others 1937: 81, Table 2.

Comments. The date from Bc-50 has generated more discussion than any other single date in Southwestern archaeology (see Bannister 1965: 132–3 for a summary of this discussion). The crux of the problem is not the interpretation of the date and the overall significance of the Pueblo II Period, which is basically the theme of all the discussions, but rather *where is Room 15?*

There is a sherd count and a list of artifacts from Room 15. Kiva 4 is reported as being adjacent to Rooms 5, 6, and *15* (Brand and others 1937: 79, Tables 1, 2); however, there is *no* Room 15 on the site map, nor do the records of the National Park Service contain any references to this room.

Obviously, not much weight can be placed on a single non-cutting date from any site, especially when it comes from a room that has been subsequently "lost." It is difficult to understand how this date could create so much confusion when its only ceramic associations are clearly given as Red Mesa Black-on-white, Escavada Black-on-white, and Exuberant Corrugated.

53k. Pueblo del Arroyo

Summary of dates. Forty-five dates range from *978* to 1117, with 23 dates after 1090 (Bannister 1965: 188–9; Judd 1959b: 55). Bannister (1959: 189) summarizes a discussion of the 45 dates by stating that " . . . the central portion of the pueblo [Rooms 33–81] was essentially completed by 1090, and that the north and south wings were added on in the 1090's and early 1100's."

Pottery types. Breternitz 1963: 129–31; Judd 1959b; Vivian and Mathews 1965.

Comments. Pueblo del Arroyo has the best quantified information available on the ceramic associations of a classic Chaco Canyon site; it should be consulted when making inferences about the ceramic content of other contemporary Chaco sites.

53l. Bc-51

Dates. Bannister 1965: 133; Kluckhohn and Reiter 1939: 43.

Summary of dates. The 1077+ date is possibly from a repair beam. Room 7 may have been reoccupied by persons from across the canyon (Kluckhohn and Reiter 1939: 43, 136).

Pottery types. Kluckhohn and Reiter 1939, Table 2.

Comments. The association of Chaco Black-on-white and Kana-a Gray with the tree-ring dates is questionable. According to Vivian and Mathews (1965), the McElmo Black-on-white is not in association with Chaco Black-on-white, and Bc-51 was abandoned before Chaco Black-on-white came into full development.

53m. Bc-59

Summary of dates. Three dates of 1110c from the ventilator shaft of the upper kiva of Kiva 2 indicate construction or repair in 1110 or shortly thereafter (Bannister 1965: 135).

Pottery types. Breternitz 1963: 131–2.

Comments. The dates for the upper kiva of Kiva 2 indicate that it is contemporaneous, at least in part, with the nearby large Chaco ruins.

53n. Casa Chiquita

Summary of dates. The single date of 1060+c is from a first floor beam of the sixth room from the southwest corner, south row (Bannister 1965: 137).

Pottery types. Breternitz 1963: 133.

Comments. Casa Chiquita is contemporaneous, from surface indications, with Kin Kletso, 53s. Neither ruin is Chaco in plan or architecture (Vivian 1959: 69).

53o. Casa Rinconada

Summary of dates. There is a single date of 919, for the SW corner post (Bannister 1965: 137).

Comments. Several factors weaken the validity of the single date. Hawley derived the date but it was never published; it may have been considered tentative (Bannister 1965: 138). Vivian and Reiter (1960: 25) discuss the pottery from four different stratigraphic levels in Casa Rinconada. Although the sherd counts show a definite change in ceramic content, it is not possible to relate the SW corner post to any of these levels. The authors (1960: 26) also suggest a reoccupation of Casa Rinconada late in the Chaco series.

53p. Chetro Ketl, East Dump

Summary of dates. The 55 dates range from 921 to 1119. Their significance is fully discussed by Hawley (1934, Protocol 2); Senter (1938: 6) and Bannister (1965: 151–3).

Pottery types. Breternitz 1963: 134; Hawley 1934.

Comments. Hawley's efforts to date pottery types by association with dated tree-ring specimens in a refuse deposit utilize the maximum amount of information available. Stratigraphic inversions, mixing, and the use of nonconstruction tree-ring dates, however, not only make accurate archaeological interpretation difficult, but also do not permit much weight to be placed on these tree-ring dates.

53q. Half House

Dates. Adams 1951: 289–91; Bannister 1965: 164.

Pottery types. Adams 1951: 278–80.

Comments. Bannister (1965: 164–5) discusses the dates from Half House and emphasizes the non-association of seven additional tree-ring dates, representing three or four specimens. These seven specimens are from the red sand fill above the floor; thus, the *691* date is the only one in definite association with Half House.

53r. Kin Chinde

Summary of dates. The six tree-ring dates range from 1019 to 1045, with five falling after 1039. No provenience is given. See Bannister (1965: 169–70, 175).

Pottery types. There is no information concerning the ceramics associated with Kin Chinde.

Comments. The six tree-ring dates are from the sites designated Fisher Mound 21 and Mound No. 20. Bannister (1965: 169, 174) believes both these sites are synonymous with Kin Chinde. Although he treats them separately, I have chosen to consider the two sites as being Kin Chinde.

53s. Kin Kletso

Summary of dates. There are 15 dates ranging from 1059c to 1178v from ten rooms, plus two dates of 1063v and 1124c from an unknown provenience (Bannister 1953; 1965: 171). Seven of the dates identified by provenience are construction beams. "Of these seven, four are from three first-story rooms with the cutting dates 1059, 1076, 1076, and 1076, and three are from three second-story rooms with the cutting dates 1123, 1124, and 1124" (Bannister 1960: 20). These dates are further interpreted in Bannister's (1965: 171) statement that "a reasonable inference from the tree-ring data is that Kin Kletso underwent at least two building periods wherein portions of the first story were constructed about 1076, and some rooms of the second story were added about 1124."

Pottery types. Breternitz 1963: 137–8; Vivian and Mathews 1965, Table 1.

Comments. Kin Kletso is not a trash-filled site. Sherds are thinly scattered through the room fill and on the floor. This would seem to indicate a short occupation (Vivian and Mathews 1965).

"Kin Kletso appears to be more nearly a pure McElmo site than any reported to date from the Mesa Verde . . ." (Vivian and Mathews 1965).

Reference should be made to the quantified ceramic information from Kin Kletso when making inferences about the ceramic content of contemporary Chaco Canyon sites, such as Casa Chiquita. Casa Chiquita, like Kin Kletso, is not typically Chaco in plan or architecture (Vivian 1959: 69).

53t. Leyit Kin

Summary of dates. Eighteen dates range from 1011 to 1045, with 11 dating from 1038+ to 1045. All specimens are from Kiva A, below bench level (Bannister 1965: 174).

Pottery types. Breternitz 1963: 139; Dutton 1938: 92–3, Tables 5–8, 12–16, 22, 24).

Comments. Since it is difficult to correlate the sherd counts for the various levels of the stratigraphic test at Leyit Kin with Kiva A and the tree-ring dates, the reader is referred to Dutton (1938, Table 29) for this information.

53u. Tri-Wall Unit, Pueblo del Arroyo

Summary of dates. The single date of 1109c is from the east wall of Room 1, one of the outer rooms of the Tri-Wall structure (Bannister 1965: 191; Vivian 1959: 67–8).

Pottery types. Breternitz 1963: 140; Vivian 1959: 68.

Comments. The Tri-Wall Unit, an archaeological entity in the literature, is also treated separately herein, because it was probably constructed later than the main ruin of Pueblo del Arroyo, 53k. Concerning the time differential between the Tri-Wall Unit and the main ruin of Pueblo del

Arroyo, Vivian (1959: 69) says "the single tree-ring date suggests that this may have been an interval of 23 years after the central house block was built and 6 years after the south wing was added."

53v. Shabik'eshchee Village

Summary of dates. There are eight dates from wall uprights of the Great Kiva and four dates from wall uprights of House H (Bannister 1965: 192). The phenomenon of clustering for these tree-ring specimens leads Bannister (1965: 192) to state that "on the basis of this feature, then, it would seem that 753 and 757 may well represent the construction dates of the Great Kiva and House H, respectively."

Pottery types. Breternitz 1963: 141; Roberts 1929: 107–24.

Comments. Shabik'eshchee Village, a Modified Basketmaker site according to Roberts' terminology, has been cited extensively in subsequent comparative publications dealing with this period.

53w. Talus Rock Shelter

Summary of dates. There is a single date of 1101(end) from a fireplace on the floor of the small cave (Bannister 1965: 193).

Comments. Hawley (1934: 8) says that the Talus Rock Shelter is contemporaneous with nearby large pueblos. To make inferences about the ceramic assemblage in the absence of associated archaeological material, we must refer to such sites as Chetro Ketl, 53e, and Pueblo del Arroyo, 53k.

53x. Talus Unit No. 1

Summary of dates. Nineteen dates range from 1008+? to 1082+ (Bannister 1965: 194). Room 3, Floor 1 shows a strong cluster of dates in the 1030–40 decade, but for the site in general, we can only infer " . . . that the pueblo was probably built, occupied, and repaired during the 11th century" (Bannister 1965: 195).

Pottery types. Breternitz 1963: 142–3; Murphey 1936; Shiner 1961b, Table 2.

Comments. The basic ceramic content of Talus Unit No. 1 is similar to that of the contemporaneous, large Chaco ruins, such as Chetro Ketl, 53e, and Pueblo del Arroyo, 53k.

53y. Bc-192, Lizard House

Summary of dates. The single date of 1104vv is from Kiva C (Breternitz 1963: 143).

Pottery types. Breternitz 1963: 143–4.

Comments. According to J. C. Maxon, Kiva C "was occupied early during the occupation of the pueblo" and "the pueblo was apparently not occupied long as there is very little difference in sherd percentages from the fill or floors of most of the rooms."

Bc-192 illustrates the misconceptions that may arise when there is no excavated pottery to use for interpretive purposes. A surface collection of 25 sherds (Pierson 1949, Appendix) shows the following percentage distribution of types: Escavada Black-on-white 56%, Gallup Black-on-white 28%, and McElmo Black-on-white 16%. The percentages for these three decorated types as recovered from the floor of Kiva C are respectively 26%, 20%, and 6%.

54. CHIHUAHUA H:11:1

54a. Chihuahua H:11:1 (GP)

Summary of dates. The single specimen dated 1374+x lacks specific provenience information (Haury 1938: 3).

Pottery types. Breternitz 1963: 145.

Comments. Recent reexamination of the dated tree-ring specimen has not verified the published date; consequently, this specimen should be ignored for interpretive purposes.

55. FORT GRANT AREA

55a. Fort Grant Pueblo

Summary of dates. Smiley (1951) cites the two dates given by Miller (1942: 24) as 1332. The Laboratory of Tree-Ring Research files show four dates of 1276, 1279, 1295, and 1311.

Comments. There is no further published information on the site, nor is it recorded in the Arizona State Museum Archaeological Survey. Fort Grant Pueblo must be disregarded for interpretation, because of the insufficient ceramic information, the unknown proveniences of the tree-ring specimens, and the actual recorded disagreement of dates.

56. TE'EWI

56a. Te'ewi, LA 252

Summary of dates. Smiley, Stubbs, and Bannister 1953: 28.

Pottery types. Breternitz 1963: 146; Wendorf 1953b: 59–61.

Comments. Hewett (1953: 24) says the site was occupied from 1250 to about 1500. The four Biscuit B period rooms with tree-ring dates were built and occupied about 1400.

57. PUYE

57a. Puye, LA 47

Comments. Smiley, Stubbs, and Bannister 1953: 19.

58. BANDELIER NATIONAL MONUMENT

58a. Frijolito, LA 78

Comments. Smiley, Stubbs, and Bannister 1953: 20.

58b. Tyuonyi, LA 82

Comments. Smiley, Stubbs, and Bannister 1953: 21.

58c. Tshirege, LA 170

Comments. Smiley, Stubbs, and Bannister 1953: 24–5.

58d. Water Canyon Ruin, LA 545

Comments. Smiley, Stubbs, and Bannister 1953: 32.

58e. Rainbow House, LA 217

Comments. Smiley, Stubbs, and Bannister 1953: 26.

58f. Group M, Bandelier National Monument

Comments. Smiley, Stubbs, and Bannister 1953: 38–9.

58g. Large Kiva, Bandelier National Monument

Comments. Hendron (1940: 10) lists nine dates for the large kiva: 1412+x, 1417+x, 1423+x, 1428+x, 1481+x, 1486+x, 1500+x, 1505+x, and 1513b. These dates are cited by Stallings (1937: 4) as being from Tyuonyi, 58b, but they may also be some of the tree-ring specimens noted by Smiley, Stubbs, and Bannister (1953: 21) as being lost since original dating.

The provenience for the tree-ring dates is uncertain; they may be from the large kiva. Other than to note that Hendron (1940, Chart 1) dates construction at 1513, this structure should not be used for interpretive purposes.

59. JEMEZ AREA

59a. Jemez Mission (San José, Giusewa)

Comments. This is a post-Spanish contact site. Smiley, Stubbs, and Bannister 1953: 41.

59b. Unshagi, LA 123

Comments. Unfortunately, Reiter (1938) does not give any specific information concerning the dating or the pottery from Unshagi. See Smiley, Stubbs, and Bannister (1953: 23–4).

59c. Kiatsekwa, LA 133

Comments. Smiley, Stubbs, and Bannister 1953: 24. The dates are all in the early 1600's.

59d. Vallecito Viejo or Policia, LA 136

Summary of dates. There are three dates, one at 1655, and two at 1657 (Stallings 1933: 805).

Pottery types. Breternitz 1963: 149.

Comments. LA 136 is a post-Spanish contact site.

59e. Seshukwa, LA 303

Comments. There is a single tree-ring date of 1597C. Smiley, Stubbs, and Bannister 1953: 30.

59f. Amoxiumqua, LA 481

Comments. Smiley, Stubbs, and Bannister 1953: 31–2.

60. CANYON LARGO AREA

60a. NA 1740

Comments. This Navajo site has a single date of 1826 (Breternitz 1963: 150).

60b. NA 1741

Comments. This Navajo site has a single date of 1739 (Breternitz 1963: 150).

60c. Rincon Largo

Comments. This Navajo site has two dates, 1618 and 1725 (Breternitz 1963: 150).

60d. H3, S13, C1

Comments. This Navajo site has a single date of 1754+, obtained by Hall (1951: 27).

60e. H5, S13, C2

Comments. This Navajo site has a single date of 1735, obtained by Hall (1951: 27).

60f. H1, S19, C5

Comments. This Navajo site has a single date of 1747, obtained by Hall (1951: 27).

61. GILA PUEBLO

61a. Gila Pueblo

Summary of dates. There is one date of *1385* from Room 68 and five dates of *1345* from Room 90 (Haury 1935: 3).

Pottery types. Breternitz 1963: 151; Gladwin 1957: 321; Shiner 1961a: 8.

Comments. Gila Pueblo is regarded as a typical late Salado site.

62. CHACO YUMA WEST

62a. Chaco Yuma West

Dates. Knipe 1942: 24.

Pottery types. Knipe 1942: 24.

Comments. Lack of additional information makes the single non-cutting date of 1274+ difficult to interpret.

63. TONTO NATIONAL MONUMENT AREA

63a. Upper Tonto Ruin

Summary of dates. The single date of 1346 is from a random log sample (Haury 1938: 3).

Pottery types. Steen 1962: 18.

Comments. Pierson (1962: 68) assigns the upper ruin to the Tonto phase, which he dates at 1350 to 1400±25 years.

63b. Lower Tonto Ruin

Summary of dates. An upright post in Room 5 gives a date of 1109vv (Breternitz 1963: 153).

Pottery types. Breternitz 1963: 153; Pierson 1962: 61–5.

Comments. The 1109+ tree-ring date certainly represents a reused beam from a previous occupation; the upper and lower Tonto ruins are contemporaneous.

64. MIDDLE VERDE RIVER AREA

64a. Tuzigoot, NA 1261

Summary of dates. A single date of 1185+ is from Group III, Room 10, an intermediate period room at Tuzigoot (Caywood and Spicer 1935: 19).

Pottery types. Caywood and Spicer 1935: 48, 63.

Comments. Both the tree-ring date and the associated pottery belong to the intermediate period at Tuzigoot – Honanki phase.

65. NUTRIA CANYON AREA

65a. Village of the Great Kivas, Small Pueblo B

Summary of dates. No specific provenience is given for the single date of 1031+ (Douglass 1938: 13; Roberts 1932: 169).

Pottery types. Breternitz 1963: 155; Roberts 1932: 104–32.

Comments. The literature of Southwestern archaeology contains numerous references calling attention to the 1031+ dates, because they appear to be too early for some of the associated pottery types.

66. KING'S RUIN

66a. King's Ruin, NA 1587

Summary of dates. Thirteen dates, one from Room 5 and 12 from Room 6, range from 1023+ to 1050+. The estimated bark dates for 9 specimens are 1028±1; for 4 specimens, 1065±15. These clusters are interpreted as representing the two building periods at the site (Baldwin 1939: 24).

Pottery types. Baldwin 1939: 23; Spicer and Caywood 1936: 29–43, 46–9; Breternitz 1963: 155–7.

Comments. The pottery types indicate a greater time span than that of the tree-ring dates. Since the site, however, was occupied after 1065, the late pottery types can be accounted for without violating the time spans of these types as they are known from other sites and site-areas.

67. KINISHBA AREA

67a. Kinishba

Dates. Baldwin 1934: 105; Baldwin 1935: 30; Breternitz 1963: 157–8.

Summary of dates. The 75 dates range from 1233+ to 1307, with 29 between 1255 and 1269, and 39 between 1270 and 1307. The latest date from each of the six rooms with tree-ring dates is 1236+, 1300, 1301+, 1302, 1306, and 1307.

Pottery types. Baldwin 1934: 59, 63, 65; Breternitz 1963: 158–9; Cummings 1940: 69–92, Pls. 1–33.

Comments. The Kinishba excavation and analysis were done before current ceramic terminology came into use. Both the bulk of the tree-ring dates and the pottery types fall within the period of roughly 1250 to 1325.

68. PINEDALE AREA

68a. Pinedale, NA 1006

Dates. Breternitz 1963: 160–1; Haury and Hargrave 1931: 46–7.

Summary of dates. There are 17(?) individual, dated beams ranging from 1131 to 1331. The kiva, which is the only architectural unit specifically dated by Haury and Hargrave (1931: 52), was in use soon after 1300.

Pottery types. Breternitz 1963: 161–2; Haury and Hargrave 1931: 62–71.

Comments. The main occupation of Pinedale is placed from about 75 years after the lower level at Showlow ruin, 69a, (Haury and Hargrave 1931: 62) into the 1300's. The time span of 1290 to 1325 probably represents the minimum period of heaviest occupation.

69. SHOWLOW AREA

69a. Showlow (Whipple) Ruin, NA 1003

Dates. Breternitz 1963: 162–4; Haury and Hargrave 1931: 14–5.

Summary of dates. There are some minor discrepancies between the published dates and the records available at the Laboratory of Tree-Ring Research. Regardless of the actual number of individual, dated beams, the original interpretations of Haury and Hargrave (1931: 15–6) still hold: the lower level at Showlow is dated tentatively at 1204; the upper level, about 1375 with a 1360 to 1375 building period apparent; and final construction at 1383.

Pottery types. Breternitz 1963: 164–5; Haury and Hargrave 1931: 27–44.

Comments. Showlow represents one of the first serious attempts to interpret tree-ring dates in a stratigraphic archaeological situation. The additional dates from the ruin (Breternitz 1963) support the original interpretations of Haury and Hargrave (1931).

70. KLAGETO AREA

70a. Klageto, NA 1016

Summary of dates. No provenience is given for the single date of 1112 (Douglass 1938: 11).

Comments. The decorated pottery types in the Museum of Northern Arizona Archaeological Survey Collection, identified by Colton as Wingate Polychrome, Kayenta Polychrome, Kintiel Polychrome, Kintiel Black-on-yellow, and Klageto Black-on-yellow, indicate occupation later than the early 1100's. This site should be disregarded for interpretive purposes.

70b. Klageto, NA 1017

Summary of dates. No provenience is given for the single date of 1126 (Douglass 1938: 11).

Comments. The Museum of Northern Arizona files indicate that the pottery is the same as for NA 1016; thus the comments for 70a also apply.

70c. Kinnazinde, NA 1018

Comments. This is a post-Spanish contact site showing Navajo occupation.

71. WIDE RUIN AREA

71a. Kin Tiel (Wide Ruin), NA 1015

Dates. Breternitz 1963: 166–7.
Summary of dates. Although there are some differences in the details of tree-ring dates as given by Breternitz (1963: 166–7) and Haury and Hargrave (1931: 94), the conclusion that Kiva 1 was built in 1276 is substantiated. Minor differences in tree-ring date details similarly appear for Kiva 2, but again, there is substantial agreement: Kiva 2 was built in 1276 and repaired in 1285.
Pottery types. Breternitz 1963: 167–8.
Comments. The cluster of tree-ring dates around 1275 applies specifically to the two kivas and presumably to the whole site.

72. SIERRA ANCHA SITES

72a. Canyon Creek Ruin, Arizona C:2:8 (GP)

Summary of dates. Twenty-nine dates range from 1323+ to *1348,* with 21 between *1337* and *1348* (Haury 1934: 55–7).
Pottery types. Breternitz 1963: 168; Haury 1934: 128–39.
Comments. The provenience and significance of all the dated tree-ring specimens are fully discussed by Haury (1934).

Canyon Creek ruin was abandoned by 1350 or very soon thereafter (Haury 1934: 58).

72b. Sierra Ancha, Arizona C:2:11 (GP)

Summary of dates. No provenience is given for the two specimens with cutting dates of *1340* and *1347* (Breternitz 1963: 169; Haury 1934: 14).
Pottery types. Breternitz 1963: 169; Haury 1934: 14.
Comments. The comments for Canyon Creek ruin, 72a, apply as well to this site.

73. SIERRA ANCHA SITES

73a. Sierra Ancha, Arizona C:1:38 (GP)

Summary of dates. No provenience is given for the single cutting date of *1340* (Breternitz 1963: 169; Haury 1934: 12).
Pottery types. Haury 1934: 12.
Comments. See the general comments for the Sierra Ancha sites, 74.

74. SIERRA ANCHA SITES

General Comments

"The construction in all ruins [Sierra Ancha sites 73, 74a–j] seems to have extended over a period beginning about 1278 and lasting to 1348" (Haury 1934: 19).

Because the tree-ring dates from all these sites represent a relatively short time span (cutting dates extend from 1288 to 1347 with the exception of a single, obviously reused timber dating 1248), and because the pottery (often represented by a small number of sherds) is almost identical, the 11 sites in question may be thought of as comprising a single temporal and cultural unit for interpretive purposes.

Canyon Creek ruin, 72a, which shows a similar range of tree-ring dates and associated pottery, should be referred to for further details and comparisons.

74a. Sierra Ancha, Arizona C:1:8 (GP)

Summary of dates. No provenience is given for the nine cutting dates, which range from *1322* to *1329* (Breternitz 1963: 170; Haury 1934: 6, 17).
Pottery types. Haury 1934: 5.

74b. Sierra Ancha, Arizona C:1:14 (GP)

Summary of dates. Three cutting dates, from two rooms and one miscellaneous location, are *1295, 1311,* and *1312* (Breternitz 1963: 170; Haury 1934: 6, 17).
Pottery types. Haury 1934: 6.

74c. Sierra Ancha, Arizona C:1:16 (GP)

Dates. Breternitz 1963: 171; Haury 1934: 8, 17.
Summary of dates. Twenty-one dates range from 1278+ to *1324,* with ten dates between *1302* and 1313.
Pottery types. Haury 1934: 8.

74d. Sierra Ancha, Arizona C:1:21 (GP)

Summary of dates. No provenience is given for the two dates of *1299* and 1313+ (Breternitz 1963: 171; Haury 1934: 8).
Pottery types. Haury 1934: 8.

74e. Sierra Ancha, Arizona C:1:25 (GP)

Summary of dates. Three dates from Room 4 range from 1294+ to 1314+, with a single cutting date of *1310* (Breternitz 1963: 172; Haury 1934: 9, 17). Six dates of uncertain provenience range from *1248* to 1323+, with additional cutting dates at *1295* and *1312.*
Pottery types. Breternitz 1963: 172; Haury 1934: 9.

74f. Sierra Ancha, Arizona C:1:30 (GP)

Summary of dates. No provenience is given for the two specimens with cutting dates of *1299* and *1308* (Breternitz 1963: 173; Haury 1934: 9, 17).
Pottery types. Haury 1934: 9.

74g. Sierra Ancha, Arizona C:1:40 (GP)

Summary of dates. The 6 specimens from two rooms and three miscellaneous locations range from 1303+ to *1347.* Two other cutting dates are both *1304* (Breternitz 1963: 173; Haury 1934: 13, 17).
Pottery types. Haury 1934: 13.

74h. Sierra Ancha, Arizona C:1:44 (GP)

Summary of dates. No provenience is given for the six specimens ranging from *1310* to *1330.* One other cutting date is *1323* (Breternitz 1963: 174; Haury 1934: 13, 17).
Pottery types. Haury 1934: 13.

74i. Sierra Ancha, Arizona C:1:45 (GP)

Summary of dates. No specific provenience is given for the three specimens with cutting dates of *1309, 1320,* and *1322* (Breternitz 1963: 174; Haury 1934: 14, 17).
Pottery types. Breternitz 1963: 174.

74j. Sierra Ancha, Arizona C:1:46 (GP)

Summary of dates. No provenience is given for the single cutting date of *1323* (Breternitz 1963: 175; Haury 1934: 14, 17).
Pottery types. Haury 1934: 14.

75. BUTLER WASH AREA

75a. Butler Wash

Summary of dates. There is no provenience or associational information for the single specimen dated 1250b (Schulman 1950b: 21).

76. KIN-LI-CHEE WASH AREA

76a. Kin-Li-Chee (Rincon Red House), Arizona K:3:1 (ASM)

Summary of dates. No provenience is given for the two non-cutting dates of 1126 and 1130 (Douglass 1938: 11).
Pottery types. Breternitz 1963: 177.
Comments. It is impossible to make an adequate interpretation of the tree-ring dates from Kin-Li-Chee without excavation or provenience information.

76b. Cross Canyon Group, NA 8013

Dates. Breternitz 1963: 177–8; Dean 1962.
Summary of dates. One hundred and twenty-six individual dates are distributed as follows: *Roomblock, subfloor* has nine dates from five different rooms, which range from 854R to 918v. There are three dates between 871vv and 875v, and three dates between 909vv and 910R. Deposition probably took place between about 875 and the early 900's; it represents fill in underlying pit houses, which were built about 875 with some additional building or repair at 910. *Kiva 2* (Pit House 5) produced a single date of 873vv from a timber in the NW post hole and was apparently coeval with the Roomblock, subfloor material. *Roomblock, house construction* has 27 tree-ring dates from the fill of four rooms, which range from 923+ to 1013+++vv, with 11 dates between 939 and 945, nine between 1000 and 1006, and a single timber from a post hole dating 952vv.

These rooms were built during two periods, one about 940 and the other about 1005. *Kiva 1* has a total of 88 individual dates, which range from 898vv to 1024R, with 40 dates at 1010 or later. Kiva 1 is contemporaneous with the latest occupation of the roomblock houses; it was built in 1011, with major roof repairs in 1024.

Pottery types. Breternitz 1963: 179–80.

Comments. The tree-ring dates, the associated pottery, and the architectural sequence all reflect a definite, complementary stratigraphic relationship.

77. JEDDITO AREA

General Comments

At the present time the Jeddito area sites (77d–771, 77n) can be mentioned only briefly because there are no published reports correlating all the tree-ring dates and the archaeological material. Information on the individual tree-ring specimens is not available at the Laboratory of Tree-Ring Research.

The published lists of dates that are available are those of Douglass (1938: 11); Hall (1951: 27); Smiley (1951); and for Awatovi, 77d, Smith (1952b: 317–8).

77a. Kokopnyama, NA 1019

Dates. Breternitz 1963: 180–1.

Summary of dates. Breternitz (1963: 180–1) lists 38 individual specimens, which range between 1255 and 1430; Haury and Hargrave (1931: 116) list 42 dates; and Smiley (1951) lists 40 specimens.

Kiva R-23 was in use after 1416 (Haury and Hargrave 1931: 117).

Kiva R-24 was constructed in either 1380 or the following year (Haury and Hargrave 1931: 117).

Room 25 seems to be earlier than Kivas R-23 and R-24 by approximately 100(?) years.

The "cut" tree-ring specimens are from the test trench in the deep trash at Kokop. There are eight dates from 1380 to 1400. It is difficult to reconcile (with the evidence) the statement in Haury and Hargrave (1931: 116) that 22 wood specimens are from dwelling or storage rooms, because the distribution and number of dates apparently apply to the "cut" specimens.

Pottery types. Breternitz 1963: 182.

Comments. Although the sherd material from Kokop has yet to be analyzed, the tree-ring dates and the pottery types both show occupation of Kokop from about 1260 to at least 1430.

77b. Chakpahu, NA 1039

Dates. Breternitz 1963: 183.

Summary of dates. Twelve dates range from 1377 to 1390.

Pottery types. Breternitz 1963: 183–4.

Comments. The tree-ring dates appear to be associated with Pueblo IV pottery types.

77c. Kawaika-a (Kawaikuh), NA 1001

Summary of dates. There are 53 dates, which range from 1284 to 1495, with 14 between 1364 and 1368, and five between 1380 and 1400 (Douglass 1938: 11; Hall 1951: 27). Specfic provenience and associational information is not available.

Pottery types. Breternitz 1963: 184.

77d. Awatovi, NA 820

Summary of dates. The 468 tree-ring dates range from 1213 to 1700. Roof beams from Room 788, a kiva under an altar of the Spanish church, have dates of 1377±5, 1415±8, 1502±5, 1503±x, and 1504±x, plus a floor specimen dated 1564±x (Smith 1952b: 317). Thirteen other tree-ring specimens from three painted kivas are also mentioned by Smith (1952b: 318).

Comments. The ceramic characteristics of part of the Western Mound are presented by Burgh (1959).

77e. Pink Arrow

Summary of dates. The 33 dates range from 1365 to 1387.

77f. Site 4

Summary of dates. There are 39 tree-ring dates between 1250 and 1255.

77g. Site 4A

Summary of dates. There are 33 tree-ring dates between 701 and 794.

77h. Site 104

Summary of dates. Ninety-six dates range from 1247+ to 1285.

77i. Site 106

Summary of dates. The four tree-ring dates are between 1255+ and 1262+.

77j. Site 107

Summary of dates. Four dated specimens range from 1180+ to 1216+.

77k. Site 111

Summary of dates. Twelve tree-ring dates fall between 1026+ and 1274.

77l. Site 169

Summary of dates. Three dates range from 1007+ to 1052.

77m. Jeddito Site 264

Dates. Daifuku 1961: 19–20, 23, 26, 28, 30.

Summary of dates. Pit Houses B and F, called Type I, have a total of 56 dates ranging from 660+x to 700±15; Pit House B has eight dates between 692±1 and 694±1.

Pit Houses A and D, called Type II, have a total of 20 dates ranging from 636+x to 816+1. Pit House A has three dates after 775+x; Pit House D has nine dates between 726±1 and 738±1.

Pottery types. Breternitz 1963: 188; Daifuku 1961: 76–9.

Comments. If we beg the question of phase assignment, we are able to classify the Type 1 pit houses as Basketmaker III and the Type II pit houses as Late Basketmaker III–Early Pueblo I.

77n. Naha Formation

Summary of dates. Twelve dates ranging from 1383+ to 1696+ from tree-ring specimens in a geologic context are used to date the Naha Formation (see Hack 1942: 53).

78. RESERVE AREA

78a. Turkey Foot Ridge

Dates. Breternitz 1963: 189; Smiley 1951.

Summary of dates. Pit Houses F and H are San Francisco phase (Martin and Rinaldo 1950: 264, 272) with a total of 15 dates ranging from 748vv to 786v.

Pit Houses E, K, and O were built and occupied during the San Francisco and Three Circle phases (Martin and Rinaldo 1950: 260, 284, 300). The eight dates range from 738+vv to 776vv.

Pit House B is a Three Circle phase structure (Martin, Rinaldo, and Antevs 1949: 106) with only two dates, 777vv and 778vv.

Pottery types. Breternitz 1963: 189–90; Martin and Rinaldo 1950: 379–80, 382, 385, 388; Martin, Rinaldo, and Antevs 1949: 190.

Comments. On the basis of tree-ring dates all six pit houses appear to be contemporary, even though the pottery types show a perceptible change in types and relative occurrences between the earliest and latest pit houses. The six dated structures were built and occupied during the last half of the 700's. The site was probably occupied into the 800's.

78b. Twin Bridges Site

Dates. Breternitz 1963: 191; Smiley 1951.

Summary of dates. The 17 dates from Pit House D range from 745vv to 784v, with ten dates falling after 759vv.

Pottery types. Martin, Rinaldo, and Antevs 1949: 191.

Comments. Pit House D is a Three Circle phase structure (Martin, Rinaldo, and Antevs 1949: 122) whose floor pottery closely resembles that from Turkey Foot Ridge, 78a. There are no cutting dates. It is postulated that construction and occupation took place in about 800.

78c. Wheatley Ridge Site

Dates. Breternitz 1963: 191–3; Rowe 1947: 47.

Summary of dates. There is a total of 23(?) dates from five houses and additional miscellaneous locations. The dates derived by J. H. Denison range from 867+ to *936*; those obtained by H. S. Gladwin, from 847+ to *951*.

Pottery types. Breternitz 1963: 193; Rowe 1947: 40, 56.

Comments. Rowe (1947: 40) compares Houses 1, 2, and 5 (the latter only tested) to the Three Circle phase houses at Harris Village, and Houses 3A and 4 to the San Francisco phase houses at Harris Village. Based on the mixture of architectural features at Wheatley Ridge, the similarity in pottery, and the short time span indicated by Denison's dates, Rowe (1947: 53) proposes that the material be lumped into a single phase called Cenaga dated 800 to 900.

Bluhm (1957: 77) apparently considers all the dates given by Rowe to belong to the Three Circle phase, because she quotes Rowe and then gives 911+ to 926+ as the range of dates for the Three Circle phase at Wheatley Ridge.

Rowe (1947: 47) lists three dates from House 3, but the original records indicate that these dates are from House 3A.

The two sets of dates, one obtained by Denison and the other by Gladwin, have not been checked or verified by the Laboratory of Tree-Ring Research. The lack of verification and the absence of information on associated intrusive pottery, which might assist in the dating situation (at least in determining relative age), suggest that it is best to disregard the Wheatley Ridge site for interpretive purposes.

79. POINT OF PINES AREA

79a. Point of Pines Ruin, Arizona W:10:50 (ASM)

Dates. Breternitz 1963: 195–7; Haury 1958: 4; Smiley 1949b: 20.

Summary of dates. There are 179 dates ranging from 1201vv (artifact) to 1308 (artifact?), with 155 between 1265vv and 1290c.

Pottery types. Breternitz 1963: 197–8.

Comments. Room 11, with a single date of 1294+, is a Canyon Creek phase room. All other dated rooms (Rooms 50–52, 61, 66–68, 70, 71, 72E, 73, 81, 84, 86, 90, 95, 96) are Maverick Mountain phase, representing occupation of the Point of Pines ruin by a group of migrants from the Kayenta-Anasazi (Haury 1958). The six tree-ring specimens having neither the Point of Pines chronology nor the ring structure, are thought to be from trees grown in the Kayenta area. All the dated tree-ring specimens from northern Arizona are small and probably represent artifacts carried to the Point of Pines region; they are not parts of construction beams.

79b. Point of Pines, Arizona W:10:51 (ASM)

Summary of dates. The single date of 1302+ is from the fill of Room 21 (Smiley 1949b: 20; Wendorf 1950: 91).

Pottery types. Breternitz 1963: 199; Wendorf 1950: 35.

Comments. Room 21 is assigned to the Point of Pines phase. The 1302+ date is too early for the archaeology. The pre-Point of Pines phase pottery is from Maverick Mountain phase pit houses, which underlie the pueblo.

80. BLOOMFIELD AREA

80a. Solomon Ruin (Bloomfield Ruin and Chaco 8:7 in the GP Survey)

Summary of dates. No specific provenience is given for the three dates of 1086+, 1089(OS), and 1089+ (Peterson 1935: 24).

Pottery types. Breternitz 1963: 200.

Comments. Solomon ruin is difficult to use for interpretive purposes without additional information about provenience and quantification.

81. BENNETT'S PEAK AREA

81a. Bennett's Peak Site, LA 8438

Dates. Breternitz 1963: 200–1; E. A. Morris 1959b: 172–3.

Summary of dates. Twelve dates range from 675+x to 857+. E. A. Morris (1959b: 172–3) says there were two building periods, one at 795 and another about 840, with construction continuing until 857.

Pottery types. E. A. Morris 1959b: 172.

Comments. Bennett's Peak, a Pueblo I period site dated at 800 to 850, is comparable to some of the Chapin Mesa phase sites (E. A. Morris 1959b: 173–4).

82. PINE RIVER AREA

82a. Pine River

Comments. The single specimen dated 634+x (Haury and Flora 1937: 7) was probably obtained by Reagan (1919), but actually no definite site provenience or location is known.

82b. Cueva Grande

Summary of dates. Schulman (1949a: 13) gives four dates which range from 921vv to 1016vv.
Comments. We know neither the exact location of this site nor the cultural material (pottery) associated with it.

83. ALKALI RIDGE AREA

83a. Alkali Ridge, Site 13

Summary of dates. Seventeen dates from three pit houses and four surface rooms range from 741 to 777B, with 13 between 759 and 772 (Brew 1946: 90). The eight dates from Room 11A, the two from Room 218A, and the one from Room 220A, which were obtained by Gila Pueblo, have not yet been verified by the Laboratory of Tree-Ring Research. The dates are, however, in the same time range and are offered as corroborative information.
Pottery types. Breternitz 1963: 202; Brew 1946.
Comments. Site 13 is the type site for the Abajo phase (Brew 1946: 93–4); all the dated structures belong to this phase. Specifically, Pit House A was abandoned, Pit House F was used and abandoned, and Pit House G was used and filled during the Abajo phase (Brew 1946: 16, 174, 176).

84. GRAND GULCH AREA

84a. Grand Gulch, Nelson's Site 74

Summary of dates. Aside from the original reference (Douglass 1938: 12) there is no further information on the single date of 1133 or the site location.

84b. Grand Gulch

Summary of dates. The comments for 84a also apply to the single date of 1135 for this site.

85. LONG MESA AREA

85a. Long Mesa Ruin (Hill Canyon No. 1)

Summary of dates. The five dated beams, with dates ranging from 957vv to 1073vv, are presumably from the first roof of the south mound building (Schulman 1948b: 5, 1951: 22).
Comments. There is no definite information on the cultural material (pottery) associated with these tree-ring dates.

85b. Hill Canyon Ruin No. 2

Summary of dates. No provenience is given for the single date of 1000 (Schulman 1951: 22).
Comments. Again, there is no further information on the archaeological content of this site.

86. FALLS CREEK AREA

General Comments

Although most of the Falls Creek area tree-ring dates are associated with Basketmaker II remains, the area (near Durango, Colorado) has been considered in some detail to clarify certain associational and interpretive data, which are often confusing and repetitious in the several original articles concerning dating in this area.

86a. Colorado B:9:1 (GP) (also designated Ignacio 12:1)

Summary of dates. Haury and Flora (1937: 7) give six dates from the four main roof-supports and two miscellaneous locations, which range from 543+x to 590+x. It is estimated that the kiva was constructed about 600.

Schulman (1949a: 13) dated one specimen from a pit house (designated Ignacio 12:1) at 349vv. (Ignacio 12:1 appears as 86e in Smiley 1951.)
Pottery types. Breternitz 1963: 205; Daniels 1940 Vol. 3: 23.
Comments. Both structures with tree-ring dates are culturally Basketmaker III. Many rings are missing from the outside of the specimen dated 349vv. These missing rings should be considered in any interpretation of the date.

The Gila Pueblo files show that H. S. Gladwin obtained dates in the late 500's and early 600's for tree-ring specimens from Ignacio 12:1.

Flora (1940) also dates some specimens in the 600's. These specimens come from other houses at Colorado B:9:1, which are also considered to be Basketmaker III. (See also Daniels 1940 Vol. 3: 2, 2*A*.)

86b. Colorado B:9:2 (GP) (also designated South Shelter and Ignacio 7:2)

Summary of dates. Douglass (1938: 12), Morris and Burgh (1954: 49), and Schulman (1949b: 27) make reference to the single specimen dated 650b from the front of the north end of the South Shelter within the Basketmaker III habitation area.

Comments. The date apparently applies to the Basketmaker III time period, but there is no specific mention of the associated cultural material.

One specimen from the Basketmaker II period, South Shelter (Morris and Burgh 1954: 49), is dated 198. Since the more recent reference by the original excavators (Morris and Burgh 1954) has been published, the provenience given simply as Falls Creek in Schulman (1949a: 13) is no longer considered valid.

See also North Shelter, 86i.

86c. Falls Creek, General

Comments. Only seven dates remain from the thirteen cited for 86c, Falls Creek, by Smiley (1951). The 13 dates are given by Schulman (1949a, 1949b) as Falls Creek, but Specimen No. 2728 is from the South Shelter (see 86b) and Specimens AC-8, AC-21, AB-1, and 2H-30 (see 86i) are from the North Shelter. Specimen AB-1 is listed in both Schulman's 1949 publications.

The remaining seven tree-ring dates within the general Falls Creek category are all from the Basketmaker II cultural horizon with dates ranging from 174vv to 243c.

The eight specimens with the site designation "?" in Schulman (1949b: 27) have been disregarded in this paper, because the dates, ranging from 502vv to 684vv, have no additional information on provenience or associations.

86d. Ignacio 7:101, Talus Village

Dates. Floor 1 (specimens prefixed with "I" in Schulman 1949a: 13, 1949b: 27) has 10 dates ranging from 197± to 324vv. Morris and Burgh (1954: 48) say the 324+ specimen is from Floor 1a which, according to Morris (1949: 34), was built soon after 322.

Floor 2 (specimens prefixed with "II" in Schulman 1949a: 13, 1949b: 27) has three dates between 184vv and 208vv. Specimen II-X is dated at 85 with possibly 100 rings missing (Schulman 1952: 33). According to Morris and Burgh (1954: 48), the two latest dates are from Floor 2a, which was built near 200 (Morris 1949: 34).

Floor 3 (specimens prefixed with "III" in Schulman 1949a: 13, 1949b: 27) has four dates between 188c and 214vv. Morris and Burgh (1954: 48) attribute these specimens to Floor 3a, which was built about 200 (Morris 1949: 34).

Area 5, Floor, has two Gila Pueblo dates of 605 and 631 (Morris and Burgh 1954: 21–3).

The provenience for Specimen FILL-1 dated 316vv (Schulman 1949a: 13) is not known.

Summary of dates. Floors 1, 2, and 3 are Basketmaker II and Area 5 is attributed to Basketmaker III occupation.

Pottery types. Breternitz 1963: 208.

86e. Ignacio 12:1

See Colorado B:9:1, 86a.

86f. Ignacio 17A:6 (also designated Colorado B:13:2 in the GP Survey)

Comments. Schulman (1949b: 27) gives a single date of 494vv, which is without provenience or associational information.

86g. Ignacio 16A:1

Comments. Neither the site location nor the specimen provenience is known for the one date of 636vv (Schulman 1949b: 27).

86h. Cornelius Cave

Comments. Neither the site location nor the specimen provenience is known for the two dates of 930+vv and 945+vv (Schulman 1949a: 13).

86i. North Shelter (also designated Ignacio 7:2A)

Dates. Specimens 2H-30 and AB-1 (dated 203b and 260vv), cited as Falls Creek in Schulman (1949b: 27), are listed as being from the North Shelter trash by Morris and Burgh (1954: 48). (AB-1 is also published in Schulman 1949a: 13.) The three pieces of the same original timber dated 46b by Schulman (1952: 33) are also from North Shelter trash (Morris and Burgh 1954: 48). Also definitely attributed to the North Shelter (cave) is Specimen 9-11-50, dated 197v (Schulman 1951: 28). All these dated specimens were associated with Basketmaker II remains.

Schulman (1952: 33) lists 38 additional dates from Durango Rock Shelters. These dates do not include the three from the same specimen dated 46b, which shows outside rings ranging from 20 B.C. to A.D. 54. These 38 specimens, which could be from either the North or the South Shelters, are not discussed by Morris and Burgh (1954), presumably because they are small charcoal specimens whose exact provenience could not be ascertained.

Two specimens (AC-8 and AC-21), listed as Falls Creek by Schulman (1949a: 13) and dated 543+vv and 575v, are identified as being from the Basketmaker III reoccupation of the North Shelter (Morris 1952: 36). Morris and Burgh (1954: 49) further state that these tree-ring dates are from the surface layer of Terrace I at the north end of the North Shelter.

Summary of dates. The forty-four dates include 42 from the Basketmaker II period and two from Basketmaker III associations.

Comments. This group of dates is not of much value for ceramic interpretation. The 42 Basketmaker II period dates come from a non-ceramic horizon. There is also no specific information on the ceramic associations of the two Basketmaker III dates.

86j. Ignacio 7:23

Summary of dates. Twelve dates obtained by Gila Pueblo range from 733 to *763*. There are additional cutting dates of *761* and two of *762*. All the dated specimens are from wall and roof poles (Carlson 1963).

Pottery types. Carlson 1963.

Comments. There are a few brownware sherds from the site, but they are not recorded as being specifically from the dated pit house.

86k. Ignacio 7:30

Summary of dates. Eight dates, again derived by Gila Pueblo, range from 732 to *761*, with one other cutting date at *760*. All the dated specimens are from wall or roof poles (Carlson 1963).

Pottery types. Carlson 1963.

86l. Ignacio 7:31

Summary of dates. None of the 12 Gila Pueblo derived dates, ranging from 735 to 759, are cutting dates; however, 11 dates fall after 751. One of the two 759 dates is from a main roof-support; the other specimens are from wall and roof poles (Carlson 1963).

Pottery types. Carlson 1963.

86m. Ignacio 7:36

Summary of dates. Gila Pueblo obtained nine dates ranging from 729 to *762*, the latter from a main roof-support. The other eight dates are from wall or roof poles (Carlson 1963).

Pottery types. Carlson 1963.

Comments. All the dated sites at Falls Creek Flats, 86j–m, are Basketmaker III.

87. YAMPA CANYON AREA

87a. Marigold Cave

Summary of dates. A single specimen, dated 690+, comes from the trash fill on the floor of Pit House I (Burgh 1950: 19–20; Schulman 1950a: 18). Schulman estimates the cutting date to be about 750±50.

Pottery types. Breternitz 1963: 213.

Comments. Burgh (1950: 20) states that the cultural material and the estimated cutting dates are in agreement.

88. MESA VERDE NATIONAL PARK AREA

General Comments

There are approximately 127 dates from 25 sites in this area, but the material culture associations are almost unknown, particularly for the latest sites. Comment and further interpretation are necessarily deferred until the material currently being excavated and analyzed as part of the Wetherill Mesa Project (jointly sponsored by the National Park Service and the National Geographic Society) is available. New tree-ring dates and new archaeological information will enable us to make inferences about the ceramic content of the majority of the Mesa Verde ruins from which we presently have tree-ring dates, but little information on the associated material culture.

The most recent summary of the Mesa Verde area is Herold (1961), and even this fine report does not include several of the sites that have produced tree-ring dates.

88a. Pit House C

Summary of dates. The six dates at 612 are interpreted as the construction date (Douglass 1938: 12).

Pottery types. Breternitz 1963: 214; Lancaster and Watson 1943: 195–6.
Comments. Pit House C is assigned to the Four Corners phase, as defined by E. A. Morris (1959a: 560).

88b. Step House

Summary of dates. No provenience is given for the single date of 610v (Schulman 1946: 20).
Comments. Recent, but as yet unreported work in Step House has resulted in the excavation of the Pueblo III unit and additional pit rooms.

O'Bryan (1950: 104) assigns Step House to his Four Corners phase. A Lino Style black-on-white or black-on-gray bowl, which presumably belongs to the same time horizon as the tree-ring date, is illustrated in Nordenskiöld (1893, Pl. 23).

88c. Pit House No. 1

Summary of dates. The 15 dates range from 684vv to 700c, with six cutting dates at 700. Smiley (1949a: 171) postulates construction at 700 to 705.
Pottery types. Smiley 1949a: 169.
Comments. The tree-ring dates and the pottery indicate a late Basketmaker III pit house of the Four Corners phase, as defined by E. A. Morris (1959a: 560).

88d. Pipe Shrine House

Summary of dates. The kiva ventilator shaft produced two dates, 898+ and 1214+ (Smiley 1947: 30–1).
Pottery types. Watson 1947:32.
Comments. The interpretation of the dates for Pipe Shrine House is difficult, if not impossible.

88e. Slab Room under Pipe Shrine House

Dates. Breternitz 1963: 216.
Summary of dates. The eight non-cutting dates suggest that the slab room was built in the early 1000's.
Comments. See the information on pottery types and the comments for Pipe Shrine House, 88d.

88f. Bone Awl House

Dates. Breternitz 1963: 216; Schulman 1946: 20.
Comments. The dates are meaningless without further information. Bone Awl House is not mentioned by Herold (1961).

88g. Mug House

Dates. Getty 1935a: 22; Schulman 1946: 20.
Summary of dates. The two dates are both 1066.
Pottery types. Breternitz 1963: 216–7.
Comments. Mug House is the scene of recent excavation by the Wetherill Mesa Project. The analysis of Mug House pottery in terms of current classifications will enable us to use this site to make inferences about the ceramics which probably occur at other Mesa Verde Pueblo III sites.

88h. Spruce Tree House

Dates. Breternitz 1963: 218; Getty 1935b: 29; Peterson 1935: 24; Schulman 1946: 20–1.
Summary of dates. Twenty-five dates range from 1020vv to 1274c. The 20 dates between 1230c and 1254c seem to indicate the period of major construction.
Comments. All we can say about Spruce Tree House is that the site was occupied in late Pueblo III and by inference, that the ceramics found at Mug House, 88g, were also present here.

88i. Balcony House

Dates. Getty 1935a: 22; Peterson 1935: 24; Schulman 1946: 20.
Comments. The ceramic component for this late Pueblo III site is inferred from the ceramics found at Mug House, 88g.

88j. Cliff Palace

Dates. Breternitz 1963: 220; Getty 1935a: 22; Schulman 1946: 20–1.
Summary of dates. The eight dates range from 1210c to 1273c, with six dates after 1264c.
Comments. We can only make inferences about the associated pottery types by referring to Mug House, 88g.

88k. Hemenway House

Summary of dates. No specific provenience is given for either the 1171v or the 1174c date (Getty 1935a: 22; Schulman 1946: 20).
Comments. There is no additional information available for this site at the present time.

88l. Kodak House

Summary of dates. No specific provenience is given for the single specimen dated 1132vv (Schulman 1946: 21).
Comments. Specific information on the ceramic content is not available.

88m. Long House

Dates. Breternitz 1963: 221; Schulman 1946: 20.
Summary of dates. The 11 dates range from 1184v to 1274c, with six dates from 1263c to 1274c.
Comments. Long House is the scene of recent excavations by the Wetherill Mesa Project; additional tree-ring dates as well as information on the associated material culture will be forthcoming. At the present time we can only suggest that the Late Pueblo III ceramic complex is the same as that of Mug House, 88g.

88n. Oak Tree House

Dates. Getty 1935a: 22; Peterson 1935: 24; Schulman 1946: 21.
Comments. No additional information from the site is associated with the two dates of 119v and 1184c.

88o. Ruin No. 16

Dates. Getty 1935a: 22; Schulman 1946: 20.
Comments. The ceramic component of Ruin No. 16, which accompanies the two dates in the middle 1200's, is inferred from our knowledge of Mug House, 88g.

88p. Spring House

Dates. Breternitz 1963: 222; Schulman 1946: 20.
Summary of dates. There are two dates, 1117vv and 1197.
Comments. Information on the specific ceramic content of Spring House is not available.

88q. Square Tower House

Dates. Getty 1935a: 22; Schulman 1946: 21.
Summary of dates. Six dates, without provenience information, range from 1066vv to 1246v, with four after 1241v.
Comments. Again, the ceramic content of this site can only be inferred from the pottery types found in other Pueblo III sites, such as Mug House, 88g.

88r. Buzzard House

Summary of dates. No provenience is given for the single date of 1273c (Getty 1935a: 22, Schulman 1946: 20).
Comments. The ceramic content is inferred to be similar to that of Mug House, 88g.

88s. New Fire House

Summary of dates. Two dates from a ledge support are 1259v and 1260v (Schulman 1946: 21).
Comments. We can make inferences about the probable ceramic content by referring to Mug House, 88g.

88t. Painted Kiva House

Summary of dates. There are three dates: 1199c, 1202c, and 1271 (Breternitz 1963: 224; Schulman 1946: 21).
Comments. In the absence of additional specific information, further interpretation of this site has not been attempted.

88u. Pit Structure No. 1

Summary of dates. Nine dates range from 538vv to 626vv, with four dates between 622vv and 626vv (Breternitz 1963: 224; Smiley 1950: 22).
Pottery types. Breternitz 1963: 224.

88v. Pit Structure No. 2

Summary of dates. Six dates range from 624+vv to 667+vv, with three between 664vv and 667+vv (Breternitz 1963: 224; Smiley 1950: 22–3).
Pottery types. Breternitz 1963: 224.
Comments. The site lacks additional information to use for interpretive purposes.

88w. Far View House, Subfloor

Dates. Smiley 1950: 22.
Summary of dates. Four dates from two locations range from 772vv to 1078+vv, with three dates after 1059.
Comments. Smiley (1951) lists five dates from Far View House, Subfloor, but the Laboratory of Tree-Ring Research files indicate that one specimen is from Room 32, listed as 88aa in this paper.

Specific information on the ceramics associated with these tree-ring dates is not available.

88x. Twin Trees Site, Deep Pit House

Summary of dates. Seven dates range from 570vv to 674c; construction soon after 674 is suggested (Lancaster and Watson 1954: 12; Schulman 1951: 28).
Pottery types. Breternitz 1963: 225; Lancaster and Watson 1954: 22.

Comments. The Deep Pit House is a late Basketmaker III structure assignable to the Four Corners phase, as defined by E. A. Morris 1959a: 560.

88y. Slab House

Summary of dates. No specific provenience is given for the single date of 847b (Breternitz 1963: 226).
Pottery types. Breternitz 1963: 226.

88z. Site 16

Summary of dates. There are two bark dates of 1074 from Kiva 1 (Lancaster and Pinkley 1954: 42, 78; Schulman 1951: 28).
Pottery types. Lancaster and Pinkley 1954: 85.
Comments. Kiva 1, which belongs to Unit Pueblo No. II at Site 16, is assigned to the Mancos phase. The bark dates of 1074 are considered to be construction dates, with occupation being postulated until about 1100 (Lancaster and Pinkley 1954: 78).

88aa. Far View House

Summary of dates. The one non-cutting date of 1039vv from Room 32 (Smiley 1950: 22) is listed as Far View House, Subfloor in Smiley (1951).
Comments. Interpretation is unwarranted at this time.

88bb. ASS 1060

Dates. Nichols 1962: 12.
Summary of dates. There are six non-cutting dates, plus one cutting date of 608. Alden Hayes informs me that "all the pieces had a definite association with the pit house."
Pottery types. Breternitz 1963: 227.
Comments. ASS 1060 is a Basketmaker III or Modified Basketmaker pit house built about 608 and assignable to the Four Corners phase, as defined by E. A. Morris (1959a: 560).

88cc. Site 145

Summary of dates. All the dates from Site 145 (O'Bryan 1950: 55–61) obtained by Gila Pueblo have not been checked or verified by the Laboratory of Tree-Ring Research.

Pit House I: Twelve dates range from 430+ to 587+ with cutting dates at *522* and *572*. Construction in the last quarter of the sixth century is probable.

Pit House II: Twenty-three dates range from 633+ to *664*, with cutting dates at *657* and *664*. Construction probably took place in 664.
Pottery types. Breternitz 1963: 228; O'Bryan 1950: 120–1.
Comments. Both O'Bryan (1950: 104) and E. A. Morris (1959a: 560) assign both pit houses to the Four Corners phase.

89. STOLLSTEIMER MESA AREA

89a. Piedra Ruin, Colorado B:15:1 (GP)

Summary of dates. The single date of 774 is from Unit C-3 (Haury 1938: 3).
Pottery types. Breternitz 1963: 229; Roberts 1930: 83–141.
Comments. Lack of additional information makes the single date of little use for interpretation.

90. JOHNSON CANYON AREA

90a. Johnson Canyon, Site 33

Summary of dates. Building II, eastern extension, has a single date of 692+x. Three of the four main corner roof posts of the great kiva are dated at 675+, 767+, and 831 (E. H. Morris 1939: 80, 84). Flora (1940) dated an unknown number of specimens from the backdirt at Site 33 and obtained dates ranging from 684 to 747.
Pottery types. Breternitz 1963: 230; E. H. Morris 1939: 80, 84, 157–84.
Comments. The dates from Site 33 belong to the Pueblo I occupation.

91. LA PLATA AREA

91a. La Plata, Site 25

Summary of dates. Douglass (1938: 12) gives dates of 836 and 845. The 836 date is from the kiva, but I can find no record in the Laboratory of Tree-Ring Research files for the 845 date nor does E. H. Morris (1939: 63) mention it.
Pottery types. The ceramic associations of the kiva, which is Pueblo I, can only be inferred from the pottery present at Johnson Canyon, Site 33, 90a.
Comments. Caution is necessary when making inferences about the ceramics associated with tree-ring dates.

92. ACKMEN-LOWRY AREA

92a. Lowry Ruin

Dates. Breternitz 1963: 231; Douglas 1938: 12; Haury 1938: 3; Martin 1936: 195; Stallings 1937: 3.
Summary of dates. Thirteen of the 14 dates are between 1085 and 1090c.
Pottery types. Martin 1936: 102, 110–1.
Comments. The Lowry ruin is generally classifiable as a Late Pueblo II site. Room 21, specifically, belongs to the McElmo phase.

92b. Cahone Canyon

1. SITE 1
Dates. Martin 1939: 495.
Summary of dates. Twenty dates range from 837 to 872, with 16 between 857 and 872.
Pottery types. Martin 1939: 481–2; Rinaldo 1950: 95.
Comments. All the dated structures similar in ceramic content and time relationship may be treated as a contemporaneous group.

Martin (1939: 460–3) dates Developmental Pueblo (Pueblo I) in the Ackmen-Lowry area from about 860 to 950. Rinaldo (1950: 94) considers Site 1 to be Abajo phase.

2. SITE 2
Dates. Martin 1939: 495.
Summary of dates. Twelve dates range from 612+ to 768, with eight dates between 761 and 768+.
Pottery types. Martin 1939: 483, 485; Rinaldo 1950: 95.
Comments. Contemporaneity of the dated structures and ceramic similarity permits treatment of Site 2 as a unit. Martin (1939: 460–3) dates Modified Basketmaker in the Ackmen-Lowry area from about 700 to 860. Rinaldo (1950: 94) treats Site 2 as Abajo phase.

93. AZTEC RUINS NATIONAL MONUMENT AREA

93a. Aztec Ruin

Dates. Breternitz 1963: 234–6; Douglass 1938: 13.
Summary of dates. Forty-nine dates range from 1110 to 1125, with 36 between 1111 and 1115. There is a single date at 1240CL.

Gila Pueblo also obtained 91 dates from Aztec ruin (Gladwin 1945: 126–7, 129), with 85 between 1103 and 1126, and six between 1225? and 1252. At least 23 of these dates (specimens also dated by the Laboratory of Tree-Ring Research) are cited in Breternitz (1963: 234–6). Although the Gila Pueblo dates are not listed here, they show a clustering in the interval between 1111 and 1115.
Pottery types. Breternitz 1963: 237; E. H. Morris 1917: 55; 1919; 1921; 1924; 1928.
Comments. Breternitz (1963: 237) briefly discusses the interpretation of most of the pottery illustrated in the various Morris publications and their relation to the so-called Mesa Verde occupation of Aztec ruin in the 1200's.

Gordon Vivian is of the opinion that the main building period at Aztec, represented by the many tree-ring dates in the early 1100's, is McElmo phase; for the amount of iron paint pottery still around is no different from the relative occurrence of iron and carbon paint pottery seen in McElmo phase sites at Mesa Verde (see O'Bryan 1950).

94. NINE MILE CANYON AREA

94a. Sky House, Nine Mile 13

Summary of dates. Twelve dates range from 768vv to 1090v, with five dates between 1086+ and 1090v (Ferguson 1949: 10; Schulman 1948b: 5).
Pottery types. Breternitz 1963: 238; Gillin 1955: 25.
Comments. Christensen's (1951: 29) estimate that Sky House was built near 1092 seems to be a reasonable assumption. Sky House, like the other known sites in Nine Mile Canyon, represents a Pueblo-type culture.

94b. Nine Mile X

Comments. The three dates of 915+vv, 924vv, and 951+v obtained by Schulman (1948b: 5) from an undesignated site (or sites) are of no value for interpretation.

94c. Upper Sky House, Nine Mile 28

Comments. No provenience is given for the single date of 1011+vv (Schulman 1951: 28).

See the comments for Sky House, 94a.

94d. Four Name House

Comments. A tree-ring specimen dated 1151b is associated with the masonry structure, but three of the other dates in the 1700's and 1800's are not associated with the structure (Schulman 1951: 28).

"The site appears to have been occupied around 1151" (Christensen 1951: 30).

94e. Olger Ranch Ruin

Comments. The single date of 1065b (Schulman 1951: 28) is associated with the masonry structure. No other information is available.

94f. Lookout House, Nine Mile 8

Comments. The date of 1145+b (Schulman 1948b: 5) is listed as Nine Mile X in Smiley (1951).

See the comments for Sky House, 94a.

95. KANAB AREA

95a. Cave Du Pont

Dates. Stallings 1941: 3.

Comments. The 217 date (with bark adhering) is associated with Basketmaker II materials.

96. PRAYER ROCK DISTRICT

96a. Broken Flute Cave

Dates. Breternitz (1963: 240–2) modifies some of the details given by E. A. Morris (1959a: 199–201.

Summary of dates. One hundred individual dates, 80 determined by the Laboratory of Tree-Ring Research and 20 obtained by Haury while at Gila Pueblo, are listed in Breternitz (1963: 240–2). The dates range from 354+x to 730, with 75 between 620 and 630. There are no doubt some duplicate dates for the same original timbers.

Sixteen additional dates that appear in the Gila Pueblo files have not been checked or verified by the Tree-Ring Laboratory; therefore they are not cited in Breternitz (1963). They do, however, range from 440+ to *626,* with eight dates between 623 and *626.*

E. A. Morris (1959a: 201) estimates that the various pit houses were constructed as follows: Pit Houses 4, 5, 6, 7, 8, 9, and 12 were built in the decade 620 to 630; Pit House 11 was built in the 640's; and Pit House 3, in the 670's or 680's.

Pottery types. E. A. Morris 1959a: 487, 501–21.

Comments. Broken Flute Cave is considered a type site for Basketmaker III in the Four Corners area. See E. A. Morris (1959a) for a description of the vast amount of material culture recovered.

97. PRAYER ROCK DISTRICT

97a. Obelisk Cave

Dates. Breternitz (1963: 243–4) modified some of the details given by E. A. Morris (1959a: 205).

Summary of dates. The 16 individual dates, ranging from 470 to 489+, represent 14? original timbers.

The Gila Pueblo files also show an additional 15 dates ranging from 436+ to *491,* with 12 dating between 472+ and *491.* These dates have not been verified by the Tree-Ring Laboratory and at least ten of these dates are from timbers noted as having been previously sampled.

Comments. E. A. Morris (1959a: 206) states that "the occupation of Obelisk Cave was either by Basketmaker III people who reused wood collected by Basketmaker II people, or who actually lived in the late 400's." Morris also adds that almost all the Obelisk Gray pottery from the Prayer Rock Caves comes from this cave.

E. A. Morris (1936: 35) states that there is no pottery in the graves in Obelisk Cave.

I consider the dates from this site to belong to the Basketmaker II horizon; unfortunately, the field notes for this very important site have not yet come to light.

98. CANYON DE CHELLY — CANYON DEL MUERTO AREA

General Comments

The University of Colorado Museum is presently engaged in a project sponsored by the National Science Foundation to study the collections made by the late Earl H. Morris. Most of the tree-ring material cited for Canyon de Chelly and Canyon del Muerto was collected by Morris. Analysis of the cultural material from the sites in this area will permit us to make a much more complete and accurate archaeological interpretation of the numerous tree-ring dates.

98a. Mummy Cave

1. TALUS SPECIMENS

Dates. Breternitz 1963: 245; Schulman 1949b: 26.

Comments. The eleven dates, ranging from 380 to 656c, with eight dates between 483±1 and 498, are without provenience or associational information.

2. POST-BASKETMAKER CISTS AND ROOMS

Dates. Breternitz 1963: 246; Schulman 1949b: 26.

Summary of dates. Ten dates from five separate cists or rooms range from 333v to 702c. There is obviously some reuse of beams from former occupation of the cave, but even so, there are six dates between 666c and 702c.

Comments. Until the archaeological content of these cists and rooms is known, any interpretation will be premature.

3. RETAINING WALLS

Summary of dates. A single date of 649 is from a retaining wall in the west center of the talus slope (Breternitz 1963: 247).

Comments. Smiley (1951) lists six dates for the retaining walls, but five of these dates are now identified as being from the Post-Basketmaker cists and rooms, 98a(2).

4. ROOM IN TALUS

Dates. Breternitz 1963: 247; Schulman 1949b: 26.

Comments. All five dates, ranging from 348b to 485vv, are from a pre-Pueblo room with a four-post roof-support and upward and outward sloping masonry walls (E. H. Morris field notes on file at the University of Colorado Museum). No further information is available at this time.

5. TIMBER FROM EAST END

Comments. There is no additional information on the specimen dated 804v (Schulman 1949b: 26).

6. CAVE 1

Summary of dates. Two posts in the north pre-kiva are dated 702+c and 787+vv (Breternitz 1963: 274; Schulman 1949b: 26).

Comments. This pre-kiva is assigned to the Post-Basketmaker period by E. H. Morris (Field Notes on file at the University of Colorado Museum). No other information is available at this time.

7. MUMMY CAVE TOWER

Dates. Breternitz 1963: 248; Douglass 1935: 51; Peterson 1935: 24.

Summary of dates. The 36 dates range from 1251 to 1284. It is conclusive that the second and third floors were built in 1284.

Comments. E. H. Morris (1941: 229) indicates that the tower dates from the Mesa Verde occupation of Mummy Cave would imply the presence of Mesa Verde Black-on-white.

8. PROVENIENCE UNKNOWN

Comments. Little can be said about the 304 and 436vv dates (Schulman 1949b: 26; 1952: 32).

98b. Twin Cave

Dates. Breternitz 1963: 249; Haury 1938: 3.

Summary of dates. The Basketmaker III houses from the west and east caves appear to have been built about 637 and 667 respectively.

Comments. Smiley (1951) lists Twin Cave as being in the Canyon de Chelly area, but the site is in Hospitibito Canyon. See also Vandal Cave, 18a, and Hospitibito, 103f.

There is no additional information on this site; however, it should not be confused with Twin Caves, NA 2536, 15f, in the Tsegi Canyon drainage.

98c. Sliding Ruin, Mindeleff No. 32

Summary of dates. The eight dates range from 834vv to 957(OS), with four dates at 956 and 957 (Douglass 1938: 12; Peterson 1935: 24; Schulman 1949b: 26).

Comments. According to David DeHarport, the site was occupied from Pueblo I through Pueblo III (St. Johns Polychrome present as trade). The beams were reused in the latest occupation; consequently, the data do not warrant further interpretation.

98d. Mindeleff No. 15

Comments. There is no provenience or pottery association information for the single specimen dated 1011+ (Douglass 1935: 51; Peterson 1935: 24).

98e. White House, NA 2187

Dates. Breternitz 1963: 250–1; Douglass 1935: 51; Peterson 1935: 24.

Summary of dates. Sixteen dates range from 957 to 1275, with eight dates between 1071 and 1075.

Pottery types. Breternitz 1963: 251.

Comments. The early pottery types indicate an earlier, underlying occupation. The bulk of the pottery is associated with the main occupation, which apparently falls between 1050 and 1100. The final occupation of White House is characterized by Mesa Verde pottery. (See Three Turkey House, 109a.)

99. MANCOS CANYON AREA

99a. Mancos Canyon, Site 1 (LA 2390)

Summary of dates. The three dates from Room H are 1185+ and two at 1192+ (Reed 1958: 199).

Pottery types. Breternitz 1963: 252; Reed 1943, 1958: 16.

Comments. Reed (1958: 16) characterizes the site as "essentially pure Pueblo II, of the Mancos phase or focus . . . occupied into the beginning of the so-called McElmo development . . ."

Room H seems to have been used around 1200.

99b. Mancos Canyon, Site 4 (LA 2387)

Summary of dates. There is a single date of 993+ from Room F (Reed 1958: 199).

Pottery types. Breternitz 1963: 253; Reed 1943, 1958: 19.

Comments. The single non-cutting date is too early for the associated ceramics even though the "plus" factor is thought to be great.

100. BLANDING AREA

100a. Five Kiva House

Summary of dates. The two bark dates of 1243 are from timbers found in fallen debris (Stallings 1936: 14).

Pottery types. Stallings 1936: 3–4.

Comments. The tree-ring dates apply to the Pueblo III occupation.

101. ALLANTOWN — WHITE MOUND AREA

101a. Allantown

Dates. Breternitz 1963: 254–5; C. F. Miller 1934: 16; 1935: 31; Roberts 1939: 48, 142, 187–8, 259.

Summary of dates. The 27 dates cited in Breternitz (1963: 254–5), ranging from 814 to 1011, include five dates that appear only in Roberts (1939).

Pottery types. Breternitz 1963: 255; Roberts 1940: 20–104, Figs. 8, 22, 43, Pls. 2 *a*, 9 *d*.

Comments. Group 1, Structure 2, constructed in 815 (Roberts 1939: 259), is a Kiatuthlanna phase pit house.

Group 1, Structure 3, built in 867 or soon thereafter (Roberts 1939: 259), is also Kiatuthlanna phase.

Group 2, Structure 12, thought to be a "ceremonial chamber" built in either 870 or 918 (Roberts 1939: 110, 261–2), is also Kiatuthlanna phase.

Group 2, Structure 15, which was built in 888, is Late Developmental Pueblo (Roberts 1939: 139, 259) and probably assignable to the Kiatuthlanna or Red Mesa phase.

Unit 1, Kiva A appears to be a Red Mesa phase structure; however, the large "plus" factor for the tree-ring date of 845+ must be taken into consideration for interpretation. Roberts (1939: 261) discusses Kiva A, but refers to it as Kiva B.

Unit 3, kiva and house are part of "a typical single-clan or unit type of the late Developmental Pueblo period, the stage usually referred to as Pueblo II" (Roberts 1939: 227). Both structures are assigned to the Wingate phase by Gladwin (1945: 76). Roberts (1939: 239) discusses the dates for both Unit 3 structures, but for our purposes it is sufficient to say that they were not only contemporaneous but they were both built within the first few years of the 1000's.

101b. White Mound Village

Summary of dates. The following summary includes only the dates obtained by Haury, as shown in Gladwin (1945: 29):

Section 1, Cist 1 has eight dates ranging from 783+ to *802*, with additional cutting dates of two each at *786*, *793*, and *801*.

Section 1, House 3 has 21 cutting dates between *781* and *790*, with 17 at *786*.

Section 1, Unit 5 has five dates ranging from 671+x to *785*.

Section 3, Post 3 is dated 713+ and Section 3, Post 5 is dated 704+x.

Pottery types. Breternitz 1963: 257–8; Gladwin 1945: 21, Pl. 5.

Comments. White Mound Village, undoubtedly occupied around 800, is the type site for the White Mound phase.

White Mound Village, appearing as 102 in Smiley (1951), has been combined with 101, Allantown, in this paper to permit the use of number 102 for the Lupton area.

102. LUPTON AREA

102a. Box Canyon

Summary of dates. The single date of 666B, from a Pueblo III cliff dwelling, is obviously a reused beam (Breternitz 1963: 258).

Comments. There is no further information for the site or the tree-ring specimen.

102b. Arizona K:12:5 (ASM)

Dates. Breternitz 1963: 258.

Summary of dates. The 17 dates show two definite clusters, one about 1011 and the other about 1119. Since there is evidence for remodeling or reconstruction in this kiva, the interval of almost 100 years between tree-ring clusters is explainable.

Pottery types. Breternitz 1963: 259.

Comments. A preliminary report on this Wingate phase site may be found in Wasley (1960a).

102c. Arizona K:12:6 (ASM)

Dates. Breternitz 1963: 259.

Summary of dates. The construction of the kiva at this Wingate phase site appears to be dated conclusively by the clustering of 12 of the 14 dates at 1123.

Comments. Also applicable to this site are the comments and the pottery type information for Arizona K:12:5, 102b.

103. RED ROCK VALLEY

General Comments

The Red Rock Valley caves (103a–e) are a series of five cave sites in the Prayer Rock district of northeastern Arizona, generally assignable to the Basketmaker III period (see also Broken Flute Cave, 96a, and Obelisk Cave, 97a).

In general, the Red Rock Valley caves appear to have been occupied during the last half of the 600's, or about 50 years later than Broken Flute Cave. See E. A. Morris (1959a) for further discussion and descriptions of other associated material culture.

103a. Red Rock Valley Cave 1

Dates. E. A. Morris 1959a: 201–5.

Summary of dates. Pit House 1: There is one date at 657. Pit House 3: Three dates range from 655 to 668.

103b. Red Rock Valley Cave 2

Dates. E. A. Morris 1959a: 201–5.

Summary of dates. Pit House 1: Twenty-three dates extend from 624 to 759, with 11 dates between 665 and 669c. Both of the 759 dates are from planks. Pit House 2: Seventeen dates range from 641 to 699, with seven between 667 and 669, and four between 673 and 676. One of the two 699 dates is from a plank. Pit House 4: Fifteen dates range from 642 to 666, with 11 between 653 and 659. West ledge and no specific provenience given: Four dates range from 645 to 670, with three dating after 667.

Fourteen of the dates cited were derived by Gila Pueblo, and there is certainly some duplication of dates for specimens also dated by the Laboratory of Tree-Ring Research.

103c. Red Rock Valley Cave 6

Dates. E. A. Morris 1959a: 201–5.

Summary of dates. No provenience is given for the 15 specimens dated from 553vv to 675. Nine dates are either 674 or 675.

103d. Red Rock Valley Cave 7

Dates. E. A. Morris 1959a: 201–5.

Summary of dates. No provenience is given for the two dates at 666 and the single date of 674.

103e. Red Rock Valley Cave 8

Dates. E. A. Morris 1959a: 201–5.
Summary of dates. No provenience is given for the five dates ranging from 637 to 704.
Pottery types. Breternitz 1963: 261.

103f. Hospitibito Canyon

Comments. The single specimen was collected by the Bernheimer Expedition of 1930. The specimen is *not* from the Red Rock Valley, but from beyond the divide in the Chinle Wash drainage. Bernheimer's (1930: 24) description makes it clear that if this tree-ring specimen is not actually from Vandal Cave, 18a, Painted Cave, or Twin Cave, 98b, it is at least from another site in the immediate vicinity. Consequently, the single date of 1229 (Douglass 1938: 12) is of little interpretive value.

103g. Prayer Rock Cove

Comments. Prayer Rock Cove is listed as Prayer Rock Cave in Smiley (1951).

Four dates from the site are 1238±, 1261?, 1273?, and 1277 (Breternitz 1963: 262; Douglass 1938: 12).

The field notes of E. H. Morris for September 9, 1931 (on file at the University of Colorado Museum) state that the pottery and the fallen roof timbers not only pertain to the Pueblo III horizon in the site but that the black-on-white pottery appears to be peripheral Mesa Verde.

104. FORESTDALE VALLEY

104a. Bluff Ruin, Arizona P:16:20 (ASM)

Dates. Douglass 1944: 13; Haury and Sayles 1947.

Information on Smiley's recent reexamination of the Bluff ruin tree-ring specimens is listed in Breternitz (1963: 263–4).

Summary of dates. A total of 12 dates, representing 11(?) trees, range from 265 to 329v. Seven dates are in the 300's. The duplicate dates for the specimens from the great kiva dating 306v, 320v, and 329v account for the 31 dates listed in Smiley (1951).
Pottery types. Haury and Sayles 1947: 15, 18, 22, 24, 54, 56, 60.
Comments. All the dated structures at the Bluff ruin are Hilltop phase. The tree-ring evidence indicates construction activity in the early 300's.

104b. Bear Ruin, Arizona P:16:1 (ASM)

Dates. Haury 1940a; 1940b.

Information on Smiley's recent reexamination of the Bear ruin tree-ring specimens is contained in Breternitz (1963: 265).

Summary of dates. Eight dates range from 641v to 713+, with five dates at 662v to 668v. Occupation of all three dated structures appears to be contemporaneous, during the last half of the 7th century and into the 8th century.
Pottery types. Haury 1940a: 20–2, 43–7, 68, 79, 120–1.
Comments. The dated structures of Bear ruin are assigned to the Forestdale phase.

104c. Arizona P:16:2 (ASM)

Dates. Haury 1940a: 33–4; Haury 1940b: 15; Smiley 1950: 23.

Dates obtained from a recent reexamination of the Arizona P:16:2 tree-ring specimens are listed in Breternitz (1963: 266–7).

Summary of dates. Thirty-one dates range from 1008vv to 1115vv, with 14 between 1070+ and 1098+, and 15 between 1100+ and 1115+. It seems safe to say that the site was built and occupied during the last quarter of the 11th century and the first quarter of the 12th century.
Pottery types. Breternitz 1963: 267–8.
Comments. Haury (1950: 34) estimates that the great kiva at Arizona P:16:2 was constructed about 1125.

105. WINGATE SITES

105a. Wingate 11:47 (GP)

Summary of dates. Five posts in the windbreak at the south end of the house (Room 4) give non-cutting dates ranging from 806+x to 872+x (Breternitz 1963: 268; Gladwin 1945: 59), with the latter date probably being the one published as 892+x (Haury 1938: 3).
Pottery types. Breternitz 1963: 268.
Comments. Occupation of the site around 900 seems likely. Gladwin (1945: 60) obtained a cutting date of *902* from another specimen, which was not verified by other tree-ring workers. Whatever the actual calendar date of construction and occupation, Wingate 11:47 is a Red Mesa phase site.

105b. Wingate 11:49 (GP)

Summary of dates. Haury's two dates from the trash mound (rubbish-filled pit?) are 863+x and 880+ (Gladwin 1945: 60; Haury 1938: 3).
Pottery types. Breternitz 1963: 269.
Comments. Gladwin (1945: 60–1), upon returning to the site, collected additional tree-ring specimens, one of which he dated at *922*. Occupation of this Red Mesa phase site (about 900) appears to be contemporaneous with Wingate 11:47, 105a.

105c. Wingate 11:60 (GP)

Summary of dates. Twenty-three dates, obtained by Gladwin (1945: 61) and not verified by other tree-ring workers, range from 868+ to *916*. The earliest cutting date is *879* with a concentration between *888* and *893*; however, no specific provenience is given for any of the dated specimens.
Pottery types. Breternitz 1963: 270.
Comments. Wingate 11:60 (a Red Mesa phase site) is, with reference to architecture, ceramics, and temporal position, a counterpart of Wingate 11:47, 105a, and Wingate 11:49, 105b.

106. MOGOLLON VILLAGE

106a. Mogollon Village, Mogollon 1:15 (GP)

Dates. Haury 1936a: 16, 18, 20, 23.
Summary of dates. Thirty-four of the 36 dates are cutting dates. Presumably construction and occupation of all four pit houses falls between 896 and 908.
Pottery types. Breternitz 1963: 271; Haury 1936a: 16, 18, 20, 101.
Comments. All four houses are assigned to the San Francisco phase, but House 2, at least, is considered to be transitional San Francisco–Three Circle phase (Wheat 1955: 172).

107. STARKWEATHER RUIN

107a. Starkweather Ruin

Dates. Breternitz 1963: 271–2; Haury 1938: 3.
Summary of dates. The three dates, from two pit houses, are all 927. Pit House I is labeled both Mogollon 3, San Francisco phase, and Mogollon 4, Three Circle phase, by Wheat (1955, Tables 5, 17), but the structure is obviously assignable to the latter phase. Pit House R is also called Mogollon 3 by Wheat (1955, Table 4), but it, too, is almost certainly a Three Circle phase pit house.
Pottery types. Breternitz 1963: 272; Nesbitt 1938: 79, 81.
Comments. The dates and the ceramics compare nicely with the information from the dated Three Circle phase structures at Wheatley Ridge, 78c, and Mogollon Village, 106a.

108. NATURAL BRIDGES NATIONAL MONUMENT AREA

108a. Natural Bridges Area

Comments. There is no site provenience or associational information for the single specimen dated 675vv (Schulman 1950b: 21).

109. THREE TURKEY HOUSE

109a. Three Turkey House, NA 1747 and NA 3467

Summary of dates. There are two bark dates, one at 1266 from the main roof beam of the kiva, and one at 1276 from a log in Room 15 (Colton 1939b: 26; 1939c: 28).
Pottery types. Colton 1939c: 29.
Comments. Three Turkey House is a Mesa Verde site (Colton 1939c: 31) from which all the associated non-Mesa Verde pottery types are designated as tradewares.

110. SHUMWAY AREA

110a. Shumway, Arizona P:12:6 (ASM)

Dates. Breternitz 1963: 274.
Summary of dates. The seven dates, all without provenience information, range from 916 to 938, with no apparent clustering.
Comments. The ASM Survey Collection has sherds representing a much longer time span than that of the tree-ring dates, but without any provenience information, the site has no interpretive value.

111. NAVAJO MOUNTAIN AREA

111a. Little Granary House, NA 4083

Summary of dates. No specific provenience is

given for the single date of 1259 (Douglass 1938: 11).

Pottery types. Breternitz 1963: 274–5.

Comments. Little Granary House may be the same site as NA 4209 or PE 7 (see Taylor 1958: 4). The single date and the doubtful identification of the site make interpretation difficult even though the pottery types and the tree-ring date appear to be coeval.

111b. Double-Walled Ruin, NA 4207

Summary of dates. The one date of 1189± is from Room 10 (Breternitz 1963: 275).

Pottery types. Breternitz 1963: 275.

Comments. Again, the single date is difficult to interpret in view of the wide range of pottery types present at the site.

A description of the unusual double-walled kiva is in preparation (Miller, Breternitz, and Euler: MS).

111c. Red House, NA 2655

Summary of dates. There is no provenience for the three dates of 1117, 1140, and 1143 (Breternitz 1963: 276).

Pottery types. Breternitz 1963: 276.

Comments. Hargrave's (1935: 40) statement that the site was apparently occupied during both Pueblo II and III is borne out by the sherd collection.

111d. Lost Mesa Ruin or Segazlin Ruin, NA 4075

Summary of dates. Six dates, which come from a room, the kiva, and an unknown location, range from 1264vv to 1284B (Breternitz 1963: 277).

Pottery types. Breternitz 1963: 277.

Comments. The tree-ring dates and the ceramics indicate occupation in the last half of the 13th century.

111e. Cactus Rock Pueblo, NA 5815

Summary of dates. All five dates, from kiva construction beams, are in the early 1260's (Breternitz 1963: 277).

Pottery types. Breternitz 1963: 277.

Comments. Both the pottery types and the tree-ring dates indicate occupation of the site in the last half of the 13th century.

111f. Lost Mesa, NA 7519A

Summary of dates. A total of 14 dates from five rooms range from 1223v to 1275v, with seven of the dates falling after 1260 (Breternitz 1963: 278).

Pottery types. Breternitz 1963: 278–9.

Comments. Both the pottery types and the tree-ring information indicate occupation in the last half of the 1200's.

111g. Lost Mesa, NA 7520B

Summary of dates. All three dates from the floor of Room 6a are 1268 (Breternitz 1963: 279).

Pottery types. Breternitz 1963: 279.

Comments. Room 6, built in 1268, and the pottery found on its floor are coeval.

111h. NA 7549

Summary of dates. One tree-ring specimen from the floor of Kiva 1 is dated 1204vv (Breternitz 1963: 279).

Pottery types. Breternitz 1963: 279.

Comments. The single date is difficult to interpret; however, Kiva 1 seems to have been used for an unknown number of years after 1204.

112. VAQUEROS CANYON SITES

112a–c. Vaqueros Canyon, Site 1 (LA 2120)

Dates. Breternitz 1963: 280–1; Hall 1944: 8, 11–4, 83.

Summary of dates. House A (112a): The 13 dates, all from roofing material, range from 777 to 855. Five of the individual dates may be from only two original timbers. Hall estimates construction at 780, with repairs to 856.

House B (112b): Eight dates range from 710 to 821+, with perhaps some duplicate dates for the same specimens. The two oldest dates, 710 and 714, are from under the latest floor; the six most recent dates, 745+ to 821+, are from fallen roof beams of the latest roof. Hall suggests reuse of an old pit house depression for the original construction about 712 to 745, with final construction and repair at 821+.

House C (112c): The 26 dates from a variety of locations within the pit house are probably roofing material for the most part; they range from 702 to 875. Hall suggests construction at 801 or 802, with repairs until 875 or 876.

Pottery types. Breternitz 1963: 281; Hall 1944: 8, 11, 13, 71.

Comments. Smiley (1951) also lists these three houses as Gob-1, 43m.

All three houses are assigned to the Rosa phase. According to Hall's interpretation, House B is the oldest, House A next in age, and House C the youngest – all with overlapping periods of occupation. The period of construction, occupation and repair for each of these houses was about 75 years.

112d–h. Vaqueros Canyon, Site 12 (LA 2122)

Dates. Breternitz 1963: 281–2; Hall 1944: 22, 25, 27, 83–4.

Summary of dates. House A (112d): The nine individual dates, which range from 811 to 866, are probably from five beams with dates of 811, 834, 863, 865, and 866. Eight of the dates have no provenience, the ninth is from the floor. Hall estimates construction at 811 or 812, with repairs until 866+.

House B (112e): The 15 dates range from 791 to 864 and may include some duplicates. Hall estimates construction at 791 or 792, with repairs up to 864 or 865.

House D (112f): There appear to be only two beams, dated 840 and 850, represented by three individual dates. The Museum of New Mexico files indicate that the fourth date (Hall 1944: 84, Specimen 202) is actually from House B. Hall's estimated construction date of 854±5 appears to be valid.

Surface Structure 1 (112g): There is a single date of 875 with no specific provenience. The Museum of New Mexico files indicate that the second date listed by Hall (1944: 84, Specimen 141) is from House A. House D is partly under Surface Structure 1 and thus earlier. There is a 25 year difference in the end dates of the tree-ring specimens from the two units.

Surface Structure 2 (112h): Four of the six dates, from the fire pit west of Surface Structure 2, are apparently from the same original timber, with 850 being the latest date. No provenience is given for the other two dates of 841 and 848. The seventh date (Hall 1944: 84, Specimen 210) is actually from House B.

Pottery types. Breternitz 1963: 283; Hall 1944: 22, 25, 27, 71.

Comments. Smiley (1951) also lists these five structures as Gob-12, 43n.

Estimated construction dates for the five dated structures, all assigned to the Rosa phase, extend from 791 to 875. Pit Houses A and B were occupied for 50 to 75 years. The dated structures are roughly contemporaneous, with the notable exception of the superposition of Surface Structure 1 over part of House D.

The tree-ring dates and the ceramic associations are very similar to those seen at Site 1, LA 2120, 112a–c.

112i. Vaqueros Canyon, Site 11 (LA 2121)

Summary of dates. Hall (1944: 18) says that for House A there are 50 individual dates from six beams, ranging from 850+x to 876, with two at 876. In a later publication, Hall (1951: 27) cites 14 dates between 779 and 874±3, but there is no explanation of the dates. It seems safe to assume construction or repair in about 875 for House A.

Pottery types. Breternitz 1963: 284; Hall 1944: 18, 71.

Comments. Both the ceramics and the tree-ring dates show that House A is coeval with the Rosa phase units at Vaqueros Canyon, Site 1, 112a–c, and Site 12, 112d–h.

113. BIG BEAD MESA

113a. Big Bead Mesa

Comments. This Navajo site has produced tree-ring dates in the 17th and 18th centuries (Hall 1951: 27).

114. RED BUTTE AREA

114a. Red Butte, NA 5166C

Dates. The dates listed by Mc.Gregor (1951: 20) have been superseded by those from Smiley's (1951) reexamination of the tree-ring material (see Breternitz 1963: 285).

Summary of dates. Nine of the 13 dates fall between 768vv and 775c, with the latter inter-

preted as the building date for the house.
Pottery types. Mc.Gregor 1951: 31–2.
Comments. NA 5166C, a Naylier phase house and the earliest structure excavated in the Red Butte area, was reoccupied at least twice after original construction (Mc.Gregor 1951: 56–7). This factor no doubt accounts for the variety of pottery types found. Although the original construction is well dated around 775, we cannot apply this date to most of the pottery types found at the site.

115. TOHATCHI AREA

115a. LA 2505

Summary of dates. The two dates, 1020c and 1047b, are from stringers covering the ventilator tunnel of Kiva B (Bullard and Cassidy 1956: 46–7, 51).
Pottery types. Bullard and Cassidy 1956: 51.
Comments. The kiva seems to have been used around 1050.

116. TESUQUE VALLEY AREA

116a. Tesuque Valley Ruin, LA 742

Comments. Smiley, Stubbs, and Bannister 1953: 35–6.

117. RIO PUEBLO COLORADO AREA

117a. NA 3941A

Dates. Breternitz 1963: 286.
Summary of dates. The 18 dates range from 546v to 639C, the latter probably indicating the construction date.
Pottery types. E. A. Morris 1959a: 574–5.
Comments. NA 3941A is a Basketmaker III pit house.

118. CANYON PADRE AREA

118a. Wilson Pueblo, NA 1139

Dates. Breternitz 1963: 287; Harlan 1962: 48.
Summary of dates. The 1176 and the two 1178 dates may be from the same original timber. There are additional dates of 1157 and 1248. None of the specimens has provenience information.
Pottery types. Colton 1946: 91.
Comments. Obviously, the tree-ring dates apply to the pueblo and not the brush shelter at NA 1139. All but the latest date, in the 1200's, are within the range of the ceramic dates of 1150 to 1200 assigned to the pueblo by Colton (1946: 92).

119. VERNON AREA

119a. Table Rock Pueblo

Summary of dates. The single date of 1331+ is from Kiva 2 (Martin and Rinaldo 1960: 288).
Pottery types. Breternitz 1963: 288.
Comments. Further details and discussion may be found in Martin and Rinaldo (1960).

120. CASAS GRANDES AREA

General Comments

This number is reserved for material from the main site at Casas Grandes (Paquime), Chihuahua D:9:1 (AF) and the Convento site, Chihuahua D:9:2 (AF). Recently, a 500 or more year chronology has been tied into known dendrochronological sequences and the Christian calendar. In the near future, a large amount of material will be available for interpretive purposes.

121. NAVAJO RESERVOIR DISTRICT

121a. LA 4086

Dates. Breternitz 1963: 289.
Summary of dates. Evidence is conclusive that Feature 14 was built in 881 and repaired in 888.
Comments. Feature 14 is a Piedra phase(?) pit house whose pottery is probably similar to that found at sites LA 4195 (121b), LA 4380 (121c), and LA 4408 (121d).

The feature numbers given here are field designations that will appear in publication with appropriate descriptive terms.

121b. Sambrito Village, LA 4195

Dates. Breternitz 1963: 290.
Summary of dates. A total of 34 dates range from 874vv to 899c, with 15 dates after 894r.
Pottery types. Breternitz 1963: 290.
Comments. LA 4195 is a Piedra phase site.

121c. LA 4380

Dates. Breternitz 1963: 291.
Summary of dates. The ten dates range from 853vv to 900r, with seven dates falling after 879+v. Dates are within the same general time

range as LA 4086 (121a), LA 4195 (121b), and LA 4408 (121d) – all Piedra phase sites.

Pottery types. Breternitz 1963: 291.

Comments. The feature numbers given in Breternitz (1963: 291) will differ somewhat in the final publication.

121d. Serrano Site, LA 4408

Dates. Breternitz 1963: 291; Hester 1963: 77.

Summary of dates. The nine dates fall within the same time range as the other Piedra phase sites in the Navajo Reservoir District. Construction in the late 800's is probable, with 898 the most likely date.

Pottery types. Breternitz (1963: 292) is superseded by Hester (1963: 58).

Comments. The tree-ring dates are from four superimposed pit houses, *all* of which are Piedra phase.

122. ZIA PUEBLO

122a. Zia Pueblo, LA 28

Comments. This is a post-Spanish contact site. Smiley, Stubbs, and Bannister 1953: 47.

THE MASTER TREE-RING DATE CHART

Table 3 summarizes the distribution of tree-ring dates from all the Southwestern archaeological sites considered in this paper. Some of the sites mentioned in Chapter 2 are not shown on Table 3 because either they have tree-ring dates associated with preceramic periods, specifically Basketmaker II, or they date from the post-Spanish contact period.

The sites are arranged from early to late on the basis of the concentrations and clusters of tree-ring dates, without regard to the order of site and site-area numbers used in Chapter 2.

Different sections or periods at the same site are shown separately when this specific information is available and useful for interpretive purposes. For example, Pueblo Largo, 4a, and the Point of Pines ruin, 79a, both have tree-ring dates associated with different groups of archaeological material; thus, these tree-ring dates are plotted separately.

When there is no specific information on the tree-ring date provenience or the associated pottery, the tree-ring dates from the particular sites are treated as a group. For example, there is specific provenience information for the tree-ring dates from Broken Flute Cave, 96a, but there is no information on the specific pottery from each of the dated pit houses. Also, it is not possible to correlate the mass of tree-ring dates from Pueblo Bonito, 53c, with specific pottery associations.

Explanation of the notes in Table 3. Notes, designated by Arabic numerals, refer to the following comments:

1. Modified after Smiley, Stubbs, and Bannister (1953: 39).
2. After Smiley, Stubbs, and Bannister (1953: 39), with new tree-ring dates.
3. Flagstaff region site which should date post-Sunset Crater eruption?
4. Flagstaff region site with ceramics indicating that it is post-Sunset Crater eruption.
5. Flagstaff region site with ceramics indicating that it is pre-Sunset Crater eruption.
6. Modified after Bannister (1965: 200).
7. After Bannister (1965: 200), with new tree-ring dates.
8. Additional information on distribution, concentrations, and provenience of tree-ring dates not available.
9. All tree-ring dates were obtained by Gila Pueblo and have not been verified by the Laboratory of Tree-Ring Research; see comments for site, Chapter 2.
10. Does not include definite Basketmaker II tree-ring dates.
11. Some, but not all, dates shown on chart were obtained by Gila Pueblo; see comments for site, Chapter 2.
12. Includes some Gila Pueblo dates not verified by the Laboratory of Tree-Ring Research; see comments for site, Chapter 2.

Key to symbols on the Master Tree-Ring Date Chart. The symbols showing tree-ring date distributions (modified after Bannister 1965: 200) are explained at the end of Table 3.

TABLE 3

MASTER TREE-RING DATE CHART

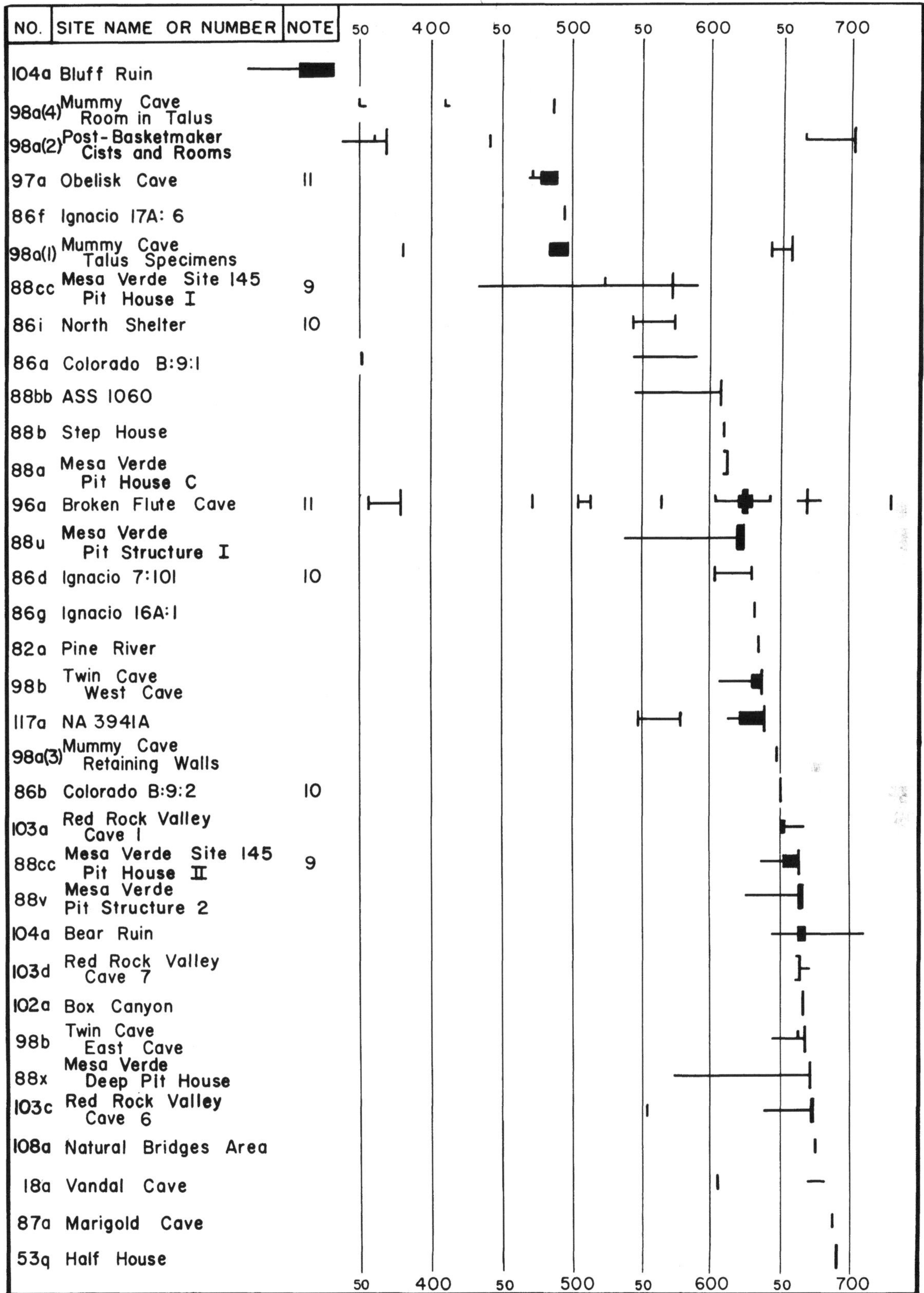

TABLE 3

MASTER TREE-RING DATE CHART (Cont.)

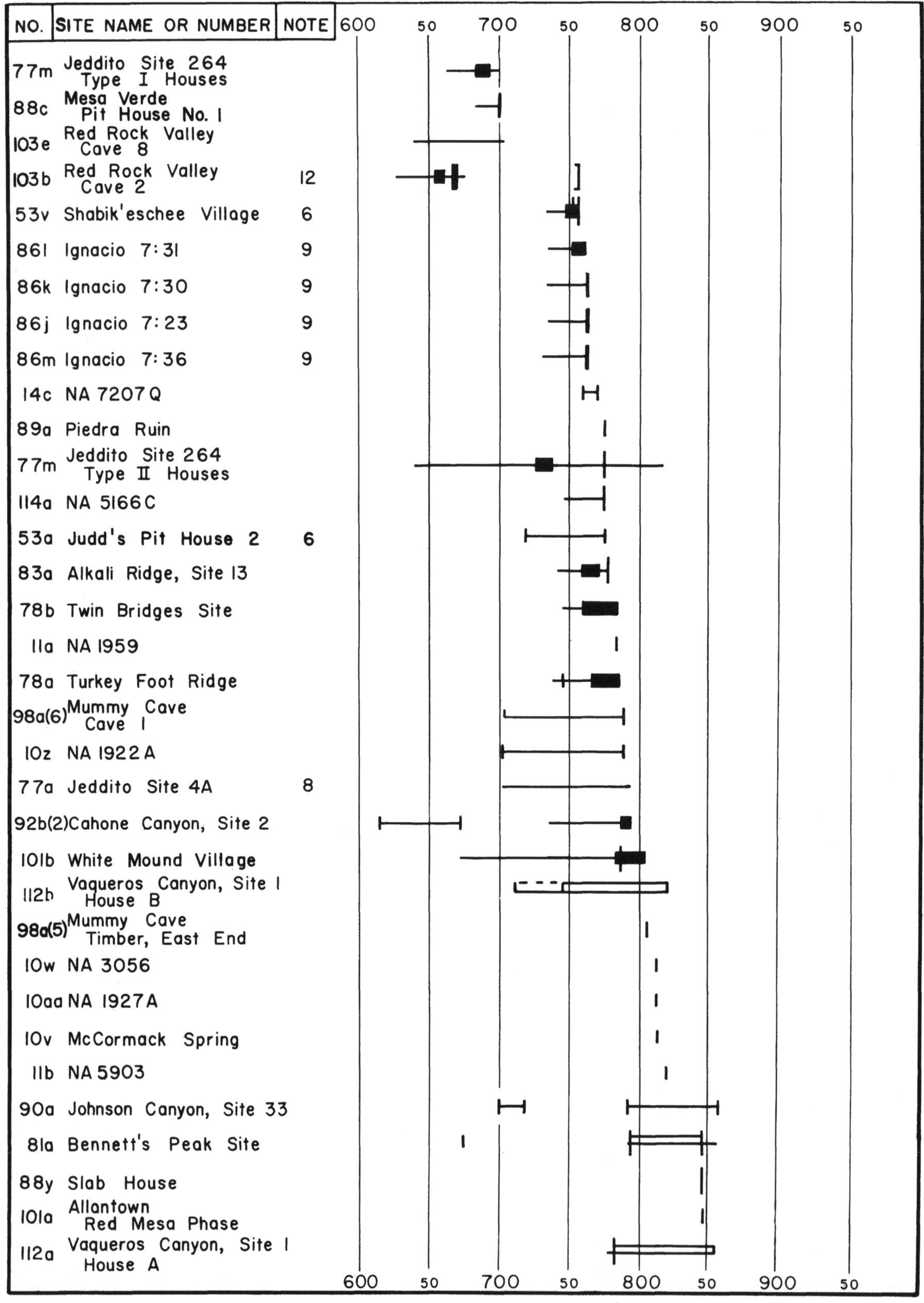

TABLE 3
MASTER TREE-RING DATE CHART (Cont.)

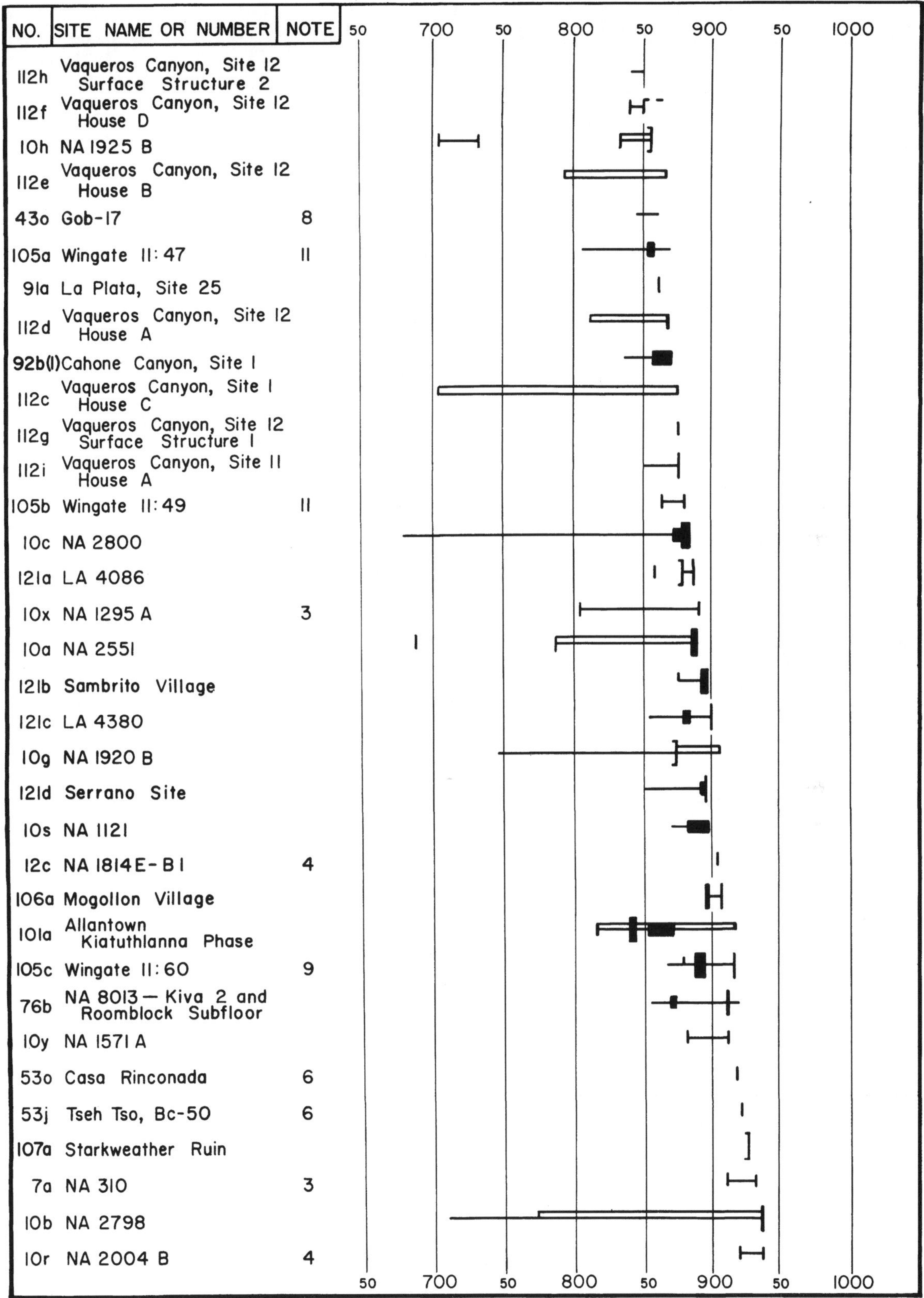

TABLE 3

MASTER TREE-RING DATE CHART (Cont.)

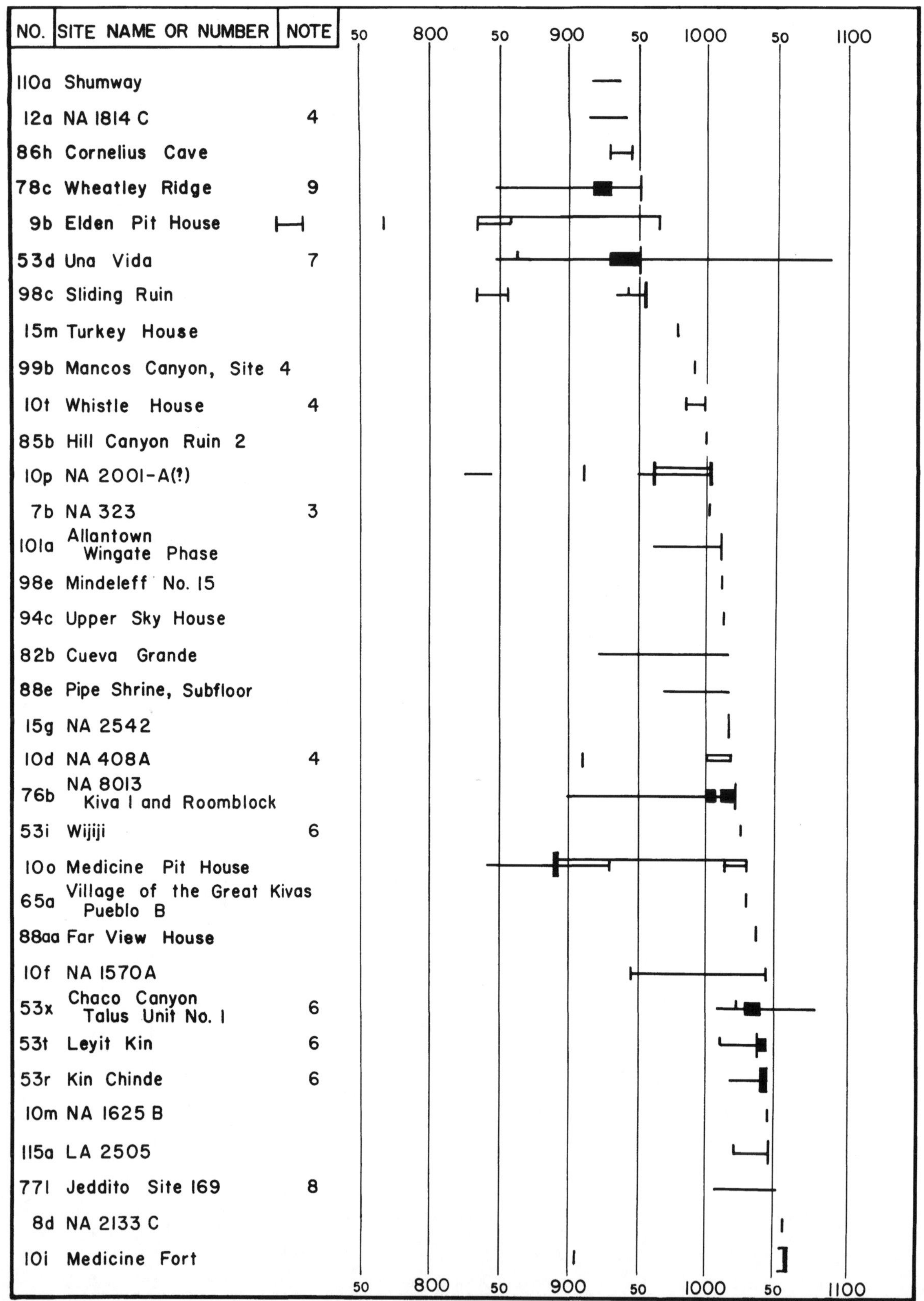

TABLE 3

MASTER TREE-RING DATE CHART (Cont.)

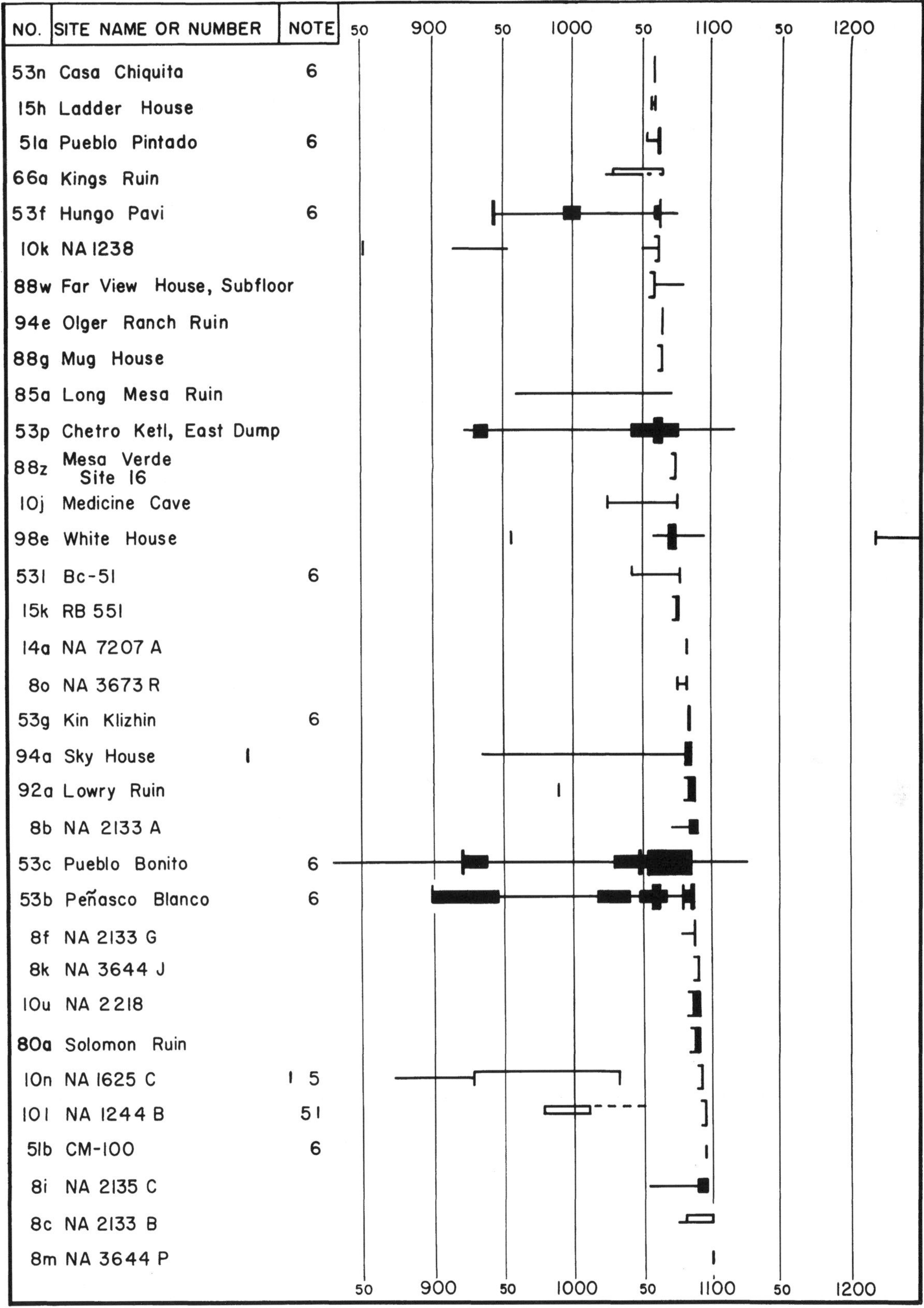

TABLE 3

MASTER TREE-RING DATE CHART (Cont.)

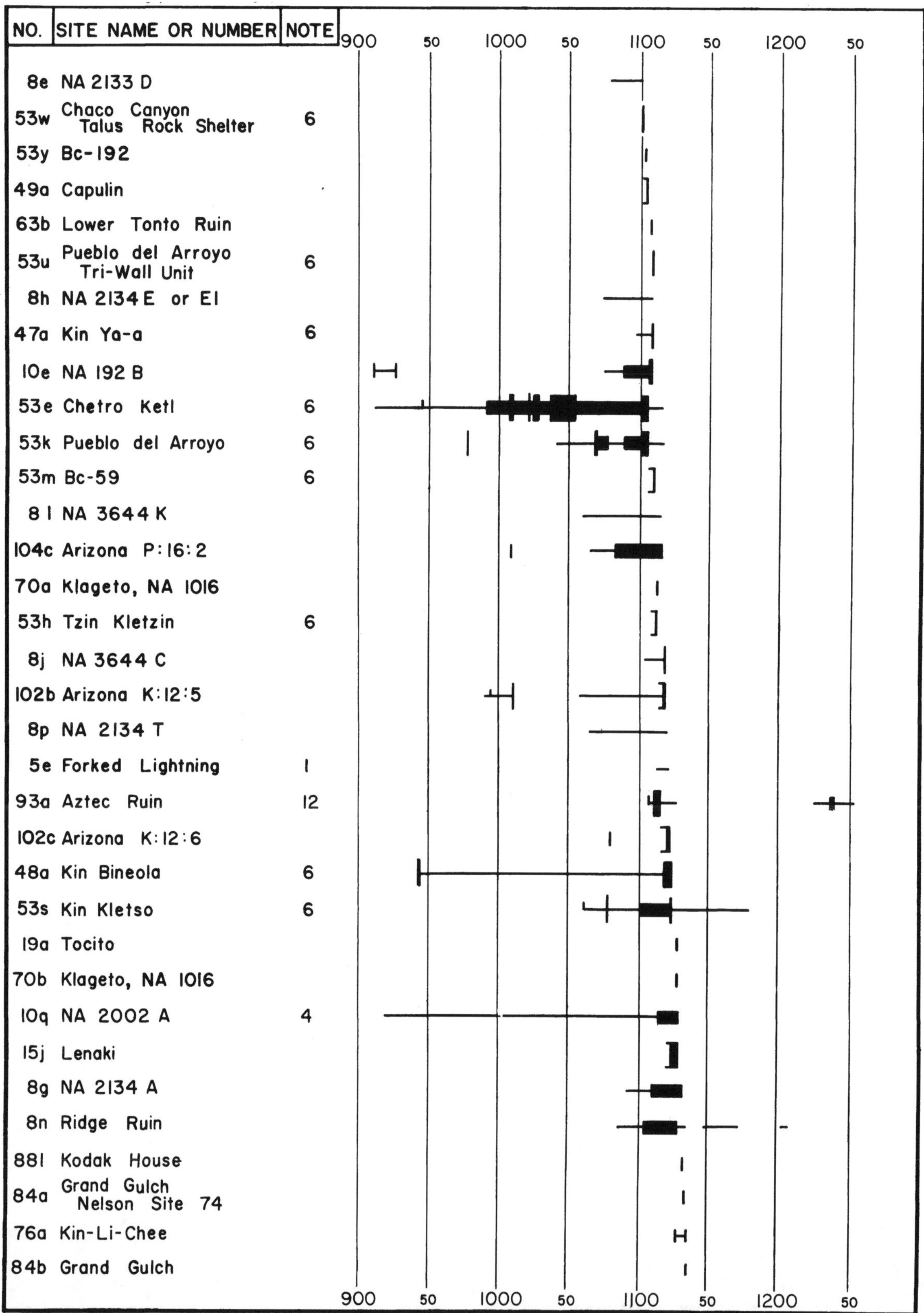

TABLE 3

MASTER TREE-RING DATE CHART (Cont.)

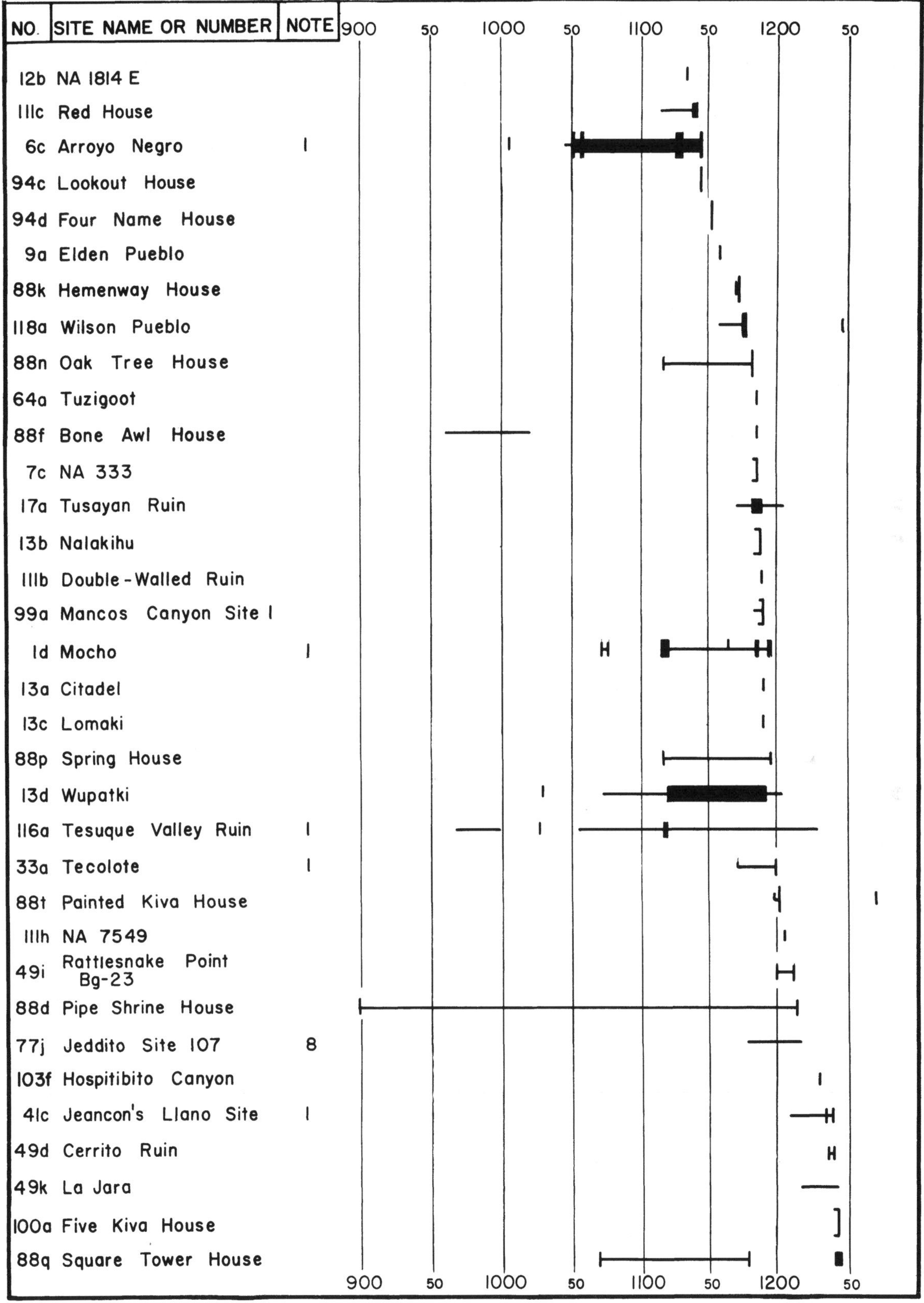

TABLE 3

MASTER TREE-RING DATE CHART (Cont.)

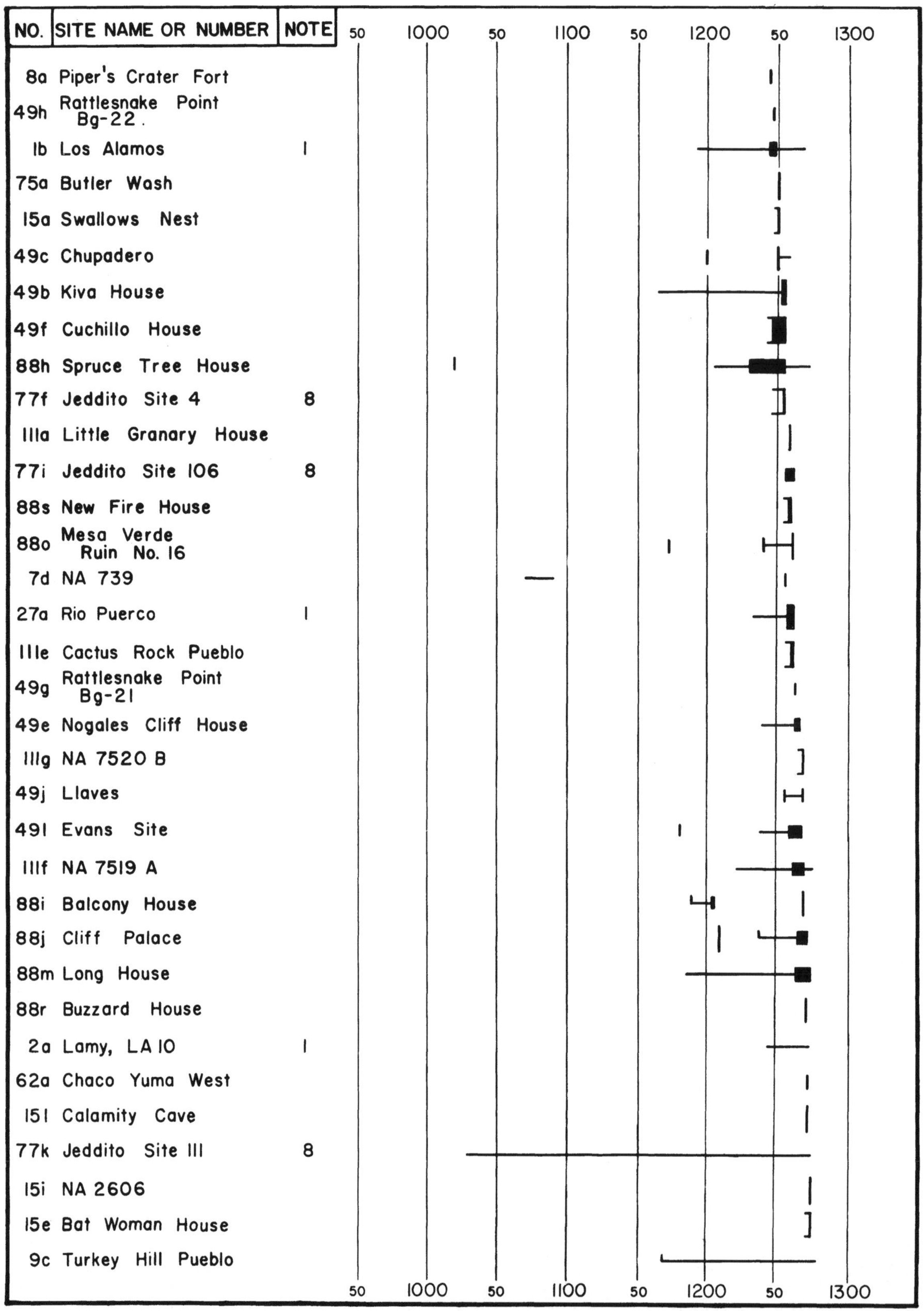

TABLE 3

MASTER TREE-RING DATE CHART (Cont.)

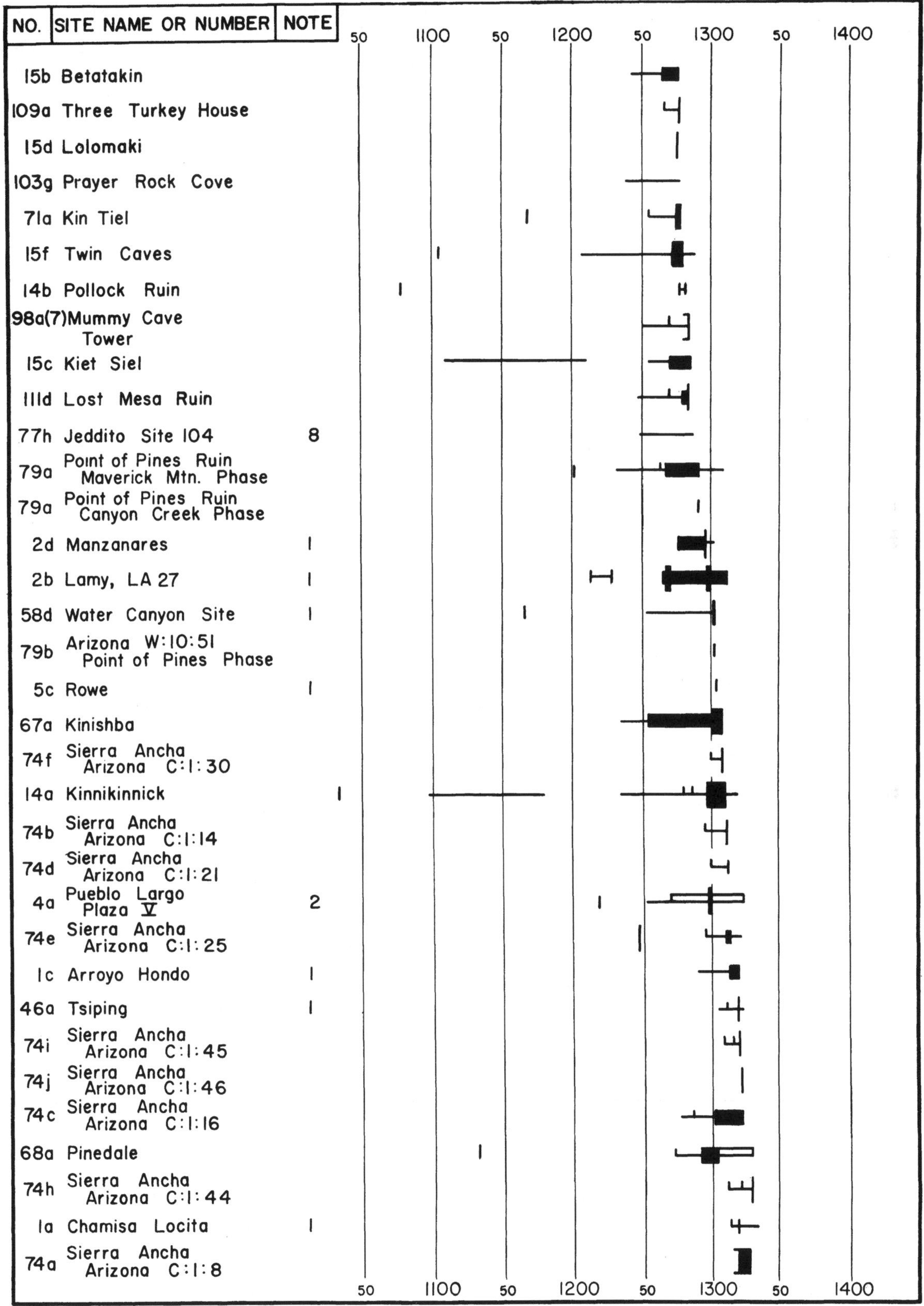

TABLE 3

MASTER TREE-RING DATE CHART (Cont.)

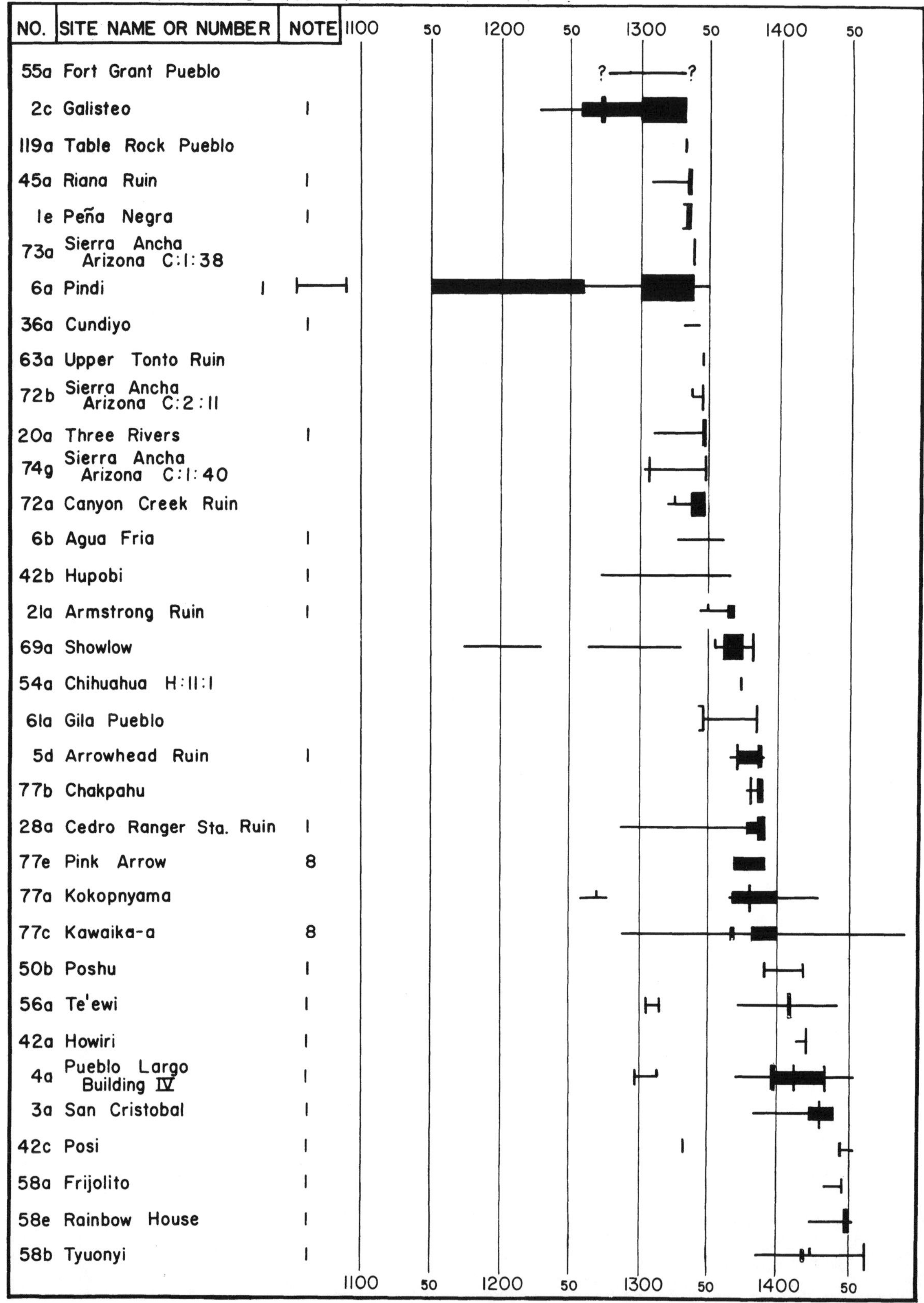

TABLE 3

MASTER TREE-RING DATE CHART (Cont.)

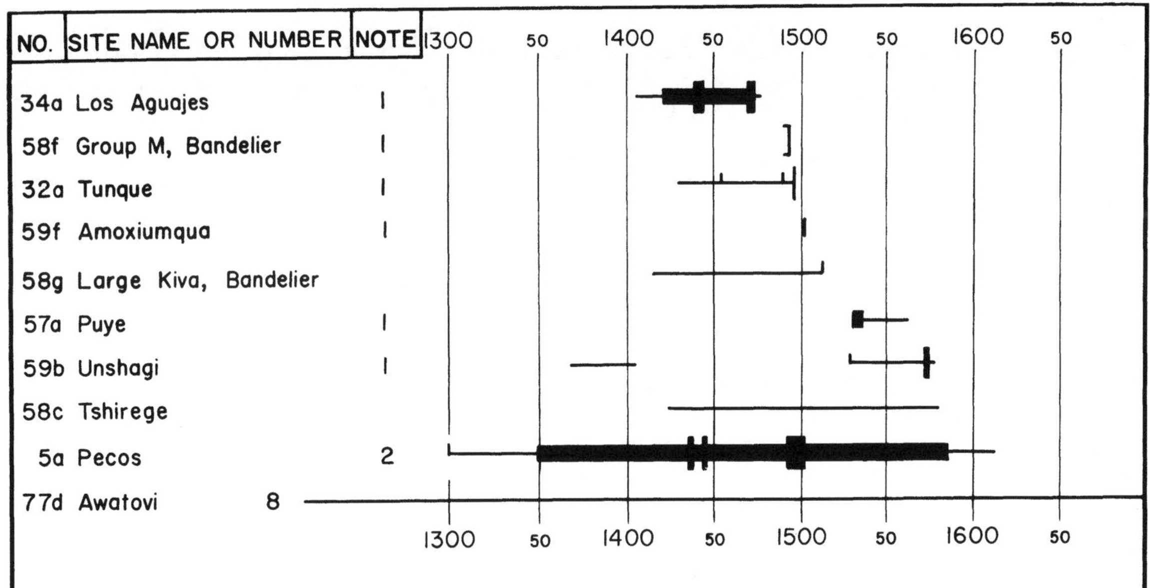

Key to Symbols (Modified after Bannister 1959)

- Single non-cutting date.
- Range of only two non-cutting dates.
- Range of more than two non-cutting dates.
- Single cutting date or latest cutting date.
- Cutting date or earliest cutting date.
- Single cluster of dates.
- Concentration of dates.
- Cluster of dates.
- Probable minimum period of occupation of site, building, pit house, or room.

3. THE USE OF ASSOCIATED TREE-RING SPECIMENS FOR DATING POTTERY TYPES AND CERAMIC STYLES

THE DENDROCHRONOLOGICAL DATA presented in Chapter 2 may now be used to illustrate certain principles and ideas concerning the possibilities for the dating of pottery types and ceramic styles. The tree-ring information from individual sites and site components may be discussed in terms of potential application as a dating tool. Examples of good and poor dating validity may be cited, utilizing the interpretation of the archaeological association of tree-ring specimens and ceramics.

The examples to be discussed indicate the range of dating validity that is presently available; graphic presentations of dating situations indicate the method used to determine the dates for the pottery considered in Chapter 4.

DATING POTTERY TYPES

A "pottery type" has already been defined as a group of vessels that are alike in every important characteristic, including techniques of manufacture, methods of decoration, and kinds of decoration. This definition also applies to potsherds, which are fragments of ceramic containers, as well as to complete vessels.

The concept of "pottery type," which is widely used in Southwestern archaeology, is the common category of classification and description used for field and laboratory analysis of archaeological ceramics. Pottery types are the common denominator for comparison and synthesis. Individual potsherds or vessels may be "typed" differently by various archaeologists, but the disagreement will be within the framework of the "pottery type" concept. In this paper the "pottery type" concept is considered to be a valid, definable unit of analysis and description.

The dating of the individual tree-ring specimens is also accepted as valid, unless qualified in the text of Chapter 2 and in Table 3.

Pottery types and tree-ring dates are the basis for the next step in analysis: determining the validity of the archaeological association of these two categories of information. The validity is determined, ranked, and quantified with varying

TABLE 4

SYMBOLS USED TO INDICATE THE TYPE OF VALIDITY-ASSOCIATION OF SPECIFIC POTTERY TYPES SHOWN IN TABLE 6 AND CHAPTER 4

Site-Area Number	*Auxiliary Symbol*	*Meaning of Auxiliary Symbol*
178	None	Pottery type present.
178	*	Dominant pottery type within either indigenous or trade category.
178	(?)	Identification of pottery type uncertain, or uncertainty as to indigenous or trade assignment; see specific text reference in Breternitz (1963: 17–306).
178	@	Presence of pottery inferred from information available from site of similar time period in vicinity *or* identified from illustrations in literature not utilizing current terminology.
178	–	Not much weight should be placed on the site or the tree-ring dates for pottery association interpretation; see specific text reference in Breternitz (1963: 17–306).

degrees of reliability primarily on the basis of the archaeological interpretation of this association.

The symbols in Table 4 indicate the kind or type of validity-association of pottery types found in archaeological situations. It should be obvious that a pottery type which is a dominant type within either the indigenous or trade category (see introductory paragraphs of Chapter 4 for discussion of the indigenous and trade categories) is much more valuable for interpretive purposes than the mere suggestion that a pottery type is probably present at a site.

The code symbols in Table 5 indicate the validity-provenience for both tree-ring specimens and pottery types. This validity is determined, in each instance, on the basis of the archaeological associations of the specific pottery and the tree-ring specimens.

The code letters and numbers in Table 5 may appear in the following combinations:

A1
A2
A3 B3 C3 } NOTE: Z may appear, but only as a
A4 B4 C4 } part of the code combinations: AZ3, AZ4, BZ3, BZ4, CZ3, CZ4.

For interpretive purposes *A* represents a higher degree of validity than either *B* or *C*; the lower the accompanying number, the more the pottery association may be emphasized. The appearance of *Z* in any of the code combinations indicates that the reliability of the association between the tree-ring dates and the pottery is in doubt; reference should be made to the pertinent notations for the site in Chapter 2 or Breternitz (1963).

The interpretation of the distribution of the tree-ring dates for any site or site component is based on the graphic presentation shown in the Master Tree-Ring Date Chart, Table 3.

St. Johns Polychrome will illustrate the application to archaeological interpretation of the validity-association of pottery types (Table 4), the validity-provenience of tree-ring dates and pottery (Table 5), and the range and clusters of tree-ring dates (Table 3).

Table 6 shows graphically the occurrences and associations of St. Johns Polychrome which are used to "date" this pottery type in Chapter 4. The recorded occurrences of St. Johns Polychrome are designated either indigenous or trade and then ranked on the basis of the validity code (Table 5), with the most valid associations (in both categories) listed first. Within any one validity code symbol, *A*1 for example, the sites where St. Johns Polychrome is present are listed in sequence from older to younger on the basis of tree-ring date concentrations. Consequently, the first sites listed are weighted more heavily for dating and interpretive purposes.

TABLE 5

SYMBOLS USED TO INDICATE THE VALIDITY-PROVENIENCE OF TREE-RING DATES AND POTTERY

Validity-Provenience Code

Tree-Ring Dates	*Pottery Types*
A – Dates for specific architectural feature, with associated pottery.	1 – Floor vessels or sherds from architectural feature with tree-ring dates.
B – Dates for specific architectural feature, *not* correlated with pottery.	2 – Pottery from specific architectural feature with tree-ring dates; generally a fill provenience but may include floor ceramics.
C – Dates from site; no specific provenience.	3 – Pottery from site collection or identified specifically in literature; no specific provenience or no specific association with tree-ring dates.
Z – Later tree-ring dates from site obviously not in association with pottery type under discussion; see text in Breternitz (1963: 17–306).	4 – Pottery inferred from similar nearby sites or from the literature.

Within the indigenous category the maximum range of tree-ring dates from sites having St. Johns Polychrome is 1031+ to 1307, with no definite concentration of tree-ring dates. The maximum range of tree-ring dates for the trade category is 963+ to 1612+ with a concentration of dates between 1200 and about 1300. Using the tree-ring evidence alone, St. Johns Polychrome is probably best dated between 1200 and 1300; however, for ultimately dating this pottery type (as presented in Chapter 4), other factors may be taken into consideration in order to arrive at a more valid date, or to qualify or justify the date that was determined on the basis of tree-ring date association only.

St. Johns Polychrome is not well dated as an indigenous product, but it is in a trade context. The indigenous category alone does not permit us to "date" St. Johns Polychrome; it is a correlate to the trade context information available.

Every pottery type "dated" in Chapter 4 has been similarly analyzed graphically; however, limitations of space do not permit presentation of each individual analysis as exemplified by St. Johns Polychrome.

Chapter 4 contains examples of the various types of dating which are possible with the tree-ring and ceramic association information available. For example, Dogoszhi Black-on-white and Sosi Black-on-white are two additional pottery types that cannot be well dated by either the indigenous or the trade category dating evidence alone, but the combination of the information within these two categories allows us to "date" these pottery types with a reasonable degree of accuracy.

Four Mile Polychrome and Holbrook Black-on-white are examples of pottery types dated primarily on the basis of tree-ring date associations in an indigenous context. Gallina Black-on-white, on the other hand, is dated solely as an indigenous product.

Gila Polychrome, Kana-a Black-on-white, and Wingate Black-on-red are dated primarily on evidence from sites where they appear as trade. Heshotauthla Polychrome is dated by tree-ring association only as a tradeware.

Chaco Black-on-white is an example of a type that is well dated indigenously, but poorly dated as a trade product. Conversely, Black Mesa Black-on-white is well dated as a trade type and poorly dated in its area of home manufacture.

Numerous examples of pottery types in Chapter 4 are poorly dated indigenously, as trade, and within both categories. This poor dating is the result of a number of situations, most important of which is the appearance of the particular pottery type in too few sites with tree-ring dates. Poor association of tree-ring dates, pottery types, or a combination of both naturally makes dating difficult. Poor ceramic identification is another delimiting factor, particularly with undecorated pottery types.

DATING CERAMIC STYLES

As previously defined, "style of design" is "a device for lumping pottery types on the basis of design" (Wasley 1959: 289). Phillips and Gifford (1959: 22) define "design style" as "a mode grouping that emphasizes aspects of any ceramic picture that concerns design element distribution through time and space."

Lino and Sosi styles are used as examples of the application of tree-ring dating to Southwestern ceramic styles.

Lino Style (Wasley 1959: 240) is made up of the following pottery types: Boulder Black-on-gray, Lino Black-on-gray, La Plata Black-on-white, Rosa Black-on-white, Abajo Red-on-orange (in part), Chapin Black-on-white, Twin Trees Black-on-white, San Marcial Black-on-white (in part), White Mound Black-on-white (in part), Piedra Black-on-white (in part). Theoretically it should be possible to take the dates for each of these types, as determined by tree-ring date associations, and combine them to "date" Lino Style. We are faced, however, with the "in part" assignment of four of the included pottery types. Piedra Black-on-white is also related "in part" to Kana-a Style (Wasley 1959: 246). The other three "in part" pottery types can not be included in the Lino Style as type entities. Consequently, there is no way to "date" the Lino Style using the dates

TABLE 6

DATING OF ST. JOHNS POLYCHROME

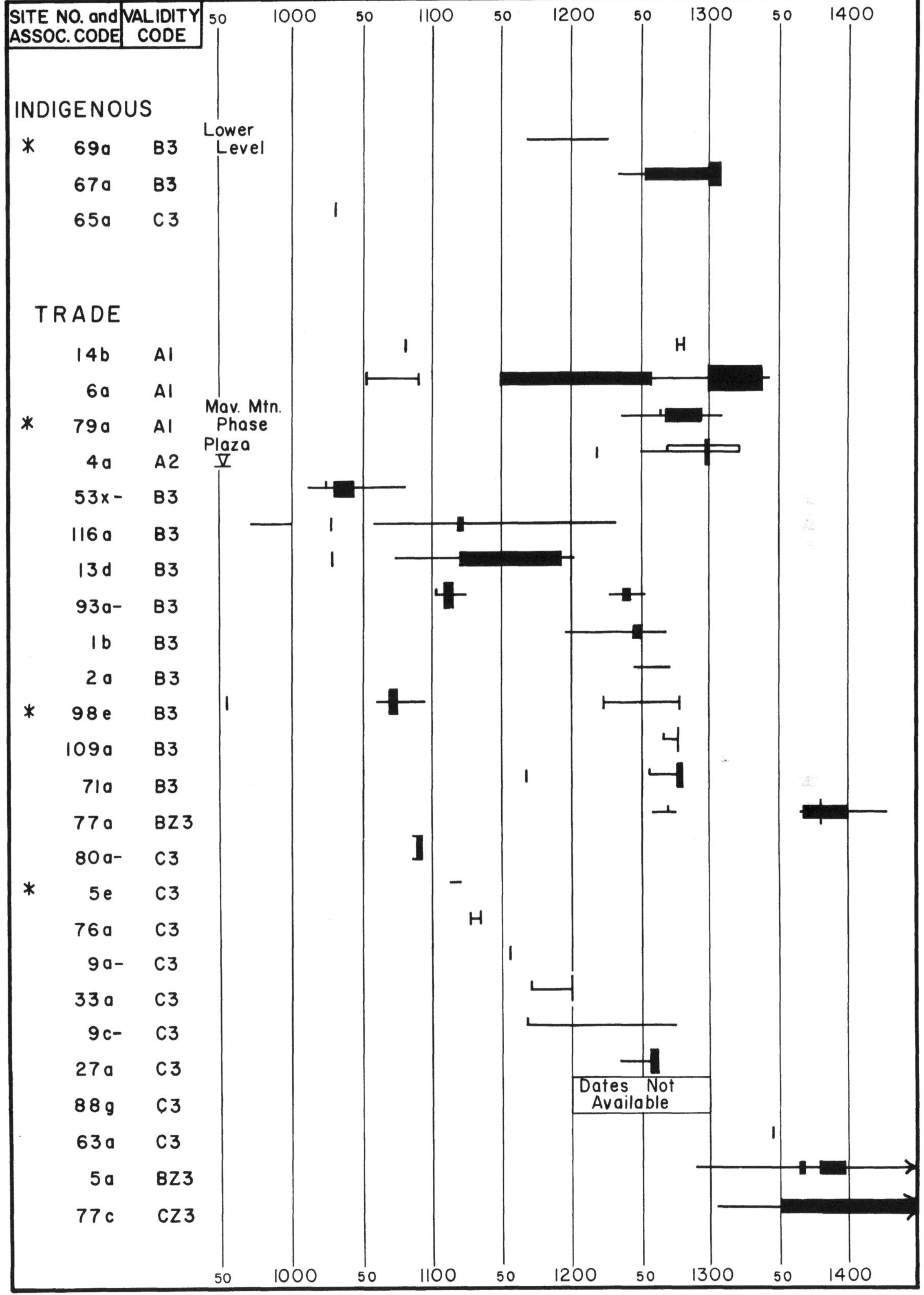

for the component types unless we eliminate the "in part" types from our discussion. The date thus obtained is not specifically applicable to the complete Lino Style as it is defined; however, enough types remain to make the date indicative of the style's overall time placement. It will be seen that this is not the case for the Sosi Style.

According to Wasley (1959: 257), the Sosi Style is made up of the following pottery types: Virgin Black-on-white, Sosi Black-on-white, Holbrook Black-on-white (in part), Snowflake Black-on-white (in part), Escavada Black-on-white, Puerco Black-on-white (in part), Mancos Black-on-white (in part), McElmo Black-on-white (in part), Kwake'e Black-on-white (in part), Socorro Black-on-white (in part), and Reserve Black-on-white (in part). When the "in part" pottery types are excluded from consideration, because they are not entities within the Sosi Style, we end up essentially with a date for the Sosi Black-on-white type, not the Sosi Style of design.

These same difficulties are encountered when attempting to date other Southwestern ceramic styles through the use of tree-ring evidence.

DISCUSSION

The preceding examples have shown that it is possible to "date" pottery types through the archaeological interpretation of tree-ring specimens to within varying degrees of reliability; however, the same degree of reliability is not obtained when attempting to date ceramic styles.

A pottery type is a concept which is not only fairly concrete and accepted by archaeologists as a valid classificatory category, but it is also a discrete enough unit to serve as a basic analytical tool for Southwestern ceramic studies.

Ceramic style, however, is not such a discrete and usable concept because it represents analysis on a higher level of abstraction. Ceramic style is not a classificatory tool, but rather one of synthesis or integration (Phillips and Gifford 1959).

Although some, but not all, Southwestern pottery types can be dated, we are unable to "date" any of the defined Southwestern ceramic styles through the use of tree-ring evidence, nor are we able to reduce them to time periods that are as well defined as those possible for dating pottery types. The "in part" use of pottery types to define ceramic styles is the greatest limitation towards using tree-ring dates for dating ceramic styles of design.

There is a future possibility that Southwestern pottery types, as discrete entities, might be combined to indicate the time period for a general or "super" style. Such an aggregate of pottery types, however, will not deal with short, specific time periods for dating prehistoric phenomena, but with larger, more general periods or stages. Quite possibly, this could be construed as actually dating ceramic styles.

A dated pottery type is similar to a "horizon marker" (see Wasley 1959: 233) in that it is more useful for dating smaller time intervals than the "horizon style" concept (Phillips and Gifford 1959: 20; Willey and Phillips 1958: 31–2), which is comparable to the "ceramic style" of the Southwest.

4. DATES FOR SOUTHWESTERN POTTERY TYPES

PRESENTATION OF DATA

THE DENDROCHRONOLOGICAL DATA of Chapter 2 may now be used as a basis for dating the Southwestern pottery types which occur at sites with tree-ring dates. The individual pottery type analysis to be presented is illustrated by the example of St. Johns Polychrome (see Chapter 3 and Table 6). It should be emphasized that the dating is done on the basis of the available tree-ring dates and does not always take into account occurrences of pottery types in other archaeological contexts which are not associated with tree-ring evidence.

The pottery types, varieties, and ceramic categories are presented in alphabetical order. The various categories of information for each pottery type are explained individually.

Reference. The references given provide sources for the descriptions of the pottery types.

Occurrence by site. Listed in either the trade or the indigenous category are the occurrences of the pottery types by sites with tree-ring dates. The indigenous category lists the sites or site-areas where the pottery is known or thought to have been made. The trade category includes those sites or site-areas where the pottery is known or thought to represent ceramic products from some other locality, *even though the distance involved may be small.* The site numbers are those used in the text of Chapter 2 and in Figure 1.

The symbols qualifying the pottery type occurrences and associations are those shown in Table 4, and are derived from the information contained for each site or site-area in Chapter 2. Pottery types which are the most numerous in both the indigenous and trade categories, and whose association is to be stressed for interpretive purposes, are designated as "dominant" types by an asterisk (Table 4). Pottery which is not designated as dominant indicates that the type is present at that particular site or site-area. When tree-ring and pottery type association evidence from a specific room or other archaeological unit is used for interpretation to obtain greater validity, it is noted parenthetically following the site number.

Range and clusters of tree-ring dates. The maximum range and clusters of tree-ring dates are shown for all the sites where the pottery is found, except when the evidence is inconclusive; then, it is discussed from the standpoint of dating validity. Any apparent clusterings or indications of concentrations of tree-ring dates are given for the pottery in both its indigenous and trade contexts.

Validity of tree-ring dating. The validity of the tree-ring dating is appraised through an examination of the association of the tree-ring dates and the pottery type under discussion. No comments are made for those pottery types or ceramic categories that cannot be dated because of obviously inadequate evidence.

ALPHABETICAL LIST OF SOUTHWESTERN POTTERY TYPES

Abajo Red-on-orange

Reference. Abel 1955.

Occurrence by site. Indigenous – *83a, 88y, 92b(1), *92b(2). Trade – 18a(?)–, 53k, 53m, *53q, 81a(?), 112c, 112d, 112e, 112f, 112g, 112h, 112i, 121d.

Range and clusters of tree-ring dates. Indigenous – 612+ to 872; best between 760's and 875. Trade – 608(?) to 1117; best between 700 and 900.

Validity of tree-ring dating. A cutting date of 691 from Half House, 53q, in Chaco Canyon, in *A*2 association with Abajo Red-on-orange, is the earliest definite date for this type – a trade product. In its area of home manufacture the tree-ring evidence indicates a beginning date in the 760's lasting until 875. As trade, small amounts show up in Chaco Canyon ruins dating in the early 1100's.

Abajo Red-on-orange is not widespread nor is it well dated, but the tree-ring evidence suggests dates of 700 to 875 or 900.

Abiquiu Black-on-gray

See Biscuit A.

Acoma Polychrome

Reference. Chapman 1933–36; Kidder and Shepard 1936.

Occurrence by site. Trade – 5a.

Adamana Brown

Reference. Hawley 1950; Wendorf 1953a.

Occurrence by site. Trade – 104a(?).

Validity of tree-ring dating. There is some question whether Adamana Brown is indigenous or trade at the Bluff site. We may say only that this pottery type is found at a single site which was occupied in the early 300's.

Alma Incised

Reference. Hawley 1950.

Occurrence by site. Indigenous – 107a.

See Alma Textured.

Alma Neck Banded

Reference. Hawley 1950; Wasley 1960b.

Occurrence by site. Indigenous – 78a, 78b, 106a. Trade – 104b.

Range and clusters of tree-ring dates. Indigenous – 738+vv to *908*; best between 760 and 908. Trade – 641v to 713+; best about 665.

Validity of tree-ring dating. Alma Neck Banded is dated earlier in a trade context than it is in an indigenous context. The tree-ring evidence suggests that this type came into existence between 665 and 700, and lasted until at least 910.

Alma Plain

Reference. Hawley 1950.

Occurrence by site. Indigenous – *78a, *78b, *78c, *106a, *107a. Trade – 101b (Section 1, House 3), 119a.

Range and clusters of tree-ring dates. Indigenous – 265+ to *951*; best between 300 and 951. Trade – *781* to 1331+; no tree-ring date clusters or concentrations.

Validity of tree-ring dating. Alma Plain and its varieties, Bluff and Forestdale, date from 300 to at least 950. Although the Bluff and Forestdale varieties have the earliest dates, there is no archaeological reason why Alma Plain will not eventually be dated back to at least the 300's in Mogollon sites. Alma Plain lasts as trade into the 1300's.

Alma Plain: Bluff Variety

Reference. Haury and Sayles 1947.

Occurrence by site. Indigenous – *104a.

See Alma Plain.

Alma Plain: Forestdale Variety

Reference. Haury 1940a.

Occurrence by site. Indigenous – *104a, *104b.

See Alma Plain.

Alma Punched

Reference. Hawley 1950.

Occurrence by site. Indigenous – 107a.

See Alma Textured.

Alma Rough

Reference. Martin and Rinaldo 1947.

Occurrence by site. Indigenous – 78a.

Validity of tree-ring dating. We cannot elaborate beyond the statement that Alma Rough occurs in two pit houses that were probably occupied during the last 50 years of the 700's.

Alma Scored

Reference. Hawley 1950.

Occurrence by site. Indigenous – 78a, 106a, 107a. Trade – 104a.

See Alma Textured.

Alma Textured

This ceramic category is a combination of the following types: Alma Incised, Alma Punched, and Alma Scored. For their occurrences by site, refer to each individual type.

Range and clusters of tree-ring dates. Indigenous – 777vv to 927; best between about 775 and 927. Trade – Bluff ruin, the only site, is dated at 300 or more.

Validity of tree-ring dating. This ceramic category is dated earlier as trade than it is indigenously; however, there is no archaeological reason to doubt the earlier dates. Alma Textured lasts from about 300 to 925 or more, with the strongest dating during the 775 to 925 period.

Angell Brown

Reference. Colton 1958.

Occurrence by site. Indigenous – 7d(?), *8b, *8c, 8d, *8f, *8h, 8i, 8j, *8k, 8l(?), *8m, 8n, 8o, 8p, 10d, 10u, 118a.

Range and clusters of tree-ring dates. Indigenous – 911+ to 1256vv; best between 1075 and 1130.

Validity of tree-ring dating. Angell Brown, a post-Sunset Crater type, is an intermediate between Rio de Flag Brown and Winona Brown (Colton 1958). The type appears about 1075 and lasts until about 1150, being most abundant for approximately the first 50 years of this period. Angell Brown is well dated considering that it is an intermediate type which is difficult to identify.

Aquarius Orange

Reference. Colton 1958.

Occurrence by site. Trade – 15b.

Arboles Black-on-white

Reference. Dittert, Hester, and Eddy 1961.

Occurrence by site. Indigenous – 121d.

Validity of tree-ring dating. Arboles Black-on-white is a local copy of Cortez Black-on-white. Since it is insufficiently dated, we can only say that it is found in a site which was apparently occupied about 900.

Ashiwi Polychrome

Reference. Mera 1939; Woodbury and Woodbury MS.

Occurrence by site. Trade – 58b.

Babicora Polychrome

Reference. Hawley 1950.

Occurrence by site. Trade – 21a.

Validity of tree-ring dating. We may state only that Babicora Polychrome is found at a site where a single room shows tree-ring dates in the middle 1300's.

Bandelier Black-on-gray

See Biscuit B.

Betatakin Black-on-white

Reference. Colton 1955.

Occurrence by site. Indigenous – 15b. Trade – 14b.

Validity of tree-ring dates. I am in agreement with Burgh (1959: 198), who has expressed doubt that Betatakin Black-on-white is a valid pottery type. Since Betatakin Black-on-white is found in association with Kayenta and Tusayan Black-on-whites, reference is made to these pottery types for indications of its dating, if indeed it is a valid pottery type.

Bidahochi Black-on-white

Reference. Colton 1955.

Occurrence by site. Trade – 9c—, 67a(?).

Range and clusters of tree-ring dates. Trade – 1168B to 1307; best(?) after 1300.

Validity of tree-ring dating. Both the associations and the identifications of Bidahochi Black-on-white are in doubt. Colton (1955) suggests dates of probably 1325 to 1400. The tree-ring evidence does not contribute greatly to either verifying or altering this range of time. The tree-ring dates no more than suggest that Bidahochi Black-on-white begins by 1300.

Bidahochi Polychrome

Reference. Colton 1956.

Occurrence by site. Trade – 14a.

Validity of tree-ring dating. The insufficient evidence does not justify comment on Colton's (1956) date of about 1320 to 1400.

Biscuit A

Reference. Hawley 1950; Kidder and Amsden 1931.

Occurrence by site. Indigenous – 36a, *42a, *42b, *42c, *46a, *50b, 57a, 58a, 58b, 58d, 58e, 58f, 116a. Trade – 3a, 4a (Plaza V), 5a, 5b, 6b, 34a.

Range and clusters of tree-ring dates. Indigenous – 963+ to 1562+; best between 1420 and 1450 or 1500. Trade – 1219vv to 1612+; best between 1300 and 1450.

Validity of tree-ring dating. The tree-ring evidence in both the indigenous and trade contexts suggests a date range of 1375 to 1450, which does not essentially alter the date given by Smiley, Stubbs, and Bannister (1953: 58).

Biscuit B

Reference. Hawley 1950; Kidder and Amsden 1931.

Occurrence by site. Indigenous – *42a, *42b, *42c, *50b, *56a (Kiva 1), 57a, 58a, 58b, 58c, 58e, 58f, 116a. Trade – 3a, 4a, 5a, 32a, 34a, 59b.

Range and clusters of tree-ring dates. Indigenous – 963+ to 1581+; best between 1411 and 1500 plus. Trade – 1219vv to 1612+; best between 1395 and 1500.

Validity of tree-ring dating. Biscuit B is quite well dated by tree-ring evidence between 1400 and 1500. Smiley, Stubbs, and Bannister (1953: 58) indicate that it is most abundant between 1450 and 1500, and extend it to 1550.

Black Falls Corrugated

Although Black Falls Corrugated is an undescribed type, it is essentially Tusayan Corrugated with black cinder temper.

Occurrence by site. Indigenous – 7d, 8a, 10u.

Validity of tree-ring dating. Because of the insufficient tree-ring evidence, we can only say that Black Falls Corrugated, a minor type or variety, post-dates the eruption of Sunset Crater.

Black Mesa Black-on-white

Reference. Colton 1955.

Occurrence by site. Indigenous – 13e, 15c, *15h, 15k, 15l, *15m, 76a(?), 77b, 111b, 111c, 118a–. Trade – 7d, 8b, *8c, *8d, *8e, *8f, *8g, *8h, 8i, *8j, *8k, *8l, *8m, *8n, *8o, *8p, 9c–, *10d, 10e, *10f, 10g, *10i, 10k, *10l, *10n, *10o, 10p, *10q, 10r, 10s, 10t, *10v–, *10w, 10x–, *10y, *10z, *11b–, 12a(?), 12b(?), 13c(?), 14c–, 53t, *66a, *92a, *98e, 104c, *114a(?).

Range and clusters of tree-ring dates. Indigenous – 977+ to 1390; best between 1060+ to 1178. Trade – 701 to 1275; best between 875 and 1130.

Validity of tree-ring dating. Black Mesa Black-on-white, one of the best dated Southwestern pottery types on the basis of tree-ring evidence, is better dated as a trade product than as an indigenous type. I do not hesitate to date it at 875 to 1130, with the strongest dating during the last 130 years of its history. It is interesting to note that Mc.Gregor's (1938a: 17) dates are identical.

Bluff Black-on-red

Reference. Abel 1955.

Occurrence by site. Indigenous – 88y. Trade – 99b(?).

Validity of tree-ring dating. The two tree-ring dates of 847B and 993+ only suggest that Bluff Black-on-red spans the 850 to 1000 time period; therefore in the absence of better evidence, it is not feasible to alter Abel's (1955) dates of 800 to 900.

Bluff Black-on-red: Bluff Variety

See Bluff Black-on-red.

"Brownware"

Occurrence by site. Indigenous – 79a, 79b, 86j(?). Trade – 77m, 86j, 86k, 86l, 86m, 88a.

Cameron Polychrome

Reference. Colton 1956.

Occurrence by site. Indigenous – 13d (Room 36C), 15h, 111c. Trade – 10q(?).

Range and clusters of tree-ring dates. Indigenous – 1057+ to 1143+; best between 1065 and 1143 plus. Trade – 918 to 1127; best between 1115 and 1127.

Validity of tree-ring dating. The poor evidence suggests a guess date for Cameron Polychrome of 1065 or 1075 to 1150, which alters the life-span of Colton's (1956) proposed date of about 1125 to 1175.

Cedar Creek Polychrome

Reference. Carlson 1961.

Occurrence by site. Indigenous – 67a, 72a, 72b. Trade – 79a, 79b.

Range and clusters of tree-ring dates. Indigenous – 1233+ to *1348*; best between 1300 and 1348. Trade – 1201vv to 1308; best between 1265 and 1302 plus.

Validity of tree-ring dating. Fairly consistent tree-ring evidence suggests a date of 1300 to 1350 for Cedar Creek Polychrome. Carlson's (1961) dates of 1300 to 1375, however, should be considered more accurate in light of his use of additional data.

Chaco Black-on-white

Reference. Hawley 1950; Gordon Vivian 1959.

Occurrence by site. Indigenous – *47a@, *48a@, *51a@, *53b@, *53c, *53f@, *53g@, *53i@, *53k, 53l(?), 53m, 53p–, *53s, *53u, *53w@, *53x, *53y. Trade – 13d(?) (Room 45A), 88g, 99a.

Range and clusters of tree-ring dates. Indigenous – 828 to 1178v; best between 1050(?) and 1125. Trade – 1066 to 1192+; best between 1066 and 1192 plus.

Validity of tree-ring dating. As an indigenous type, Chaco Black-on-white is well dated between about 1050 and 1125. It is found as a trade type until about 1200.

Chaco Corrugated

Reference. Hawley 1950.

Occurrence by site. Indigenous – *53l, *53m, *53n, *53y(?).

Range and clusters of tree-ring dates. Indigenous – 1043c to *1110*; best between 1043 and 1110.

Validity of tree-ring dating. Chaco Corrugated was apparently made between about 1050 and 1110 or more. This date would no doubt be strengthened if some of the "Grayware Corrugateds" could be classified by type.

Chaco II Black-on-white

Occurrence by site. Indigenous – 1d, 6a, 6c, 33a, 57a, 116a. Trade – 21a, 99b.

See also Red Mesa and Escavada black-on-whites.

Chaco III Black-on-white

Occurrence by site. Trade – 116a.

See also Gallup and Chaco black-on-whites.

Chapin Black-on-white

Reference. Abel 1955.

Occurrence by site. Indigenous – 90a@(?), 91a@(?)–, 88a, 88u, 88v, 88x, 88y, 96a, 103a@, 103b@, 103c@, 103d@, 103e@.

Range and clusters of tree-ring dates. Indigenous – 354+x to 847B; best between 610 and 847.

Validity of tree-ring dating. There is no tree-ring evidence to indicate that Chapin Black-on-white begins before about 600, although Abel (1955) suggests about 500. The Fifth Southwestern Ceramic Conference (1963) has proposed dates of 587vv to 900; however, the present tree-ring evidence suggests that this type lasted until 850, and was most abundant in the 600's.

Chapin Gray

Reference. Abel 1955.

Occurrence by site. Indigenous – *88a, 88c, 88g, 88u, 88v, 88x, 88y, *88bb, 96a, 103a@, 103b@, 103c@, 103d@, 103e@. Trade – 121d.

Range and clusters of tree-ring dates. Indigenous – 354+x to 847B; best between 610 and 847. Trade – There is a single occurrence from a site occupied about 900.

Validity of tree-ring dating. The tree-ring evidence indicates that Chapin Gray dates from at least 610 until about 850. Chapin Gray lasted as trade in a site occupied about 900. Abel's (1955) beginning date of 450 is not supported by the tree-ring evidence.

Chapin Gray: Chapin Variety

Occurrence by site. Indigenous – *88a, *88u@, *88v@, 88x, 88y.

See Chapin Gray for comments on dating.

Chapin Gray: Moccasin Variety

Occurrence by site. Indigenous – 88y.

See Moccasin Gray for comments on dating.

Chapin Gray: Mummy Lake Variety

Occurrence by site. Indigenous – 88g.

Chavez Brown

Reference. Colton 1958.

Occurrence by site. Indigenous – *14a, 14b (Room 11).

Validity of tree-ring dating. The tree-ring evidence is insufficient to alter the dates of 1200 to 1400 proposed by Colton (1958).

Chupadero Black-on-white

Reference. Hawley 1950; Kidder and Shepard 1936.

Occurrence by site. Indigenous – *20a, 21a. Trade – 1b, 2a, 2b, 4a (Plaza V), 5a, 5c, 5e, 6a, 6b, 28a, 33a.

Range and clusters of tree-ring dates. Indigenous – 1310 to 1366C; best between 1345 and 1366. Trade – 1051 to 1612+; best between 1150 and 1393.

Validity of tree-ring dating. This pottery type is better dated as trade than it is in an indigenous context. Chupadero Black-on-white begins at 1150 and lasts until at least 1400, with the tree-ring evidence strongest between 1250 and 1400. Since this paper is not concerned with the post-Spanish contact period, no comment shall be made on the end date of about 1675 shown by Smiley, Stubbs, and Bannister (1953: 58).

Cibicue Polychrome

Reference. Haury 1934 .

Occurrence by site. Indigenous – 72a, 72b. Trade – 14b (Room 11).

Range and clusters of tree-ring dates. Indigenous – 1323+ to *1348*; best between 1337 and 1348. Trade – The 1078 date from the Pollock site, Room 11, does not appear to be associated with this pottery type.

Validity of tree-ring dating. Cibicue Polychrome is poorly dated. The tree-ring evidence suggests only that it was being made around 1350.

Citadel Polychrome

Reference. Colton 1956.

Occurrence by site. Indigenous – 13d (Room 36C), 15c, 15h, 15j, *17a. Trade – 7d, 8a, 8j, 8n, 9a–, 9c–, 10d, 10q, 10r, 10t, 12a(?), 12b(?), 13a(?), 13b(?), *48a@, 53k, *53s, 66a, 99a.

Range and clusters of tree-ring dates. Indigenous – 1057+ to 1285; best between 1124 and 1200. Trade – 911+ to 1279; best between 1115 and about 1200.

Validity of tree-ring dating. Citadel Polychrome is quite well dated, considering the fact that sherds are often difficult to distinguish from those of Tusayan Polychrome. The tree-ring evidence suggests a date of 1115 to about 1200, which differs slightly from Colton's (1956) date of about 1125 to 1175.

Clear Creek Brown

Reference. Colton 1958.

Occurrence by site. Trade – 99a(?).

Coconino Gray

Reference. Colton 1955.

Occurrence by site. Trade – *10f, *10i, 10y, 14c.

Range and clusters of tree-ring dates. Trade – 760 to 1061; best between 890 and 1061.

Validity of tree-ring dating. Because Coconino Gray and Medicine Gray are contemporary pottery types which differ only in the decorative techniques of the neck corrugations, these two "types" are considered together for more definite dating. Both types occur during the time period of 890 to 1060.

Coconino Red-on-buff

Reference. Colton and Hargrave 1937.

Occurrence by site. Indigenous – *8b, 8d, 8p, 10v–.

Range and clusters of tree-ring dates. Indigenous – 813+ to 1119; best between 1080 and 1100.

Validity of tree-ring dating. For stronger dating Coconino Red-on-buff is considered along with its contemporary, Winona Red-on-buff. Both types are short-lived, with good tree-ring evidence for dating them between about 1080 and 1100.

"Corrugated, Brownware"

Occurrence by site. Indigenous – 72a, 72b, *79b, *104c. Trade – 99a.

"Corrugated, Grayware"

Occurrence by site. Indigenous – 53c, 65a, *88z.

Cortez Black-on-white

Reference. Abel 1955.

Occurrence by site. Trade – 121d.

Validity of tree-ring dating. Since the only comment possible is that Cortez Black-on-white occurs as trade in a site occupied around 900, no improvement can be made on Abel's (1955) date of 900 to 1000.

See also Arboles Black-on-white.

Deadmans Black-on-gray

Reference. Colton 1958.

Occurrence by site. Indigenous – 10d, 10i, 10k, 10m–, 10n, 10p, 10s, 10t, 10w, 12a, 114a. Trade – 8h, 8l, 8o.

Range and clusters of tree-ring dates. Indigenous – 746vv to 1093; best between about 900 and about 1100. Trade – 1058 to 1115; best between 1080 and 1115.

Validity of tree-ring dating. Deadmans Black-on-gray is well dated between 900 and 1115 plus, with the best dating between 960 and 1100.

Deadmans Black-on-red

Reference. Colton 1956.

Occurrence by site. Indigenous – 92b(1). Trade – 9b, 10a, 10b, 10c, 10e, 10f, 10g, 10h, *10i, *10k, *10n, *10o, *10p, 10v–, 10w, 10y, 10aa, 11a, 11b–, 14c, 66a(?), 89a(?)@, 98e, 105c, 114a.

Range and clusters of tree-ring dates. Indigenous – 837 to 872; best between 860 and 872. Trade – 678 to 1106; best between 775 and 1066.

Validity of tree-ring dating. I do not hesitate to date Deadmans Black-on-red at 775 to 1066. This type was not made in the Flagstaff region after the eruption of Sunset Crater.

As a result of discussions held at the Sixth Southwestern Ceramic Conference (1964), it now appears feasible to regard La Plata Black-on-red as a regional variety of Deadmans Black-on-red. Archaeologists working with the Kayenta branch of the Anasazi are confident that at least some Deadmans Black-on-red was manufactured in the Tsegi Canyon area.

Deadmans Fugitive Red

Reference. Colton 1958.

Occurrence by site. Indigenous – *10a, *10b, *10c, *10d, *10e, 10f, *10g, *10h, *10i, *10k, *10l, *10m–, *10n, 10o, *10p, *10q, *10r, *10s, *10t, *10v–, *10w, *10y, *10z, *10aa, *12a, *12b, 13b, 13c, 13d (Room 36C), 13e, 114a. Trade – *8b, 8c, 8d, *8e, 8f, 8g, *8h, 8j, 8k, 8l, 8n, 8o, 8p, 9b, 66a.

Range and clusters of tree-ring dates. Indigenous – 687 to 1192; best between 775 and 1150. Trade – 687 to 1207; best between 850 *or* 1025 and 1130.

Validity of tree-ring dating. Deadmans Fugitive Red dates between 775 and 1150, with its period of greatest abundance between 850 and 1150. There is no tree-ring evidence to verify Colton's (1958) proposed "pre-700" beginning date.

Deadmans Fugitive Red is associated with Deadmans Gray at all but three sites (10x, 13a, and 17a) where Deadmans Gray is reported.

Deadmans Gray

Reference. Colton 1958.

Occurrence by site. Indigenous – *10a, *10b, *10c, *10d, *10e, 10f, *10g, *10h, *10i, *10k, *10l, *10m–, *10n, *10o, *10p, *10q, *10r, *10s, *10t, 10v–, *10w, *10x–, *10y, *10z, *10aa, *12a, *12b, 13a, 13b, 13c, 13d (Room 36C), 13e, 17a, *114a. Trade – 8b, 8c, 8d, 8e, 8h, 8k, 8m, 8o, 8p, 9b, 11a.

Range and clusters of tree-ring dates. Indigenous – 687 to 1205; best between 775 and 1200. Trade – 687 to 1121; best between about 850 and 1100.

Validity of tree-ring dating. We may state with some certainty that Deadmans Gray was made during the period from 775 to 1200; it was apparently most abundant between 850 and 1150.

The beginning date of 775 alters Colton's (1958) proposed "pre-700" date. Deadmans Gray is usually associated with Deadmans Fugitive Red.

Dogoszhi Black-on-white

Reference. Colton 1955.

Occurrence by site. Indigenous – 13d (Room 36C), 15c, 15k, 15m, 17a, 77b, 111a, 111b, 111c. Trade – 7d, 8d, 8h, *8j, 8k, 8m, 9c–, *10d, 10q, 10r, 10u, 10v–, 12a(?), *12b(?), 13a(?), 13b(?).

Range and clusters of tree-ring dates. Indigenous – 977+ to 1390; best between 1137 and 1200. Trade – 813+ to 1279; best between 1085 and 1200.

Validity of tree-ring dating. The strong suggestion from the tree-ring evidence that Dogoszhi Black-on-white exists as a type between 1085 and 1200 alters Colton's (1955) proposed dates of about 1070 to about 1150.

Dogoszhi Polychrome

Dogoszhi Polychrome is considered to be incompletely slipped Tusayan Black-on-red.

See Tusayan Black-on-red.

Elden Corrugated

Reference. Colton and Hargrave 1937.

Occurrence by site. Indigenous – 7d, *9a—, 9c—, 10u, 13d. Trade – 66a.

Range and clusters of tree-ring dates. Indigenous – 1028+ to 1279; best between 1085 and 1200. Trade – 1023+ to 1050+; probably best at 1050 plus.

Validity of tree-ring dating. Elden Corrugated is not well dated because the validity of the tree-ring date association is poor. Dates of about 1085 to about 1200 are simply suggested dates for this type; Colton and Hargrave's (1937) dates of probably between 1125 and 1225 should be kept in mind.

El Paso Polychrome

Reference. Hawley 1950.

Occurrence by site. Indigenous – 20a. Trade – 74h.

Range and clusters of tree-ring dates. Indigenous and trade – 1310 to *1347;* construction at the two sites probably took place in 1330 and 1347.

Validity of tree-ring dating. There is no indication for the beginning date of El Paso Polychrome; however, the tree-ring evidence is in agreement with Hawley's (1950) statement that it lasted until 1350.

Escavada Black-on-white

Reference. Hawley 1950; Gordon Vivian 1959.

Occurrence by site. Indigenous – 47a@, *48a@, 51a@, 53b@, 53c, *53e, 53f@, 53g@, 53i@, *53j, *53k, *53l, 53m, 53n, 53p—, *53s, *53u, 53w@, 53x, *53y, 76a(?), 98e, 101a(?) (Wingate phase), 105a(?), 115a. Trade – 99b.

Range and clusters of tree-ring dates. Indigenous – 806+x to 1275; best between 925 and 1125. Trade – 993+; site probably occupied about 1000.

Validity of tree-ring dating. Escavada Black-on-white apparently lasted from 925 to 1125, but it should be borne in mind that this pottery type is variously identified by different workers. The Chaco II Black-on-white category probably also contains some Escavada Black-on-white.

Exuberant Corrugated

Reference. Kluckhohn and Reiter 1939.

Occurrence by site. Indigenous – 53j, *53l, 105a, 105c.

Range and clusters of tree-ring dates. Indigenous – 806+x to 1077+; best between 890 and 1075.

Validity of tree-ring dating. Exuberant Corrugated is not well dated, but 890 to 1075 is suggested as the range of dates, with the best dating between 925 and 1050.

"Fiber-Tempered, Unfired"

Occurrence by site. Indigenous – 18a—, 86j, 86k, 86l, 86m, *96a, *103a@, *103b@, *103c@, *103d@, *103e@.

"Fine-Banded, Smudged"

Occurence by site. Trade – 53s.

Fine Paste Brown

Reference. Haury and Sayles 1947.

Occurrence by site. Indigenous – 104a.

Validity of tree-ring dating. It is possible to state only that Fine Paste Brown occurs at the Bluff ruin, which was occupied in the early 300's.

Flagstaff Black-on-white

Reference. Colton 1955.

Occurrence by site. Indigenous – *13d, 15c, 15e, 15f, 15i, 15m, *17a, 77b, 111a, 111b, 111c, 111e, 111f, *118a. Trade – *7d, 8j, 8k, 8o, *9a—, *9c—, 10u, *12a(?), *12b(?), *13a(?), 13b(?), *13c(?), 14a, 14b, *64a, *66a, 88g(?), *92a(?), *98e.

Range and clusters of tree-ring dates. Indigenous – 977+ to 1390; best between 1120 and 1285. Trade – 914+ to 1320; best between 1066 and 1200.

Validity of tree-ring dating. In both indigenous and trade contexts, Flagstaff Black-on-white is identifiable by 1085, or 1100 at the latest, retaining its type identity until at least 1275. Flagstaff Black-on-white, part of a stylistic entity which bridges Sosi and Kayenta styles, was probably most abundant between 1100 and 1200.

Floyd Black-on-gray

Reference. Colton 1958.

Occurrence by site. Indigenous – 10a, 10b. Trade – 11a.

Range and clusters of tree-ring dates. Indigenous – 687 to 937; best between 775 and 937. Trade – There is a single date of 784+.

Validity of tree-ring dating. Dates of 775 to 940 are suggested on the basis of rather insufficient evidence. Floyd Black-on-gray is the Cohonina variant of Kana-a Black-on-white. The more complete evidence for the dating of Kana-a Black-on-white may be cited as supplementary information.

Floyd Gray

Reference. Colton 1958.

Occurrence by site. Indigenous – 10m–.

Validity of tree-ring dating. The evidence is insufficient for dating Floyd Gray. Since this type is the Cohonina variant of Kana-a Gray, the dates for Kana-a Gray may suggest the maximum range of dates for Floyd Gray.

Forestdale Red

Reference. Haury 1940a.

Occurrence by site. Indigenous – 104b.

Validity of tree-ring dating. Forestdale Red is a synonym for Woodruff Red. Since the tree-ring evidence is poor, it is possible to say only that Forestdale Red is found at a site which was probably occupied during the late 600's and the early 700's.

Forestdale Smudged

Reference. Haury 1940a.

Occurrence by site. Indigenous – 104b. Trade – 53m, 88a(?).

Range and clusters of tree-ring dates. Indigenous – 641v to 713+; best(?) about 675. Trade – 612 to *1110;* no concentration of dates.

Validity of tree-ring dating. Forestdale Smudged is a synonym for Woodruff Smudged. Because of the poor tree-ring dating evidence, we can only state, until further evidence is available, that Forestdale Smudged appears at sites dated from about 300 until about 1150.

Four Mile Polychrome

Reference. Carlson 1961.

Occurrence by site. Indigenous – *67a, 68a, *69a (upper level), *72a, *72b, 73a, 74b, 74g, 74h, 74i@. Trade – 14a, 61a, 63a, 63b–, *79a (Room 11), 79b, 119a.

Range and clusters of tree-ring dates. Indigenous – 1131+ to 1385; best between 1300 and 1385. Trade – 1031 to 1385; best between 1300 and 1385.

Validity of tree-ring dating. Carlson (1961: 192) dates Four Mile Polychrome between 1325 and 1400; however, I believe the tree-ring evidence indicates a beginning date of 1300. The areal distribution of Four Mile Polychrome at sites with tree-ring dates is not great; it is most accurately dated as an indigenous product.

Four Mile Polychrome: Kinishba Variety

Reference. Cummings 1940.

Occurrence by site. Indigenous – 67a.

Validity of tree-ring dating. Because this type is identified from illustrations in Cummings (1940), its validity as a type is tenuous. Although the tree-ring evidence is not sufficient to postulate any dates, they are probably similar to the dates for Four Mile Polychrome.

Four Mile Polychrome: Showlow Variety

See Showlow Polychrome.

"Fremont Basket Maker Pottery"

Occurrence by site. Indigenous – *87a.

Galisteo Black-on-white

Reference. Stubbs and Stallings 1953.

Occurrence by site. Indigenous – 1a, 1b, 1c, 1e, 2a, 2b, 2c, 2d, 3a, *4a (Plaza V), 5a, 5c, 5d, 5e, 6a, 6b, 28a, 33a. Trade – 58b.

Range and clusters of tree-ring dates. Indigenous – 1051 to 1612+; best between 1300 and 1393. Trade – 1385 to 1466C; best between 1418 and 1466.

Validity of tree-ring dating. As an indigenous type, Galisteo Black-on-white is dated by the tree-ring evidence between 1300 and 1393. Indications are that it lasts into the 1400's as trade. This type is dated 1300 to 1350 or more by Smiley, Stubbs, and Bannister (1953: 58).

Gallina Black-on-gray

See Gallina Black-on-white.

Gallina Black-on-white

Reference. Hawley 1950; Hibben 1949.

Occurrence by site. Indigenous – *49a@, *49b@, *49c@, *49d@, *49e@, *49f@, *49g@, *49h@, *49i@, *49j@, *49k@, *49l.

Range and clusters of tree-ring dates. Indigenous – 1106 to 1268+; best between 1248 and 1268.

Validity of tree-ring dating. Gallina Black-on-white occurs only as an indigenous type. There is good evidence to indicate that it was abundant around 1250; however, the tree-ring material inadequately indicates its total time range.

Gallina Plain

See Gallina Utility.

Gallina Utility

Reference. Hibben 1949.

Occurrence by site. Indigenous – *49a@, *49b@, *49c@, *49d@, *49e@, *49f@, *49g@, *49h@, *49i@, *49j@, *49k@, *49l.

Validity of tree-ring dating. Gallina Utility occurs at the same sites as Gallina Black-on-white; thus, we can only state that it was apparently abundant around 1250.

Gallup Black-on-white

Reference. Hawley 1950; Gordon Vivian 1959.

Occurrence by site. Indigenous – 47a@, 48a@, 51a@, 53b@, 53c, 53e, 53f@, 53g@, 53i@, 53k, *53l, *53m, 53n, 53p–, 53s, 53t, 53u, 53w@, 53x, 53y, 65a, 76a, *76b (Kiva 1), 80a–, 98e, 102b, 102c, 105a, *115a. Trade – 99a.

Range and clusters of tree-ring dates. Indigenous – 806+x to 1275; best between 1000 and 1125. Trade – 1185+ to 1192+; probably indicates date of about 1200.

Validity of tree-ring dating. Gallup Black-on-white may be dated at 1000 to 1125 as an indigenous type. There is a possibility that it lasts until about 1200 as a trade product.

Gila Black-on-red

Reference. Haury 1945.

Occurrence by site. Trade – 68a, 72a, 72b, *79a (Canyon Creek phase).

Range and clusters of tree-ring dates. Trade – 1131+ to *1348*; best between 1300 and 1348.

Validity of tree-ring dating. Gila Black-on-red is present during the 1300 to 1350 period; however, there is insufficient evidence concerning its actual range of time. At the Sixth Southwestern Ceramic Conference (1964) dates of 1300 to 1375(?) were proposed for Gila Black-on-red.

Gila Butte Red-on-buff

Reference. Gladwin and others 1937.

Occurrence by site. Trade – 104b.

Validity of tree-ring dating. It is possible to state only that Gila Butte Red-on-buff occurs as trade in a site occupied in the late 600's and early 700's.

Gila Plain

Reference. Gladwin and others 1937.

Occurrence by site. Trade – 8h, *61a, 63a, 74e, 104a.

Range and clusters of tree-ring dates. Trade – 265+ to 1385; best(?) between 300 and 1345 plus.

Validity of tree-ring dating. The tree-ring evidence indicates that Gila Plain occurs as trade pottery for over 1000 years, beginning about 300.

Gila Polychrome

Reference. Hawley 1950.

Occurrence by site. Indigenous – *61a, *63a, *63b–, 67a(?), 119a. Trade – 20a, 21a, *67a, 68a, 69 (upper level), 72a, 72b, 74h, 74i@, 74j, 77b(?), 79a, *79b, 119a.

Range and clusters of tree-ring dates. Indigenous – 1109vv to *1385*; best between 1250 and 1385. Trade – 1131+ to 1390; best between 1265 and 1385.

Validity of tree-ring dating. Although the evidence utilized in this paper suggests that Gila Polychrome dates 1250 to 1400 in both indigenous and trade contexts, the dating is strongest after 1300 – the traditionally accepted beginning date for Gila Polychrome in the literature of Southwestern archaeology. Steen (1962: 28) dates Gilo and Tonto polychromes from perhaps 1250 to after 1400. Although I acknowledge the present evidence for beginning Gila Polychrome at 1300, I believe future work may show that this type begins between 1250 and 1300.

Recent work with tree-ring material from Casas Grandes indicates that Gila Polychrome occurs earlier in northern Chihuahua than in the southwestern United States. In fact, it may be a type which was introduced into the Southwest from the Casas Grandes region (Charles C. DiPeso, personal communication).

Because post-Spanish contact sites are not included in this paper, no comments shall be made on the question of whether the manufacture of Gila Polychrome was continued into historic times.

The dates for Gila Polychrome are also applicable to Tonto Polychrome (see Tonto Polychrome).

Gila Red

Reference. Haury 1945; Schroeder 1940.

Occurrence by site. Trade – 63a, 63b–.

Gila Redware

Reference. Hawley 1950.

Occurrence by site. Trade – 72a, 72b.

Validity of tree-ring dating. The scanty evidence available allows us to say only that Gila Redware occurs as a trade product in the first half of the 14th century.

Gila Smudged

Reference. Haury 1945.

Occurrence by site. Indigenous – 61a. Trade – 63a.

Validity of tree-ring dating. Gila Smudged is poorly dated; we can only say that it occurs in the 1300's.

Gila White-on-red

Reference. H. S. and Winifred Gladwin 1930.

Occurrence by site. Indigenous – 61a.

Validity of tree-ring dating. We cannot be more specific than to state that Gila White-on-red occurs at a site occupied in the last half of the 1300's.

Gobernador Polychrome

Reference. Keur 1941; Kidder and Shepard 1936.

Occurrence by site. Trade – 5a.

"Hawikuh Glaze"

Occurrence by site. Trade – 5a.

Heshotauthla Polychrome

Reference. Carlson 1961; Woodbury and Woodbury MS.

Occurrence by site. Trade – 1a, 1c, 2b, 2c(?), 2d(?), 5a, 5c, 6a, 21a, 28a, 46a, 58a.

Range and clusters of tree-ring dates. Trade – 1051 to 1612+; best between 1300 and 1393.

Validity of tree-ring dating. The tree-ring evidence from sites where Heshotauthla Polychrome occurs as tradeware indicates a date of 1275 or 1300 to about 1400; however, Carlson's (1961) dates of 1300 to 1375, which include comparisons from sites without tree-ring dates, are probably more accurate.

Hohokam Buff

Reference. Colton 1941.

Occurrence by site. Trade – 74e.

"Hohokam Red-on-buff, Pioneer(?) Period"

Occurrence by site. Trade – 104a(?).

Holbrook Black-on-white

Reference. Colton 1955.

Occurrence by site. Indigenous – *8d, 8e, *8g, 8h, 8i, 8j, *8k, *8l, *8n, 8o, 9c–, 10v–, 10z, 76a, 118a. Trade – 66a, 104c (Room 16, Floor 3).

Range and clusters of tree-ring dates. Indigenous – 701 to 1279; best between 1075 and 1130. Trade – 1023+ to 1061+; no concentration of dates.

Validity of tree-ring dating. The dates of 1075 to 1130 indicated by the tree-ring evidence differ only slightly from Colton's (1955) dates of about 1070 to 1110.

Homolovi Black-on-red

Reference. Colton 1956.

Occurrence by site. Trade – 14a.

Validity of tree-ring dating. Colton's (1956) dates of between 1300 and 1400 still stand.

Homolovi Polychrome

Reference. Colton 1956.

Occurrence by site. Trade – *14a, 14b(?).

Validity of tree-ring dating. Homolovi Polychrome is another name for Winslow Polychrome. Although the poor tree-ring evidence suggests, more or less, a beginning date of 1300, Colton's (1956) dates of between 1300 and 1400 cannot be improved upon.

Honani Tooled

Reference. Colton 1955.

Occurrence by site. Trade – 81.

Validity of tree-ring dating. Colton (1955) dates Honani Tooled about 900; whereas the tree-ring evidence from NA 3644K places it at approximately 1100. This type, consequently, cannot be considered "dated."

"Hopi Geometric"

Reference. Called Early Sityatki Polychrome by Colton (1956).

Occurrence by site. Indigenous – 77a, 77b, 77c.

Validity of tree-ring dating. Reference to Sityatki Polychrome may give an indication of the dating for this "type."

Houck Polychrome

See Wingate Polychrome.

"Indented Corrugated, Brown"

Occurrence by site. Indigenous – 61a, *79a, 79b.

"Indented Corrugated, Gray"

Occurrence by site. Indigenous – 92a, *99a, 115a.

"Indented Neck Corrugated, Gray"

Occurrence by site. Indigenous – 92a, 105b.

Validity of tree-ring dating. Reference to Tohatchi Banded and Medicine Gray may suggest the possible dating for this generalized ceramic category.

Jeddito Black-on-orange

Reference. Colton 1956.

Occurrence by site. Indigenous – 77b. Trade – 14a, 14b.

Range and clusters of tree-ring dates. Indigenous – 1377 to 1390; best(?) near 1390. Trade – 1031+ to 1320; best between 1276 and 1320.

Validity of tree-ring dating. The tree-ring evidence suggests dates of about 1275 to 1400.

Jeddito Black-on-yellow

Reference. Colton 1956.

Occurrence by site. Indigenous – 69a (upper level), 72a, 72b, 74d(?), *77a, 77b. Trade – 5a, 14a, 14b, 59b, 67a(?), 68a–, 69a– (upper level), *119a.

Range and clusters of tree-ring dates. Indigenous – 1255+ to 1430; best between 1300 and 1400. Trade – 1031+ to 1612+; best between 1300 and 1400.

Validity of tree-ring dating. The commonly accepted date of 1300 remains the most plausible beginning date for Jeddito Black-on-yellow; however, since this paper is not concerned with sites dating after the Spanish Entrada into the Southwest, no end date is suggested.

Jeddito Corrugated

Reference. Colton 1956.

Occurrence by site. Indigenous – 77c.

Jeddito Plain

Reference. Colton 1956.

Occurrence by site. Indigenous – 77b.

Jemez Black-on-white

Reference. Hawley 1950.

Occurrence by site. Indigenous – *59b, *59c, 59d, *59f. Trade – 4a (Plaza V), 57a, 58c.

Range and clusters of tree-ring dates. Indigenous – 1362 to 1657; best between 1570 and 1657. Trade – 1219+ to 1581+; best between 1300 and 1581.

Validity of tree-ring dating. The tree-ring evidence indicates a beginning date of 1300, but since this paper is not concerned with post-Spanish contact sites, an end date is not given. Smiley, Stubbs, and Bannister (1953: 58) give a date of 1300 to 1750 for Jemez Black-on-white.

Jornada Plain (Brown)

Reference. Mera 1943.

Occurrence by site. Indigenous – 20a.

Validity of tree-ring dating. No further comment can be made except to say this pottery type occurs at a site occupied about 1350.

Kana-a Black-on-white

Reference. Colton 1955.

Occurrence by site. Indigenous – 15c, 15f, 15h, 15m, 53k, 77m (Type II houses). Trade – *9b, 10a, 10b, 10c, 10g, 10h, 10v–, *10w, 10z, 10aa, *11a, 14c, 66a, 98e–, 101a, 101b (Section 1, Unit 5), 114a, 115a.

Range and clusters of tree-ring dates. Indigenous – 636+x to 1285; best between 725 and 816 plus. Trade – 671+x to 1275; best between 775 and 950.

Validity of tree-ring dating. The overall dating of Kana-a Black-on-white appears to be 725 to 950; it is most abundant between 800 and 900. Kana-a Black-on-white, which begins as a trade product about 775, is better dated as a trade type than it is indigenously.

Kana-a Gray

Reference. Colton 1955.

Occurrence by site. Indigenous – *53a, 53c, 53l(?), 81a, 83a, 89a@, 90a@, 91a@–, *92b(1), 101a, 101b (Section 1, House 3), 105a, 105b, 105c, 111b. Trade – 9b, 10h, *10w, 10y, 10z, 11a, 14c, 121d.

Range and clusters of tree-ring dates. Indigenous – 675 to 1189+; best between 760 and about 900. Trade – 687 to 965; best between 775 or 825 and 965.

Validity of tree-ring dating. Kana-a Gray begins about 760 and lasts until 900; it occurs as tradeware in sites occupied until at least 965.

Kayenta Black-on-white

Reference. Colton 1955.

Occurrence by site. Indigenous – 15a, *15b, *15c, 15d, *15e, 15f, 15i, *15l, 77a, 77b, 77c, 111b, 111c, 111f, *111g. Trade – 8a, 9c–, 10u, 14a, 14b, 66a(?), 67a, 79a (Maverick Mountain phase).

Range and clusters of tree-ring dates. Indigenous – 1104+ to 1495; best between 1262 and 1285. Trade – 1023+ to 1320; best between 1255 or 1265 and 1310.

Validity of tree-ring dating. The tree-ring evidence given here indicates that Kayenta Black-on-white begins about 1260 and lasts until about 1300, being most abundant during the first 25 years of its existence.

See Tusayan Black-on-white for further discussion of Kayenta Black-on-white and associated pottery types.

Kayenta Polychrome

Reference. Colton 1956.

Occurrence by site. Indigenous – 15b, 15c, 15e, 15f, 15l, 71a, 77a, 77b, 77c, 111c. Trade – 9c–, 66a, 70a, 70b.

Range and clusters of tree-ring dates. Indigenous – 1104+ to 1495; best between 1265 and 1285. Trade – 1023+ to 1279; no concentration of dates.

Validity of tree-ring dating. Although the dating evidence is not conclusive, minimum dates of 1265 to 1285 are suggested. These dates correlate with the dates for Kayenta Black-on-white, mainly because the two pottery types usually occur together in the same sites. Kayenta Polychrome may have been most abundant during the 1265 to 1285 period, but it no doubt has an earlier beginning date than that of 1265.

Kiatuthlanna Black-on-white

Reference. Cibola White Ware Conference 1958; Hawley 1950.

Occurrence by site. Indigenous – *53a(?), 53k (pre-1090 rooms), *76b (Kiva 2 and Roomblock subfloor), 101a (Group 2, Structure 15), 105a. Trade – 106a– (House 4).

Range and clusters of tree-ring dates. Indigenous – 720+x to about 1090; best between about 850 and 910. Trade – There is a single date of *896.*

Validity of tree-ring dating. Kiatuthlanna Black-on-white is not well dated; however, the period 825 or 850 to about 910 seems to be the likely date for this type. By comparison, Gladwin (1945) dates the type at 800 to 870.

Kiet Siel Black-on-red

Reference. Colton 1956.

Occurrence by site. Indigenous – 17a(?).

Kiet Siel Gray

Reference. Colton 1955.

Occurrence by site. Indigenous – *15a, *15b, *15c, 15d, *15f, 15h, *15i, 15m, 111a, *111b, *111c, 111d (Room 6), *111e, *111f, *111g, 111h. Trade – 7d, 10u, 14b.

Range and clusters of tree-ring dates. Indigenous – 977+ to 1285; best between 1250 and 1285. Trade – 1070 to 1282; no concentration of dates.

Validity of tree-ring dating. The tree-ring evidence suggests dates of 1250 to 1285 or more; however, recent archaeological material not cited here indicates that the actual dates of Kiet Siel Gray are probably nearer 1200 to 1300.

Kiet Siel Polychrome

Reference. Colton 1956.

Occurrence by site. Indigenous – 15a, 15b, 15c, 15f, 15i, 15m, 111e. Trade – 9c—, 14b, 71a.

Range and clusters of tree-ring dates. Indigenous – 1104+ to 1285; best between 1250 plus and 1285. Trade – 1078 to 1282; dates concentrated in the early 1280's.

Validity of tree-ring dating. Although the beginning date for Kiet Siel Polychrome is not indicated by the tree-ring evidence, the period of abundance appears to be from about 1250 until 1285 or more.

Kinishba Polychrome

Reference. Wendorf 1950.

Occurrence by site. Indigenous – 67a. Trade – 72a, 72b, 79a.

Range and clusters of tree-ring dates. Indigenous – 1233+ to 1307; best between 1300 and 1307. Trade – 1302+ to *1348*; best between 1337 and 1348.

Validity of tree-ring dating. Although the tree-ring evidence is not strong, dates of 1300 to 1350 are suggested for Kinishba Polychrome.

Kinishba Red

Reference. Wendorf 1950.

Occurrence by site. Indigenous – *67a, *79b. Trade – 72a(?), 72b(?).

Range and clusters of tree-ring dates. Indigenous – 1233+ to 1307; best about 1300 plus. Trade – 1323+ to *1348*; best about 1350.

Validity of tree-ring dating. The poor tree-ring evidence suggests dates of 1300 to 1350.

Kinishba White-on-red

Reference. Second Southwestern Ceramic Seminar 1959.

Occurrence by site. Indigenous – 67a(?).

Kinnikinnick Brown

Reference. Colton 1958.

Occurrence by site. Indigenous – *14a, 14b.

Validity of tree-ring dating. The tree-ring evidence suggests that Kinnikinnick Brown occurs around 1300; however, its total life-span is not indicated. Colton (1958) dates this type at 1200 to 1400.

Kintiel Black-on-yellow

Reference. See description of Kintiel Black-on-orange in Colton 1956.

Occurrence by site. Indigenous – 70a, 70b, 71a.

Range and clusters of tree-ring dates. Indigenous – 1112+ to *1276*; best about 1275.

Validity of tree-ring dating. The meager tree-ring evidence indicates a date of about 1275, which corroborates Colton's (1956) date of about 1275 to 1300.

Kintiel Polychrome

Reference. Colton 1956.

Occurrence by site. Indigenous – 70a, 70b, 71a. Trade – 9c—.

Range and clusters of tree-ring dates. Indigenous – 1112+ to *1276*; best about 1275. Trade – 1168B to 1279; no concentration of dates.

Validity of tree-ring dating. The poor tree-ring evidence suggests a date for Kintiel Polychrome of about 1275.

Klageto Black-on-orange

Reference. Colton 1956.

Occurrence by site. Indigenous – *71a. Trade – 9c—.

Range and clusters of tree-ring dates. Indigenous and trade – 1168B to 1280(OS); best about 1275 to 1280.

Validity of tree-ring dating. The weak tree-ring and association evidence suggests that this pottery type occurs during the last half of the 1200's.

See also Klageto Black-on-yellow.

Klageto Black-on-white

Reference. Colton and Hargrave 1937.

Occurrence by site. Indigenous – 77b. Trade – 9c—.

Validity of tree-ring dating. It is not only impossible to date this pottery type, but there is also some question of its identity as a type (Cibola White Ware Conference 1958).

Klageto Black-on-yellow

Reference. Colton 1956.

Occurrence by site. Indigenous – 70a, 70b, 71a. Trade – 109a.

Range and clusters of tree-ring dates. Indigenous – 1112+ to 1280; best between 1276 and 1280. Trade – Two cutting dates of 1266 and 1276.

Validity of tree-ring dating. The tree-ring evidence indicates a date of 1250 or more, with no suggestion of the total life-span for this pottery type. Colton (1956) gives a date of around 1250 for Klageto Black-on-yellow. These comments probably apply equally well to Klageto Black-on-orange.

Kokop Black-on-orange

Reference. Colton 1956.

Occurrence by site. Trade – 15b.

Validity of tree-ring dating. Burgh (1959) suggests a beginning date of 1200 to 1225; whereas Colton (1956) dates Kokop Black-on-orange at probably 1250 to 1300. The tree-ring evidence does not improve our knowledge of the dating.

Kokop Black-on-white

Reference. Colton and Hargrave 1937.

Occurrence by site. Indigenous – 77b.

Validity of tree-ring dating. Not only it is impossible to date Kokop Black-on-white, but it is also inadequately described (Cibola White Ware Conference 1958).

Kwahe'e Black-on-white

Reference. Hawley 1950.

Occurrence by site. Indigenous – 1d, 2a, 5e, 6a, 6c, 33a, 58a, 58b, 116a.

Range and clusters of tree-ring dates. Indigenous – 963+ to 1466C; best between 1115 and 1200 plus.

Validity of tree-ring dating. The information given above is the same used by Smiley, Stubbs, and Bannister (1953: 58) to date this type at about 1125 to 1200 or more.

Kwakina Polychrome

See Pinnawa Polychrome and Wallace Polychrome.

La Plata Black-on-red

Reference. Abel 1955.

Occurrence by site. Indigenous – 89a@, 90a@, 91a@—, 92b(1). Trade – 77m— (Type II houses), 99b, 105a(?), 112c, 112e, 121d.

Range and clusters of tree-ring dates. Indigenous – 675 to 872; best between about 850 and 872. Trade – 636+x to 993+; best(?) between 850 and 900.

Validity of tree-ring dating. The dates that Abel (1955) gives for La Plata Black-on-red of about 800 to 1000 may be correct, but the tree-ring evidence indicates 850 to 900 as the period of greatest abundance.

The striking similarities between La Plata Black-on-red and Deadmans Black-on-red were noted by participants at the Sixth Southwestern

Ceramic Conference (1964). La Plata Black-on-red is now considered to be a regional variety of Deadmans Black-on-red.

La Plata Black-on-white

Reference. Cibola White Ware Conference 1958; Hawley 1950.

Occurrence by site. Indigenous – *53q, 53v@, 81a, 83a, 88a, 88b(?), 88x, 88bb, 88cc, 89a@, 90a@, 91a@–, 92b(1), 92b(2), *96a, *103a@, *103b@, *103c@, *103d@, *103e@. Trade – 77m (Type II houses), 112h.

Range and clusters of tree-ring dates. Indigenous – 430+ to 872; best between 572 and 872. Trade – 636+x to 850; best between 725 and 850 plus.

Validity of tree-ring dating. The most realistic dates for La Plata Black-on-white, particularly in an indigenous context, appear to be about 575 to 875. The period of greatest abundance is between about 600 and about 800. I believe these dates, determined on the basis of tree-ring evidence, are more realistic than the published dates of 500 to 700 (O'Bryan 1950) quoted by the Cibola White Ware Conference (1958).

La Plata Black-on-white is Hawley's name for Chapin Black-on-white and consequently, the Fifth Southwestern Ceramic Conference (1963) assigns both types the same date, 587vv to 900.

Leupp Black-on-white

Reference. Colton 1955.

Occurrence by site. Indigenous – 9c–, 10u.

Range and clusters of tree-ring dates. Indigenous: 1086 to 1279; no concentrations of tree-ring dates.

Validity of tree-ring dating. The evidence is insufficient to alter Colton's (1955) dates of 1200 to 1300.

Lincoln Black-on-red

Reference. Hawley 1950.

Occurrence by site. Indigenous – 20a, 21a.

Range and clusters of tree-ring dates. Indigenous – 1310 to 1366C; best between 1347 and 1366.

Validity of tree-ring dating. The tree-ring evidence indicates a date of about 1350 for Lincoln Black-on-red; whereas Smiley, Stubbs, and Bannister (1953: 58) show a date of about 1300 to 1400 for this type.

Linden Corrugated

Reference. Colton and Hargrave 1937.

Occurrence by site. Indigenous – 14b(?), 68a. Trade – 13d, 63b(?)–.

Range and clusters of tree-ring dates. Indigenous – 1078 to 1331; best(?) between 1282 and 1331. Trade – 1028+ to 1205; best(?) between 1130 and 1190.

Validity of tree-ring dating. The tree-ring evidence, though poor, suggests that Linden Corrugated lasted until about 1300, with no beginning date indicated. Colton and Hargrave (1937) give a date of probably 1050 to 1250.

Lino Black-on-gray

Reference. Colton 1955.

Occurrence by site. Indigenous – 18a–, 53q, 53v@, 77m, 83a, 86a, 88a, 88b(?), 88c, 88cc, 89a@, 92a (great kiva), 92b(1), 92b(2), 98e–. Trade – 9b, 96a, 103a@, 103b@, 103c@, 103d@, 103e@, 104b, 112c, 114a.

Range and clusters of tree-ring dates. Indigenous – 430+ to 1275; best between 572 and 872. Trade – 354+x to 965; best between 620 and 875.

Validity of tree-ring dating. Good tree-ring evidence indicates a life-span of about 575 to about 875 for Lino Black-on-gray, with its period of greatest abundance between about 610 and 800.

It should be borne in mind that the early dates within the indigenous category were obtained by Gila Pueblo, and that the earliest dates cited for the trade category may be associated with Basketmaker II remains.

Compared with Colton's (1955) dates for Lino Black-on-gray of about 500 to 750, those mentioned above indicate that this type begins some 75 years later and lasts for an additional 100 or 125 years. The dates of 575 to 875, derived from the tree-ring evidence, appear to be more realistic when the overall archaeological situation is considered.

Lino Black-on-gray: Durango Variety

Reference. Carlson 1963.

Occurrence by site. Indigenous – 86j, 86k, 86l, 86m.

Range and clusters of tree-ring dates. Indigenous – 729+ to *763*; best between 761 and 763.

Validity of tree-ring dating. Lino Black-on-gray: Durango Variety occurs at four sites which were built in the 760's. These dates fall about midway between the range of dates cited for Lino Black-on-gray.

All the tree-ring dates cited above were obtained by the Gila Pueblo tree-ring dating method.

Lino Fugitive Red

Reference. Colton 1955.

Occurrence by site. Indigenous – 53q, *77m (both Type I and Type II houses), 86a, 88c, 88x, 88cc, 92b(2)(?), 96a, 103a@, 103b@, 103c@, 103d@, 103e@, *117a.

Range and clusters of tree-ring dates. Indigenous – 354+x to 816; best(?) between 572 and 775.

Validity of tree-ring dating. Lino Gray occurs at every site that has Lino Fugitive Red; thus, the dates for Lino Gray may be used for making inferences about the dating of Lino Fugitive Red. Taken as a separate entity, the suggested dates for Lino Fugitive Red are 572 to 775.

Lino Gray

Reference. Colton 1955.

Occurrence by site. Indigenous – 18a, *53q, 53v@, *77m (both Type I and II houses), 81a, *83a, 86a, 86d, *88a, 88c, *88x, *88cc, 89a@, 90a@, 91a@–, *92b(1), *92b(2), *96a, 98e, 101a (Group 2, Structure 15), *101b, *103a@, *103b@, *103c@, *103d@, *103e@, *117a. Trade – 10m(?)–, 112a, 112b, 112c, 112d, 112h, 112i, 114a.

Range and clusters of tree-ring dates. Indigenous – 354+x to 1275; best between 572 and 872. Trade – 702 to 1045; best between 702 and 875.

Validity of tree-ring dating. Lino Gray occurs at a sufficient number of sites with tree-ring evidence to date it with considerable reliability. It begins about 575 or 600, lasts until 875, and is most abundant between 600 and 800. The range of dates and period of abundance are almost identical to those outlined for Lino Black-on-gray, which is not surprising because the two types usually occur together.

Lino Gray: Durango Variety

Reference. Carlson 1963.

Occurrence by site. Indigenous – *86j, *86k, *86l, *86m.

Validity of tree-ring dating. The tree-ring dates, ranges, validity, and comments for Lino Black-on-gray: Durango Variety also apply to this pottery type.

Lino Red

Reference. Daifuku 1961; Wendorf 1953a.

Occurrence by site. Indigenous – 53v@, 77m (Type II houses), 96a, 103a@, 103b@, 103c@, 103d@, 103e@.

Validity of tree-ring dating. The tree-ring evidence indicates probable dates of about 620 to 775 for Lino Red. Lino Red is always associated with Lino Black-on-gray and Lino Fugitive Red, but unlike the latter two, it is not recorded from as many sites.

Lino Red, sometimes referred to as Tallahogan Red, is probably a variety of Lino Gray.

Lino Smudged

Reference. Haury 1940a; E. A. Morris 1959a.

Occurrence by site. Indigenous – 53q(?), *77m (Type II houses), 96a, 103a@, 103b@, 103c@, 103d@, 103e@.

Validity of tree-ring dating. Lino Smudged, a variety of Lino Gray, is always associated with Lino Black-on-gray and Lino Fugitive Red. Because it appears at practically the same sites as Lino Red, I suggest that it be dated tentatively the same as Lino Red, between 620 and 775.

Little Colorado Corrugated

Reference. Colton 1955.

Occurrence by site. Indigenous – 8c, 8e, 8h, 8j, 8l, 8m, 8o, 8p, 14b(?), *71a, 118a. Trade – *109a.

Range and clusters of tree-ring dates. Indigenous – 1058 to 1282; best between 1080 and 1120. Trade – Two cutting dates of 1266 and 1276.

Validity of tree-ring dating. The tree-ring evidence indicates that Little Colorado Corrugated is a post-Sunset Crater pottery type, which is at variance with Colton's (1955) beginning date of probably 900. The inconclusive tree-ring dating suggests that Little Colorado Corrugated appears between about 1080 and, perhaps, 1275. The beginning date may be valid, but the end date is speculative.

"Little Colorado Glaze V"

Occurrence by site. Trade – 58c.

Little Colorado White Ware

Reference. Colton 1955.

Occurrence by site. Trade – 111g.

Los Lunas Coil

See Los Lunas Smudged.

Los Lunas Smudged

Reference. Hawley 1950.

Occurrence by site. Trade – 2a, 21a.

Validity of tree-ring dating. Los Lunas Smudged appears as tradeware at sites occupied between the 1270's and the 1370's. Evidence of the overall dating is unavailable.

McDonald Corrugated

Reference. Colton and Hargrave 1937.

Occurrence by site. Indigenous – 79b. Trade – 13d.

Validity of tree-ring dating. Although the tree-ring evidence is too sketchy to shed light on the time span of this type, it probably lasted until about 1300.

See the comments for McDonald Patterned Corrugated.

McDonald Painted Corrugated

Reference. Gifford 1957; Olson 1959.

Occurrence by site. Indigenous – 67a, 68a, 69a (lower level), *79a, 104c.

Range and clusters of tree-ring dates. Indigenous – 1008+ to 1331; best between 1200 and 1300 plus.

Validity of tree-ring dating. The McDonald Corrugated category should probably also be included here. As an entity, McDonald Painted Corrugated can be assigned approximately to the 1200 to 1300 time period.

See comments for McDonald Patterned Corrugated.

McDonald Patterned Corrugated

Reference. Olson 1959.

Occurrence by site. Indigenous – *79a, 104c.

Range and clusters of tree-ring dates. Indigenous – 1008+ to 1308; best between 1100 and 1290.

Validity of tree-ring dating. The tree-ring evidence for all three varieties of McDonald Corrugated suggests a beginning date of about 1100, which is a weak date. All three varieties lasted until at least 1300.

McElmo Black-on-white

Reference. Abel 1955.

Occurrence by site. Indigenous – 80a–, 88g, 88h@, 88i@, 88j@, 88m@, 88o@, 88q@, 88r@, 88s@, *92a, 93a (Room 224), 98e(?), *99b.

Range and clusters of tree-ring dates. Indigenous – 957+ to 1275; best from about 1090 to 1275.

Validity of tree-ring dating. The tree-ring evidence suggests a life-span for McElmo Black-on-white from about 1090 until at least 1250, and possibly until 1275; this agrees essentially with the dates of 1050 to 1250 proposed by the Fifth Southwestern Ceramic Conference (1963).

McElmo Black-on-white: Chaco Variety

Reference. Gordon Vivian 1959; Vivian and Mathews 1965.

Occurrence by site. Indigenous – *47a@, *48a@, *51a@, 51b, *53b@, *53c, *53e, *53f@, *53g@, *53i@, *53k, 53l, *53m, *53n, 53p–, *53s, 53t, *53u, *53w@, *53x, 53y.

Range and clusters of tree-ring dates. Indigenous – 828 to 1178v; best between about 1025 and 1125.

Validity of tree-ring dating. The Chaco variety of McElmo Black-on-white apparently begins about 1025 and lasts until at least 1125. Of particular note is the fact that the Chaco Canyon variety is earlier than the McElmo Black-on-white from the Mesa Verde area.

Mancos Black-on-white

Reference. Abel 1955; Gordon Vivian 1959.

Occurrence by site. Indigenous – 48a@, 53e, 53s, 53u, 53y, 80a–, 88g, *88z, *92a, *93a (Room 224), *99a, 99b.

Range and clusters of tree-ring dates. Indigenous – 911+ to 1192+; best between 1075 and 1125.

Validity of tree-ring dating. The beginning date of Mancos Black-on-white is not well established by the tree-ring evidence, but it apparently begins in the 1000's – at least by 1075. It lasts until about 1200 with its period of greatest abundance between 1075 and 1125.

The Fifth Southwestern Ceramic Conference (1963) gives dates of 950 to 1200 for Mancos Black-on-white in the Mancos area and 1050 to 1200 for the type on Wetherill Mesa.

Mancos Corrugated

Reference. Abel 1955.

Occurrence by site. Indigenous – 88g, *88z, 92a(?).

Range and clusters of tree-ring dates. Indigenous – 1066 to 1090C.

Validity of tree-ring dating. All the tree-ring dates are in the late 1000's; consequently, there is no indication of the total time span for this type.

Mangus Black-on-white

See Mimbres Bold Face Black-on-white.

Maverick Mountain Black-on-red

Reference. E. A. Morris 1957.

Occurrence by site. Indigenous – 79a.

Validity of tree-ring dating. Maverick Mountain Black-on-red is no longer considered to be a valid pottery type – black-on-red sherds previously classified are actually from Maverick Mountain Polychrome vessels (Sixth Southwestern Ceramic Conference 1964). See Maverick Mountain Polychrome.

Maverick Mountain Polychrome

Reference. E. A. Morris 1957; Wasley 1962.

Occurrence by site. Indigenous – 67a, *79a, 79b.

Range and clusters of tree-ring dates. Indigenous – 1201+ to 1308; best between 1265 and 1290.

Validity of tree-ring dating. The tree-ring material strongly suggests a date of 1265 to 1290.

Medicine Black-on-red

Reference. Colton 1956.

Occurrence by site. Indigenous – 15j, 15k, 15l, 15m. Trade – 8h, 9a—, 10e.

Range and clusters of tree-ring dates. Indigenous – 977+ to 1274; best between 1078 and 1129(?). Trade – 910 to 1160; best about 1100.

Validity of tree-ring dating. The status and actual identification of Medicine Black-on-red was discussed by the Sixth Southwestern Ceramic Conference (1964), but seemingly no agreement was reached. Medicine Black-on-red is considered by some workers to be a design variety of Tusayan Black-on-red (it is indeed placed in the Tsegi Orange Ware category), and by others, to be a design holdover of Deadmans Black-on-red, which is in the San Juan Red Ware category.

Recent data from the Kayenta branch material indicate that Medicine Black-on-red does not last as late as Tusayan Black-on-red (Ambler, Lindsay, and Stein 1964: 77).

Medicine Black-on-red is not well dated; however, dates of 1075 to 1125 are offered.

Medicine Gray

Reference. Colton 1955.

Occurrence by site. Trade – *10o, 14c, 98e.

Range and clusters of tree-ring dates. Trade – 760 to 1275; best(?) between 890 and 1031.

Validity of tree-ring dating. Because Medicine Gray and Coconino Gray are contemporary pottery types which differ only in the decorative techniques of the neck corrugations, these two "types" are considered together for more definite dating. See Coconino Gray.

Mesa Verde Black-on-white

Reference. Abel 1955.

Occurrence by site. Indigenous – 27a, 48a@, *51b, 53c, 53k, 53m(?), 53t, 53u, 53x, 80a—, 88g, 88h@, 88i@, 88j@, 88m@, 88o@, 88q@, 88r@, 88s@, *92a(?), 98a(7)@, 98e, 100a@, 103g@, *109a. Trade – 2c, 4a (Plaza V), 5a, 5e, 6a, 28a, 77a(?) (Kiva Room 25).

Range and clusters of tree-ring dates. Indigenous – 828 to 1284; best between 1030 and 1284. Trade – 1051 to 1612+; best between 1270 and 1340 plus or minus.

Validity of tree-ring dating. Although a good number of sites that produce Mesa Verde Black-on-white also have tree-ring dates, this pottery type is not well dated because of poor information regarding its archaeological associations. The available tree-ring material corroborates Abel's (1955) dates of about 1200 to 1300, but there is a possibility that it begins before 1200.

Mesa Verde Black-on-white: McElmo Variety

See McElmo Black-on-white.

Mesa Verde Black-on-white: Mesa Verde Variety

See Mesa Verde Black-on-white.

Mesa Verde Corrugated

Reference. Abel 1955.

Occurrence by site. Indigenous – 88g, 88h@, 88i@, 88j@, 88m@, 88o@, 88q@, 88r@, *99a, *99b.

Range and clusters of tree-ring dates. Indigenous – 993+ to 1274; best between about 1200 and 1274.

Validity of tree-ring dating. Abel's (1955) dates of about 1200 to 1300 are substantiated by the tree-ring evidence.

Mesa Verde Corrugated: Mancos Variety

See Mancos Corrugated.

Mesa Verde Corrugated: Mesa Verde Variety

See Mesa Verde Corrugated.

"Mica Culinary"

Occurrence by site. Indigenous – *56a.

Mimbres Black-on-white

Reference. Hawley 1950.

Occurrence by site. Indigenous – 20a. Trade – 2a, 5e.

Validity of tree-ring dating. The total range of tree-ring dates is from 1113+ to 1347. There is no good evidence for determining the beginning date of Mimbres Black-on-white, but it apparently persisted until some time after 1250.

Mimbres Bold Face Black-on-white

Reference. Hawley 1950.

Occurrence by site. Indigenous – *78a (Pit Houses O, K, E, and B), *78b, 78c(?) (Houses 1 and 2), 106a (House 2), 107a.

Range and clusters of tree-ring dates. Indigenous – 738+ to 927; best between 775 and 927.

Validity of tree-ring dating. This pottery type is not well dated; however, the tree-ring evidence suggests dates of 775 to 927 or more.

Moccasin Gray

Reference. Abel 1955.

Occurrence by site. Indigenous – 88y. Trade – 121d.

Validity of tree-ring dating. Although all the tree-ring dates are in the last half of the 800's, which would indicate that Moccasin Gray was present between 850 and 900, Abel's (1955) dates of 800 to 900 should be considered as more accurate for the total life-span of the type.

Moenkopi Corrugated

Reference. Colton 1955.

Occurrence by site. Indigenous – *13d, 13e(?), 15a, 15b, 15c, 15d, 15f, 15h, 15j, 15k, 15m, 17a, 77b, 111a, 111b, 111c, *111e, 111f, 111g, *111h, 118a. Trade – 7d, 8a, 8j, 8k, 8l, 8o, 8p, *10d, 10q, 10u, 10v–, *12a(?), 12b(?), *13a(?), *13b(?), *13c(?), 14b, 80a–, *98e.

Range and clusters of tree-ring dates. Indigenous – 977+ to 1390; best between 1078 and 1285. Trade – 813 to 1282; best between about 1080 and about 1200.

Validity of tree-ring dating. The tree-ring evidence sheds more light on the beginning date of Moenkopi Corrugated than on its terminal date. This pottery type begins about 1075 – it is definitely post-Sunset Crater eruption – and lasts until 1285 or 1300.

Mogollon Red-on-brown

Reference. Hawley 1950.

Occurrence by site. Indigenous – 78a (Pit Houses F, H, E, and B), 78c(?), 106a, *107a. Trade – 14b, 104b.

Range and clusters of tree-ring dates. Indigenous – 748vv to *951*; best between 775 and 951. Trade – 641+ to 1282; no concentration of dates.

Validity of tree-ring dating. Although not well-dated, Mogollon Red-on-brown apparently begins at 775 or 800 and lasts until at least 950; it is probably most abundant between 875 and 925. This pottery type is dated primarily in an indigenous context.

Morfield Black-on-gray

Reference. Abel 1955.

Occurrence by site. Trade – 121d.

Validity of tree-ring dating. LA 4408 was occupied about 900; this may indicate that Morfield Black-on-gray begins about 900. Until further information on this pottery type is available, Abel's (1955) dates of about 950 to 1100 still stand.

Morfield Black-on-gray was discarded from the Mesa Verde pottery typology by the Fifth Southwestern Ceramic Conference (1963).

"Mud Ware"

See Fiber-Tempered, Unfired.

Nantack Polychrome

Reference. E. A. Morris 1957.

Occurrence by site. Indigenous – 79a.

Validity of tree-ring dating. This type has the same date as Maverick Mountain Polychrome, 1265 to 1290.

"Neck Corrugated, Gray"

Occurrence by site. Indigenous – 65a(?), 101a(?).

Obelisk Gray

Reference. Colton 1955.

Occurrence by site. Indigenous – 96a(?), *97a, 103a@(?), 103b@(?), 103c@(?), 103d@(?), 103e@(?), 117a.

Range and clusters of tree-ring dates. Indigenous – 354+x to 759; best between 620 and 675.

Validity of tree-ring dating. The associational evidence shows this pottery type to be the earliest grayware in the Four Corners region. Although there is a possibility that Obelisk Gray began as early as 475, the most direct tree-ring evidence suggests a beginning date of about 620. Obelisk Gray decreased in abundance after 675, but it may have lasted until about 750.

"Obliterated Corrugated, Brownware"

Occurrence by site. Indigenous – 61a, 69a, 79b.

Padre Black-on-white

Reference. Colton 1955.

Occurrence by site. Indigenous – 9a–, 9c–, 10u, 13b. Trade – 98e.

Range and clusters of tree-ring dates. Indigenous – 1086 to 1279; best(?) between about 1100 and about 1200. Trade – 957+ to 1275; tree-ring dates concentrated around 1075, but the ceramic associations are not established.

Validity of tree-ring dating. Padre Black-on-white is not well dated, but since it is Dogoszhi Black-on-white made with Little Colorado White Ware paste, we can use the more complete information from Dogoszhi Black-on-white to infer a similar date of 1085 to 1200.

"Panhandle Paddled"

Occurrence by site. Trade – 5a.

Patterned Corrugated

Reference. Olson 1959.

Occurrence by site. Indigenous – 79b.

Piedra Black-on-white

Reference. Hawley 1950; Reed 1958.

Occurrence by site. Indigenous – 88y, 89a@, *121a@, *121b, *121c, *121d.

Range and clusters of tree-ring dates. Indigenous – 774+ to 900r; best between 847 and 900.

Validity of tree-ring dating. The tree-ring evidence indicates the presence of Piedra Black-on-white during the 850 to 900 period. Reed (1958) dates this type from about 750 to perhaps 900. The Fifth Southwestern Ceramic Conference (1963) gives dates of 700 to 900.

Piedra–Gallina Transitional Black-on-white

Reference. Hall 1944.

Occurrence by site. Indigenous – 121c.

Validity of tree-ring dating. We can say only that this pottery type occurs at a site occupied about 900.

Pindi Black-on-white

Reference. Stubbs and Stallings 1953.

Occurrence by site. Indigenous – 1a, 1b, 1c, 1e, 5a, 5e, 6a, 6b.

Range and clusters of tree-ring dates. Indigenous – 1050 to 1612+; best between 1300 and 1340.

Validity of tree-ring dating. There is no new evidence to change the date of about 1300 to about 1350 given by Smiley, Stubbs, and Bannister (1953: 58).

Pinedale Black-on-red

Reference. Carlson 1961 .

Occurrence by site. Indigenous – 67a, 68a. Trade – 63a, *79a, 79b, 80a—, 98e.

Range and clusters of tree-ring dates. Indigenous – 1131+ to 1331; best between 1273 and 1331. Trade – 957+ to 1346; no concentration of dates.

Validity of tree-ring dating. The tree-ring dates for this pottery type in a trade context are erratic. Carlson's (1961) dates of 1275 to 1325 seem to be the best that can be offered for Pinedale Black-on-red at this time.

Pinedale Black-on-white

Reference. Colton and Hargrave 1937.

Occurrence by site. Indigenous – *68a, 72a, 72b. Trade – 9c—, 14b(?).

Range and clusters of tree-ring dates. Indigenous – 1131+ to *1348*; best between 1275 and 1348. Trade – 1078 to 1282; no concentration of dates.

Validity of tree-ring dating. It seems prudent, because of the scanty tree-ring evidence, to place Pinedale Black-on-white within the *minimum* time span of 1300 to 1350, keeping in mind that Colton and Hargrave (1937) date this pottery type as about 1290 to 1375.

Pinedale Polychrome

Reference. Carlson 1961.

Occurrence by site. Indigenous – *67a, *68a, 72a, 72b, 74b, 74d, 74g. Trade – 5e(?), 63a, 63b—, 71a, 79a (Room 11), 79b.

Range and clusters of tree-ring dates. Indigenous – 1131+ to *1348*; best between about 1300 and 1348. Trade – 1113+ to 1346; best between 1275 and 1300 plus.

Validity of tree-ring dating. Corroborating evidence from both indigenous and trade contexts indicates that Pinedale Polychrome has a date of about 1275 to 1350, which extends the end date 25 years longer than that proposed by Carlson (1961).

Pinnawa Polychrome

Reference. Colton and Hargrave 1937; described as Kwakina Polychrome in Woodbury and Woodbury MS.

Occurrence by site. Trade – 119a.

Pinto Black-on-red

Reference. Gifford 1957.

Occurrence by site. Indigenous – 61a. Trade – 9c—, 67a, 68a, 79a (Maverick Mountain phase).

Range and clusters of tree-ring dates. Indigenous – *1345* to *1385*; best between 1345 and 1385. Trade – 1131+ to 1331; best between 1265 and 1331.

Validity of tree-ring dating. Although not recorded from a large number of sites, Pinto Black-on-red is fairly well dated as beginning about 1265 and lasting until about 1350. The Sixth Southwestern Ceramic Conference (1964) has suggested dates of 1275 to 1350 for this pottery type.

Pinto Polychrome

Reference. Hawley 1950.

Occurrence by site. Indigenous – 61a, 63a(?), 63b(?)—. Trade – 67a, 69a (lower level), 72a, 72b, 74g.

Range and clusters of tree-ring dates. Indigenous – 1109+ to *1385*; best(?) between 1345 and 1385. Trade – 1174 to 1383; best between about 1200 and 1348.

Validity of tree-ring dating. Colton and Hargrave (1937) date Pinto Polychrome as probably 1150 to 1250. The tree-ring evidence does not suggest a beginning date before about 1200, or slightly later, with an end date of 1385 to 1400. According to Steen (1962: 28), the Pinto style is most popular during the period 1200 to 1250.

Both Gila and Tonto polychromes are also dated by tree-ring evidence at 1250 to 1400. See comments for Gila Polychrome.

"Plain Brown"

Occurrence by site. Indigenous – 72a, 72b, 74a, 74e, 74f, 74g, 74h, *104c.

"Plain Corrugated, Brownware"

Occurrence by site. Indigenous – *79a, 79b.

"Plain, Gray"

Occurrence by site. Indigenous – 99a, 109a.

"Plainware"

Occurrence by site. Indigenous – *119a.

Poge Black-on-white

Reference. Stubbs and Stallings 1953.

Occurrence by site. Indigenous – 1a, 1c, 1e, 2d, 3a, 4a (Plaza V), 5a, 5e, 6a, 6b.

Range and clusters of tree-ring dates. Indigenous – 1050 to 1612+; best between about 1275 and 1350.

Validity of tree-ring dating. Smiley, Stubbs, and Bannister (1953: 58) date Poge Black-on-white at 1325 to 1360. New tree-ring evidence from Pueblo Largo suggests that it began at 1300 and lasted until at least 1350.

Point of Pines Polychrome

Reference. E. A. Morris 1957; Olson 1959.

Occurrence by site. Indigenous – *79b.

Validity of tree-ring dating. Point of Pines Polychrome is not dated on the basis of tree-ring evidence. The single tree-ring date of 1302+ is approximately 100 years too early when the overall archaeological situation is considered.

Polacca Black-on-white

Reference. Colton 1955.

Occurrence by site. Indigenous – 15c(?), 15f(?). Trade – 14b.

Range and clusters of tree-ring dates. Indigenous – 1104+ to 1289+; best between 1269 and 1285. Trade – 1078 to 1282; no concentration of dates.

Validity of tree-ring dating. Polacca Black-on-white is not well dated. We may say only that it appears in sites during the last half of the 1200's; it is a regional variety of Kayenta Black-on-white with White Mountain area influence.

See Tusayan Black-on-white for comments by Smith (1962) concerning this pottery type.

Potsuwi'i Incised

Reference. Hawley 1950.

Occurrence by site. Indigenous – 42a, 42b, 42c, *50b, 57a, 58b, 58c. Trade – 5a.

Range and clusters of tree-ring dates. Indigenous – 1271+ to 1581+; best between about 1425 and 1525 plus(?). Trade – 1299 to 1612+; no concentration of dates.

Validity of tree-ring dating. The tree-ring evidence suggests a guess date for Potsuwi'i Incised of about 1425 to 1525 or more.

Prescott Grayware

Reference. Colton 1958.

Occurrence by site. Trade – 13a, 13c, 13d.

See Verde Gray.

Prieto Indented Corrugated

Reference. Gifford 1957; Olson 1959.

Occurrence by site. Indigenous – 79b.

Validity of tree-ring dating. We may say only that this type appears in a site occupied after 1300.

Prieto Polychrome

Reference. E. A. Morris 1957.

Occurrence by site. Indigenous – 79a (Maverick Mountain phase).

Validity of tree-ring dating. This type is found associated with Maverick Mountain and Nantack polychromes, which date from about 1265 to 1290.

Puerco Black-on-red

Reference. Carlson 1961.

Occurrence by site. Indigenous – 65a. Trade – *48a@, 53m, 53p–, 53s, 53t, *53u, 53x, 98e.

Range and clusters of tree-ring dates. Indigenous – There is a single date of 1031+. Trade – 921+ to 1275; best between 1030 and 1124.

Validity of tree-ring dating. The tree-ring evidence suggests dates of 1030 to 1175, with 1050 to 1125 representing the period of greatest abundance. Carlson (1961) dates Puerco Black-on-red at 1000 to 1200, with the middle part of this period representing its greatest abundance.

Puerco Black-on-red is a variety of Wingate Black-on-red (Second Southwestern Ceramic Seminar 1959).

Puerco Black-on-white

Reference. Cibola White Ware Conference 1958; Hawley 1950.

Occurrence by site. Indigenous – 53p–, 53t, 65a, *76b (Kiva 1), 101a(?) (Wingate phase), 102b, 102c, 105a(?). Trade – 14c (House A?), 67a(?).

Range and clusters of tree-ring dates. Indigenous – 806+x to 1123; best between 1010 and 1123. Trade – 1083+ to 1307; no concentration of dates.

Validity of tree-ring dating. The tree-ring evidence for Puerco Black-on-white in an indigenous context suggests dates of 1010 to 1125, thereby altering the dating of 1050 to 1150 given at the Cibola White Ware Conference (1958).

"Punched Corrugated"

Occurrence by site. Indigenous – 119a.

Querino Polychrome

See Wingate Polychrome.

Ramos Polychrome

Reference. Sayles 1936.

Occurrence by site. Indigenous – 54a–. Trade – 20a.

Validity of tree-ring dating. We may state only that Ramos Polychrome is found in two sites which have tree-ring dates falling in about the last 50 years of the 1300's.

Red Mesa Black-on-white

Reference. Cibola White Ware Conference 1958; Hawley 1950.

Occurrence by site. Indigenous – 1d, 6c, 47a@, 51a@, 53a, 53b@, 53c, 53f@, 53g@, 53i@, *53j, 53k, 53m, 53n, 53s, 53w@, *76b, 101a (Unit 3, kiva), 102b, 102c, *105a, *105b, *105c, *115a, 116a. Trade – 15c, 99b.

Range and clusters of tree-ring dates. Indigenous – 720+x to 1231; best between 850 to 900 and about 1125. Trade – 993+ to 1285; no concentration of dates.

Validity of tree-ring dating. The beginning date for Red Mesa Black-on-white is not definite; however, it probably begins soon after 850. This type lasts until 1125 as "Late Red Mesa Black-on-white," which verges on Puerco Black-on-white. "Late Red Mesa" probably begins about 1050.

The Cibola White Ware Conference (1958) quotes Gladwin's dates of 870 to 930 for Red Mesa Black-on-white, but recent archaeological studies indicate that it has a longer life-span than 60 years.

"Red-Slipped Corrugated"

Occurrence by site. Indigenous – *79a.

"Redware"

Occurrence by site. Indigenous – 79a, 104c.

"Redware, Smudged Interior"

Occurrence by site. Trade – 47a@, *48a@, 51a@, 53b@, 53c@, 53f@, 53g@, 53i@, 53k, *53s, *53u, 53w@, 93a, 101b, 105c.

Reserve Black-on-white

Reference. Cibola White Ware Conference 1958; Martin and Rinaldo 1950.

Occurrence by site. Indigenous – 98e(?), 104c@, 107a. Trade – 8o, 9c–, 53x(?), 92a(?) (Room 21).

Range and clusters of tree-ring dates. Indigenous – 927 to 1275; best(?) between 1071 and 1115. Trade – 1008+ to 1279; best between 1032 and 1090.

Validity of tree-ring dating. The beginning date for Reserve Black-on-white is not indicated by the tree-ring evidence; however, the 940 date suggested by the Cibola White Ware Conference (1958) seems plausible. This type lasts into the early 1100's and appears to be most abundant around 1075.

"Reserve Brownware"

Occurrence by site. Trade – 53y.

Reserve Smudged

Reference. Martin, Rinaldo, and Antevs 1949.

Occurrence by site. Indigenous – *78a.

Validity of tree-ring dating. We may say only that Reserve Smudged appears at a site with tree-ring dates that fall in the last half of the 700's.

Rio de Flag Brown

Reference. Colton 1958.

Occurrence by site. Indigenous – *7d, 8c, 8l, *9b, 10a, 10b, 10c, *10d, 10e, *10f, *10g, *10h, 10i, *10l, *10m–, *10n, *10o, *10p, *10r, *10s, *10t, 10v–, *10w, *10x–, *10y, *10z, 10aa, *11a, *11b–, 14c, 118a. Trade – 114a.

Range and clusters of tree-ring dates. Indigenous – 687+ to 1256; best between about 800 and 1061. Trade – 746vv to 775c; concentrated at 775.

Validity of tree-ring dating. There is no good tree-ring evidence to begin Rio de Flag Brown before about 775; it lasts until the eruption of Sunset Crater, 1065 plus or minus a year. The later tree-ring dates are from sites where post-Sunset Crater pottery types, such as Winona Brown, are dominant and where Rio de Flag Brown seemingly represents intrusions or holdovers from its actual period of manufacture.

Rio Grande Glaze I

This "type" includes Rio Grande Glaze I Red, Rio Grande Glaze I Yellow, and Rio Grande Glaze I Polychrome.

Reference. Kidder and Shepard 1936.

Occurrence by site. Indigenous – *4a (Plaza V), 28a, 58b, 58e, 58f. Trade – 5c, 6a, 20a, 21a, 36a, 42b, 42c, 46a, 59f, 116a.

Range and clusters of tree-ring dates. Indigenous – 1219+ to 1493C; best between 1299 and 1425 plus. Trade – 963+ to 1502; best between 1310 and 1366(?).

Validity of tree-ring dating. The weak tree-ring dating evidence suggests a beginning for Glaze I of about 1300 and an end date of about 1450. These dates are at odds with the published dates of 1375 to 1425 (Kidder and Shepard 1936) and 1375 to 1400 (Hewett 1953).

See also the separate categories for Rio Grande Glaze I Polychrome, Rio Grande Glaze I Red, and Rio Grande Glaze I Yellow.

Rio Grande Glaze I Polychrome

Reference. Hawley 1950; Kidder and Shepard 1936.

Occurrence by site. Indigenous – *4a (Plaza V), *5d.

Range and clusters of tree-ring dates. Indigenous – 1219+ to 1392. Tree-ring concentrations uncertain.

Validity of tree-ring dating. Although the tree-ring evidence is weak, a beginning date of 1300 and an end date of 1390 or more are suggested. See comments for Rio Grande Glaze I Yellow.

Rio Grande Glaze I Red

Reference. Hawley 1950; Kidder and Shepard 1936.

Occurrence by site. Indigenous – 2c, 3a, *4a (Plaza V), 5a, *5d, 6b, 28a, 32a, 34a, 58a. Trade – 1a, 2b, 46a.

Range and clusters of tree-ring dates. Indigenous – 1219+ to 1612+; best between 1300 and 1500(?). Trade – 1212+ to 1333+; best about 1320.

Validity of tree-ring dating. A beginning date of 1300 is suggested; the end date seems to be post-1425. See also Rio Grande Glaze I Yellow.

Rio Grande Glaze I Yellow

Reference. Hawley 1950; Kidder and Shepard 1936.

Occurrence by site. Indigenous – 2c, 3a, *4a (Plaza V), 5a, *5d, 6b, 32a, 34a, 58a.

Range and clusters of tree-ring dates. Indigenous – 1219+ to 1612+; best between 1300 and about 1450.

Validity of tree-ring dating. Dates of 1300 to 1450 are suggested for Rio Grande Glaze I Yellow.

On the basis of rather weak tree-ring and archaeological association evidence, the Rio Grande Glaze I "group" seems to have been present between 1300 and 1450.

Rio Grande Glaze II

Reference. Kidder and Shepard 1936.

Occurrence by site. Indigenous – 3a, 4a (Building IV), 5a, 32a, 34a, 58a, 58b, 58e, 58f. Trade – 59b.

Range and clusters of tree-ring dates. Indigenous – 1298+ to 1612+; best between about 1400 and about 1500. Trade – 1362 to 1577; best(?) between 1570 and 1573.

Validity of tree-ring dating. The tree-ring evidence suggests that Glaze II occurs between 1400 and 1500, but the published dates for this type should be kept in mind – 1400 to 1425 (Hewett 1953) and 1425 to 1475 (Kidder and Shepard 1936).

Rio Grande Glaze III

Reference. Kidder and Shepard 1936.

Occurrence by site. Indigenous – 3a, 4a (Building IV), 5a, 32a, 34a, 58a, 58b, 58e, 58f. Trade – 57a, 58c, 59b, 59f.

Range and clusters of tree-ring dates. Indigenous – 1298+ to 1612+; best between about 1425 and 1500. Trade – 1362 to 1581+; best about 1550.

Validity of tree-ring dating. The tree-ring evidence suggests dates of about 1425 to 1500 or 1550, a time period which spans the combined dates previously published for this type – 1425 to 1475 (Hewett 1953) and 1475 to 1550 (Kidder and Shepard 1936).

Rio Grande Glaze IV

Reference. Kidder and Shepard 1936.

Occurrence by site. Indigenous – 3a, 4a (Building IV), 5a, 32a, 34a, 58b, 58e, 58f. Trade – 42a, 42b, 42c, 50b, 57a, 58c, 59b, 59f.

Range and clusters of tree-ring dates. Indigenous – 1298+ to 1612+; best between about 1425 and 1500 plus. Trade – 1271+ to 1581+; best between 1420 plus and 1573.

Validity of tree-ring dating. The dating of this pottery type is not good; however, the tree-ring evidence suggests that it begins at 1425 and ends at 1575 or later. The published dates of 1475 to 1500 (Hewett 1953) and 1550 to 1600 (Kidder and Shepard 1936) should be kept in mind.

Rio Grande Glaze V

Reference. Kidder and Shepard 1936.

Occurrence by site. Indigenous – 3a, 5a, 32a, 58b, 58e, 58f. Trade – *42a, *42c, 50b, 57a, 58c, 59b, 59d, 59f.

Range and clusters of tree-ring dates. Indigenous – 1200 to 1612+; best between about 1425 and 1500. Trade – 1334 to 1657; no apparent concentration of dates.

Validity of tree-ring dating. The tree-ring evidence suggests a beginning date of 1425 or more and a post-1650 end date; however, the dating is weak because this paper is not primarily concerned with post-1550 sites. The published dates of 1500 to 1700 (Hewett 1953) and 1600 to 1700 (Kidder and Shepard 1936) should be kept in mind.

Rio Grande Glaze VI

Reference. Kidder and Shepard 1936.

Occurrence by site. Indigenous – 3a, 5a, 32a, 58b. Trade – 57a, 58c, 59b, 59c, 59d, 59f.

Range and clusters of tree-ring dates. Indigenous – 1299 to 1612+; no good indication of date concentrations. Trade – 1422 to 1657; no good date concentrations.

Validity of tree-ring dating. Since this paper is not concerned with post-1550 tree-ring dates and sites, no attempt has been made to date this type. Hewett (1953), however, dates Rio Grande Glaze VI at 1700 to 1838.

Roosevelt Black-on-white

Reference. Hawley 1950; Pomeroy 1962.

Occurrence by site. Indigenous – 63a(?), 63b(?)–, 67a, 74d, 74e, 74g.

Range and clusters of tree-ring dates. Indigenous – 1109+ to *1348*; best between 1300 and 1348.

Validity of tree-ring dating. Pomeroy (1962) dates Roosevelt Black-on-white at 1200 to 1350; whereas Steen (1962: 28) says "it was developed possibly as early as A.D. 1150 and persisted through the 14th century." The tree-ring evidence indicates a date of 1300 to 1350 for Roosevelt Black-on-white.

Rosa Black-on-white

Reference. Hall 1944; Hawley 1950.

Occurrence by site. Indigenous – 112a, 112b, 112c, 112d, 112e, 112f, 112g, 112h, 112i.

Range and clusters of tree-ring dates. Indigenous – 702 to 876; best between 775 and 876.

Validity of tree-ring dating. Rosa Black-on-white occurs between at least 775 and 875, with the possibility that it begins around 700 and the probability that it lasts until 900.

Rosa Brown

Reference. Dittert, Hester, and Eddy 1961.
See Rosa Plain.

Rosa Glaze Black-on-white

Reference. Dittert, Hester, and Eddy 1961.

Occurrence by site. Indigenous – 121d.

Validity of tree-ring dating. It is possible to say only that this pottery type is found in a site occupied about 900.

Rosa Gray

Reference. Dittert, Hester, and Eddy 1961.

See Rosa Plain.

Rosa Neck Banded

Reference. Dittert, Hester, and Eddy 1961.

See Rosa Neck Coil.

Rosa Neck Coil

Reference. Hall 1944.

Occurrence by site. Indigenous – 112a, 112b, 112c, 112h, 112i, 121d.

Range and clusters of tree-ring dates. Indigenous – 702 to 898r; best between 702 and 898.

Validity of tree-ring dating. Rosa Neck Coil is not as strongly dated as Rosa Black-on-white and Rosa Plain, because it is not present in as many sites with tree-ring dates. The only feasible dates are between 700 and 900.

Rosa Plain

Reference. Hall 1944; Hawley 1950.

Occurrence by site. Indigenous – *112a, *112b, *112c, *112d, *112e, *112f, *112g, *112h, 112i, 121d.

Range and clusters of tree-ring dates. Indigenous – 702 to 898r; best between 702 and 898.

Validity of tree-ring dating. This pottery type is well dated between 700 and 900, but only as an indigenous product.

Rosa Scored

Reference. Hall 1944.

Occurrence by site. Indigenous – 112a, 112b, 112c, 112d, 112e, 112f, 112g, 112h, 112i.

Validity of tree-ring dating. Rosa Scored occurs at exactly the same sites as Rosa Black-on-white; hence, dating is considered to be the same, 700 to 900, with 775 to 875 the probable period of abundance.

Rosa Smoothed

See Rosa Plain.

Rowe Black-on-white

Reference. Hawley 1950.

Occurrence by site. Indigenous – 5a, 5d, 5e.

Range and clusters of tree-ring dates. Indigenous – 1113+ to 1612+; no apparent concentration of dates.

Validity of tree-ring dating. The associated tree-ring dates are erratic. Rowe Black-on-white is a late subtype of Galisteo Black-on-white; consequently, it probably dates in the late 1300's.

Sacaton Red-on-buff

Reference. Gladwin and others 1937.

Occurrence by site. Trade – 66a(?).

St. Johns Black-on-red

Reference. Carlson 1961.

Occurrence by site. Trade – 13d (Room 45A), 61a, 79a (Maverick Mountain phase).

Range and clusters of tree-ring dates. Trade – 1137+ to *1385*; no apparent concentration of dates.

Validity of tree-ring dating. Although this type is inadequately dated, sherds of St. Johns Black-on-red can be expected to exist throughout the life-span of St. Johns Polychrome, which is dated 1175 to 1300.

St. Johns Polychrome

Reference. Carlson 1961.

Occurrence by site. Indigenous – 65a, 67a, *69a (lower level). Trade – 1b, 2a, 4a (Plaza V), 5a, *5e, 6a, 9a–, 9c–, 13d, 14b, 27a, 33a, 53x–, 63a, 71a, 76a, 77a, 77c, *79a (Maverick Mountain phase), 80a–, 88g, 93a–, 109a, 116a.

Range and clusters of tree-ring dates. Indigenous – 1031+ to 1307; no concentration of dates. Trade – 963+ to 1612+; best between 1200 and about 1300.

Validity of tree-ring dating. Although St. Johns Polychrome is one of the most widespread trade products in the Southwest, it is still not well dated by the tree-ring evidence. The best dates presently available are those of 1175 to 1300 proposed by Carlson (1961).

See Chapter 3 for a discussion and Table 6 for a graphic presentation of the dating of St. Johns Polychrome on the basis of tree-ring and ceramic associations and their validity.

St. Johns Polychrome: Kinishba Variety

Reference. Cummings 1940.

Occurrence by site. Indigenous – 67a.

Validity of tree-ring dating. Even though there is obviously inadequate dating evidence for this undescribed ceramic variety, it can be anticipated that its life-span will fall within the range of dates for St. Johns Polychrome.

St. Johns Polychrome: Springerville Variety

See Springerville Polychrome.

Salado Red

Reference. Hawley 1950.

Occurrence by site. Indigenous – 61a, *63a(?), *63b(?)–.

Validity of tree-ring dating. Since the tree-ring and associational evidence is poor, we can only suggest that Salado Red occurs from 1350 to about 1400; however, this is not necessarily the total time span of the pottery type.

Salado Redware

Reference. Hawley 1950.

Occurrence by site. Indigenous – *72a, *72b, *73a, *74a, *74b, *74c, *74f, *74g, *74h, *74j. Trade – 67a(?).

Range and clusters of tree-ring dates. Indigenous –1278+ to *1348*; best between 1304 and 1348. Trade – 1233+ to 1307; best between 1300 and 1307.

Validity of tree-ring dating. There is good evidence that Salado Redware is abundant between 1300 and 1350, even though these dates may not represent its total life-span.

Salado Scored

Reference. Pierson 1962.

Occurrence by site. Indigenous – 63a.

Salado White-on-red

Reference. Colton and Hargrave 1937.

Occurrence by site. Indigenous – 63a(?), 63b(?)–.

Validity of tree-ring dating. This pottery type may date around 1300, but the tree-ring and associational evidence is open to question.

Salt Red

Reference. Haury 1945; Schroeder 1940.

Occurrence by site. Indigenous – 63a.

Salt Smudged

Reference. Haury 1945.

Occurrence by site. Indigenous – 63a.

San Carlos Red-on-brown

Reference. Olson 1959.

Occurrence by site. Indigenous – 61a, 63a. Trade – 79a (Maverick Mountain phase).

Range and clusters of tree-ring dates. Indigenous – *1345* to *1385*; best between 1345 and 1385. Trade – 1201+ to 1308; best between 1265 and 1290.

Validity of tree-ring dating. San Carlos Red-on-brown is present in sites that have tree-ring dates between the late 1200's and the late 1300's. A guess date, based on insufficient evidence, suggests that this pottery type dates from about 1275 to 1400.

San Francisco Red

Reference. Hawley 1950.

Occurrence by site. Indigenous – 78a, 78b, *78c, *106a, *107a.

Range and clusters of tree-ring dates. Indigenous – 738+v to *951;* best between about 760 and 951.

Validity of tree-ring dating. San Francisco Red is found in sites that were occupied during the period from about 750 to 950, but these dates probably do not represent the actual beginning and end dates.

Sankawi Black-on-cream

Reference. Hawley 1950; Mera 1939.

Occurrence by site. Indigenous – 42a, 42c, 57a, 58b, 58c, 58e, 58f. Trade – 3a, 5a.

Range and clusters of tree-ring dates. Indigenous – 1334 to 1581+; best between 1425 plus and 1550 plus. Trade – 1299 to 1612+; no concentration of dates apparent.

Validity of tree-ring dating. Since the dating evidence is weak, only a beginning date in the late 1400's is suggested. Smiley, Stubbs, and Bannister (1953: 58) indicate a date of about 1500 to about 1600 for Sankawi Black-on-cream.

Santa Fe Black-on-white

Reference. Stubbs and Stallings 1953.

Occurrence by site. Indigenous – 1a, 1b, 1c, 1d, 1e, 2a, 2b, 2c, 2d, 3a, *4a (Plaza V), 5a, 5c, *5d, 5e, 6a, 6c, 27a, 28a, 33a, 36a, 41c, 45a, 46a, 57a, 58a, 58b, 58c, 58d, 116a.

Range and clusters of tree-ring dates. Indigenous – 963+ to 1612+; best between 1200 and 1350.

Validity of tree-ring dating. The present information is the same as that used by Smiley, Stubbs, and Bannister (1953: 58) to date Santa Fe Black-on-white at 1200 to 1350.

Shato Black-on-white

Reference. Colton 1955.

Occurrence by site. Indigenous – 15c, 118a. Trade – 8b, 8c, 8d, 8h, 8l, 8n, 8o.

Range and clusters of tree-ring dates. Indigenous – 1109+ to 1285; no apparent concentration of dates. Trade – 1059 to 1207; best between 1080 and 1130.

Validity of tree-ring dating. The tree-ring evidence indicates a date of 1080 to 1130; however, Shato Black-on-white is poorly dated and mainly as a trade product.

The validity of Shato Black-on-white as a separate type has been questioned by Breternitz (1962) who considers it as an exotic variety of Black Mesa, Dogoszhi, and Sosi black-on-whites.

Showlow Black-on-red

Reference. Colton and Hargrave 1937.

Occurrence by site. Indigenous – 69a(?) (lower level). Trade – 7d, 9c–, 10u, 13d (Room 45A), 53x, 118a.

Range and clusters of tree-ring dates. Indigenous – At the Showlow ruin, Showlow Black-on-red(?) is associated with the lower level, dated about 1204. Trade – 1108+ to 1270; best between 1030 and 1175.

Validity of tree-ring dating. The tree-ring evidence, although not strong, supports a pre-1200 date, with a beginning date of perhaps 1050.

Showlow Polychrome

Reference. Carlson 1961.

Occurrence by site. Indigenous – 67a, 68a, 69a (upper level), 72a, 72b.

Range and clusters of tree-ring dates. Indigenous – 1174 to 1383; best between 1300 and 1383.

Validity of tree-ring dating. The tree-ring evidence suggests a beginning date of about 1300 and an end date soon after 1383. Carlson (1961) dates Showlow Polychrome, which might well be considered a variety of Four Mile Polychrome, at 1325 to 1400.

Showlow Red

Occurrence by site. Indigenous – 69a (upper level).

Validity of tree-ring dating. This ceramic category is probably made up of the plain red body sherds of various vessels of White Mountain Redware (Second Southwestern Ceramic Seminar 1959).

Sityatki Polychrome

Reference. Colton 1956.

Occurrence by site. Indigenous – 77a, 77b, 77c. Trade – 3a, 5a.

Range and clusters of tree-ring dates. Indigenous – 1255 to 1495; best between about 1375 and 1400. Trade – 1299 to 1612+; best about 1425(?).

Validity of tree-ring dating. Not only is the tree-ring dating poor, but the associational evidence is lacking during the supposed upper end of the range of time for Sityatki Polychrome. A beginning date of 1375 is suggested; Colton (1956) dates the type at probably 1400 to 1625.

"Smudged Ware"

Occurrence by site. Trade – 77m (Type II houses).

Validity of tree-ring dating. This nonspecific ceramic category is found in architectural units which are thought to have been occupied from about 725 until about 825.

Snowflake Black-on-white

Reference. Colton 1941; Martin and Willis 1940.

Occurrence by site. Indigenous – *69a (lower level), 104c@. Trade – 9c–, 14b, 111b(?).

Range and clusters of tree-ring dates. Indigenous – 1008+ to 1228; best(?) between 1100 and 1200. Trade – 1078 to 1282; no concentration of dates.

Validity of tree-ring dating. Snowflake Black-on-white is poorly dated as both an indigenous and a trade type. Colton's (1941) dates of 1100 to 1200 still stand.

Socorro Black-on-white

Reference. Hawley 1950.

Occurrence by site. Trade – 2a, 6c, 27a, 28a, 33a.

Range and clusters of tree-ring dates. Trade – 1004+ to 1393; best between 1050 and about 1300(?).

Validity of tree-ring dating. This type, which occurs only in a trade context, is not well dated. There is no new evidence to change the previous dates of about 1050 to about 1275 (Smiley, Stubbs, and Bannister 1953: 58).

Sosi Black-on-white

Reference. Colton 1955.

Occurrence by site. Indigenous – 13d, *13e, 15c, 15j, *15k, *15m, 76a(?), 77b, 111c. Trade – 7d, 9a–, 9c–, *10r, *10t, 10u, 10v–, 12a(?), 12b(?), *13a(?), 13c(?), *98e, 99a.

Range and clusters of tree-ring dates. Indigenous – 977+ to 1285; best between 1095 and 1190. Trade – 813+ to 1279; best between about 1075 and about 1200.

Validity of tree-ring dating. Neither the indigenous nor the trade categories are well dated, but they are similar. The tree-ring evidence leaves little choice except to date Sosi Black-on-white at about 1075 to about 1200.

Springerville Polychrome

Reference. Carlson 1961.

Occurrence by site. Trade – 2c, 2d, 5a, 6a, 13d, 21a, 33a, 79a (Maverick Mountain phase).

Range and clusters of tree-ring dates. Trade – 1028+ to 1612+; best between 1150 and about 1325.

Validity of tree-ring dating. The appearance at Wupatki of Springerville Polychrome, which is dated only as a trade product, strongly suggests a beginning date of about 1200 with a logical end date of about 1325. Carlson (1961) dates Springerville Polychrome at 1250 to 1300.

Sunset Brown

Reference. Colton 1958.

Occurrence by site. Indigenous – 14c.

Validity of tree-ring dating. No attempt is made to date this pottery type; in fact there is not enough evidence to comment on whether it is pre- or post-Sunset Crater. Mc.Gregor (1958) indicates that Sunset Brown is pre-eruptive; whereas Colton (1958) dates it as post-eruptive.

Sunset Red

Reference. Colton 1958.

Occurrence by site. Indigenous – *7d, 8a, *8b, 8c, 8d, 8e, *8g, *8h, *8i, 8j, *8k, *8l, 8m, *8n (Room 11), *8o, *9a–, *9c–, *10u, 10v–, 12a, 12b, 13a, 13b, *13d (Room 36C), 13e(?), 14b, 14c, *118a.

Range and clusters of tree-ring dates. Indigenous – 813+ to 1282; best between about 1075 and about 1140.

Validity of tree-ring dating. Even though the tree-ring dates are concentrated between 1075 and about 1140, there is no reason to alter Colton's (1958) dates of about 1065 to about 1200. This pottery, dated only as an indigenous product, is definitely a post-Sunset Crater type.

Sunset White-on-red

Reference. Colton 1958.

Occurrence by site. Indigenous – 9c–.

Tallahogan Red

See Lino Red.

Tanque Verde Red-on-brown

Reference. Hayden 1957.

Occurrence by site. Indigenous – *62a.

Validity of tree-ring dating. The single date of 1274+ is of little value for dating this pottery type.

Taos Black-on-white

Reference. Hawley 1950.

Occurrence by site. Indigenous – 41c.

Validity of tree-ring dating. The tree-ring evidence is inadequate to alter the dates of 1150 to 1250 given by Smiley, Stubbs, and Bannister (1953: 58).

Taos Incised

Occurrence by site. Indigenous – 41c.

Tewa Polychrome

Reference. Hawley 1950; Mera 1939.

Occurrence by site. Indigenous – 5a, 59d(?).

Validity of tree-ring dating. Tewa Polychrome is a post-1550 type, a time period not dealt with in this paper.

Three Circle Neck Corrugated

Reference. Hawley 1950.

Occurrence by site. Indigenous – *78a (Pit Houses O, K, and B), 78c.

Range and clusters of tree-ring dates. Indigenous – 738+ to *951;* best between about 750(?) and 951.

Validity of tree-ring dating. Although Three Circle Neck Corrugated is not well dated, we can say that it occurs during the period of 750 or 775 to 950 or more.

Three Circle Red-on-white

Reference. Hawley 1950.

Occurrence by site. Indigenous – *78a (Pit Houses F, O, K, E, and B), 78b, *78c, 107a.

Range and clusters of tree-ring dates. Indigenous – 738+ to *951;* best between about 775 and 951.

Validity of tree-ring dating. This type is not well dated, but it apparently occurs at the same time as Three Circle Neck Corrugated, about 750 or 775 to 950 or more.

Three Rivers Red-on-terracotta

Reference. Hawley 1950.

Occurrence by site. Indigenous – 20a, 21a. Trade – 6a.

Range and clusters of tree-ring dates. Indigenous – 1310 to 1366C; best between 1345 and 1366. Trade – 1050+ to 1349; best between 1150 and 1250 and also between 1300 and 1333.

Validity of tree-ring dating. The tree-ring evidence is insufficient to comment upon the beginning date of this pottery type, but there is a suggestion that it lasts until about 1350. Since the tree-ring associations are poor, the Smiley, Stubbs, and Bannister (1953: 58) dates of 1150 to 1300 are probably the best available.

Tizon Brownware

Reference. Colton 1958.

Occurrence by site. Trade – 15b.

Tohatchi Banded

Reference. Wendorf, Fox, and Lewis 1956.

Occurrence by site. Indigenous – 65a(?), 101a(?) (Wingate phase), 105c.

Range and clusters of tree-ring dates. Indigenous – 868+ to 1031+; no concentration of dates.

Validity of tree-ring dating. Tohatchi Banded is not well dated. For comparison we might include the "Indented Neck Corrugated, Gray" category with a range of tree-ring dates from 863+ to 1090, which corroborates the scanty information on the dating of Tohatchi Banded. We may, however, say only that Tohatchi Banded is found at some sites which were apparently occupied during the period from about 900 to about 1050(?).

Tonto Brown

See Tonto Red.

Tonto Polychrome

Reference. Hawley 1950.

Occurrence by site. Indigenous – *61a, 63a, 63b—. Trade – *67a, 72a, 72b, 74h, 74i@, 77b(?), 79a(?) (Maverick Mountain phase), 79b.

Range and clusters of tree-ring dates. Indigenous – 1109vv to *1385;* no concentration of dates. Trade – 1210+ to 1390; best between 1265 and 1385.

Validity of tree-ring dating. Tonto Polychrome occurs with Gila Polychrome at every site noted above, although not always in equal abundance; consequently, Tonto Polychrome is dated the same as Gila Polychrome, but not as strongly. Traditionally, Tonto Polychrome is considered to be later than Gila Polychrome. This should be borne in mind when referring to the comments for Gila Polychrome, which are pertinent to this discussion.

I agree with Steen's (1962: 28) proposal that Tonto Polychrome "be stricken from the rolls of Southwestern pottery types," because if Tonto Polychrome is to be recognized as an entity, it should be considered as a late variety of Gila Polychrome, not a separate type.

Tonto Red

Reference. Colton 1958, Pierson 1962.

Occurrence by site. Indigenous – *63a, *63b—. Trade – 8b, 8c, 8e, *8f, 8h, 8j, 8l, 8m, 9a—, 13d, 14b.

Range and clusters of tree-ring dates. Indigenous – 1109vv to 1346; no concentration of dates. Trade – 1028+ to 1282; best between 1085 and 1190.

Validity of tree-ring dating. Tonto Red is not well dated. The tree-ring material indicates a beginning date of at least 1085, but the evidence is insufficient to postulate an end date.

Colton (1958) gives a date of probably 1150 to 1275 for Tonto Red. Pierson (1962: 68) says that although Tonto Red is a trait of the Tonto phase, 1350 to 1400, the pottery probably lasts from 1150 to 1400.

Tonto Red is a long-lived type, of little value for dating purposes. Steen (1962: 29) points out, correctly I believe, that it should be called Tonto Brown, not Tonto Red.

Tonto Ribbed

Reference. Shiner 1961a.

Occurrence by site. Indigenous – *61a.

Validity of tree-ring dating. Tonto Ribbed is recorded from a site occupied in the middle and late 1300's. Further comment is not possible at this time.

Tsegi Black-on-orange

Reference. Colton 1956.

Occurrence by site. Indigenous – 15b, 15c, 15d, 15e, 15f, 15j, 15m, 111c, 111g.

Range and clusters of tree-ring dates. Indigenous – 977+ to 1289+; best between about 1125 and 1285.

Validity of tree-ring dating. The tree-ring evidence supports Colton's (1956) end date of 1300; however, Tsegi Black-on-orange may have begun before his beginning date of about 1225, perhaps even by 1125. The tree-ring dates are concentrated at the upper end of the total time range.

See comments for Tsegi Orange.

Tsegi Orange

Reference. Colton 1956.

Occurrence by site. Indigenous – *15c, 15d, 15e, *15f, 15j, 17a, 111a, 111b, *111c, 111d (Room 6), 111e, *111f, 111g, 111h.

Range and clusters of tree-ring dates. Indigenous – 1104+ to 1289+; best between about 1125 and 1285.

Validity of tree-ring dating. Colton's (1956) end date of 1300 is supported by the tree-ring evidence, but his beginning date of 1250 seems to be too late – Tsegi Orange is present by at least 1200, and possibly earlier.

Tsegi Black-on-orange and Tsegi Red-on-orange may be expected to have a similar time range. Until a firmer beginning date for these three types is obtained, I propose that on the basis of the tree-ring evidence, they all date from about 1150 or 1200 to 1300.

Tsegi Red-on-orange

Reference. Colton 1956.

Occurrence by site. Indigenous – 15b, 15c, 15m, 111d (Room 6), 111f.

Range and clusters of tree-ring dates. Indigenous – 977+ to 1285; best between 1262 and 1285.

Validity of tree-ring dating. Although Tsegi Red-on-orange occurs at fewer sites than Tsegi Black-on-orange and Tsegi Orange, the same sites are involved; thus, the overall dating should be the same.

See comments for Tsegi Orange.

Tucson Polychrome

Reference. Hayden 1957.

Occurrence by site. Trade – 79b.

Validity of tree-ring dating. We can only say that Tucson Polychrome is apparently a post-1300 pottery type.

Tularosa Black-on-white

Reference. Cibola White Ware Conference 1958; Rinaldo and Bluhm 1956.

Occurrence by site. Indigenous – 65a. Trade – 6a, 13d (Room 45A), 14b, 27a, 28a, 33a, 67a, 79a (Maverick Mountain phase), 98e.

Range and clusters of tree-ring dates. Indigenous – There is a single date of 1031+. Trade – 957+ to 1393; best between 1150 and about 1300.

Validity of tree-ring dating. The tree-ring evidence suggests a date of 1150 to about 1300 for Tularosa Black-on-white as a trade product; however, since it is not well dated, it is probably best to use Rinaldo and Bluhm's (1956) date of about 1100 to 1250 for this type.

Tularosa Fillet Rim

Reference. Martin and others 1952; Wendorf 1950.

Occurrence by site. Indigenous – 79a (Maverick Mountain phase), 79b. Trade – 53s, 67a(?).

Range and clusters of tree-ring dates. Indigenous – 1201+ to 1308; best between 1265 and 1300 plus. Trade – 1059 to 1307; best between 1100 and 1300 plus.

Validity of tree-ring dating. The scanty tree-ring evidence suggests a date of about 1100 to about 1300 for Tularosa Fillet Rim.

Tularosa White-on-red

Reference. Rinaldo and Bluhm 1956.

Occurrence by site. Indigenous – 79a (Maverick Mountain phase), 79b. Trade – 67a(?).

Range and clusters of tree-ring dates. Indigenous and trade – 1201+ to 1308; best between 1265 and 1300 plus.

Validity of tree-ring dating. There is no tree-ring evidence to indicate the beginning date nor is the suggested end date of about 1300 or more conclusive. Rinaldo and Bluhm (1956) date this type at about 1100 to 1200.

Tularosa White-on-red, Fillet Rim

See Tularosa White-on-red.

Turkey Hill Red

Reference. Colton 1958.

Occurrence by site. Indigenous – 7d, 8d, 8e, 8h, 8j, 8k, 8l, 8n, 8p, *9a—, *9c—, 10u, 10v—, 12b, *13b, 13d, 118a. Trade – 14b.

Range and clusters of tree-ring dates. Indigenous – 813+ to 1279+; best between 1090 to 1190 plus. Trade – No concentration of dates.

Validity of tree-ring dating. Turkey Hill Red begins a few years before 1100, about 1090, and lasts until at least 1200. There are no tree-ring dates which positively verify Colton's (1958) proposed end date of about 1275.

Tusayan Black-on-red

Reference. Colton 1956.

Occurrence by site. Indigenous – 13d, *13e, 15a, 15b, 15c, 15f, 15h, 15i, *15j, 15k, 15l, *15m, 111a, 111b, 111c. Trade – 7d, 8d, 8e, 8g, 8h, 8j, *8l, 8m, 8o, 8p, 9a—, 9c—, *10d, 10e, 10i, 10p, 10q, *10r, *10t, 10u, 10v—, 10x—, *12a(?), *12b(?), *13a(?), 13b(?), *48a@, 53s, 53x, 64a, 66a, 88g, 98e, 99a, 99b, 109a.

Range and clusters of tree-ring dates. Indigenous – 977+ to 1289+; best between about 1090 and 1285. Trade – 805+ to 1279+; best between about 1050 and about 1200.

Validity of tree-ring dating. Tusayan Black-on-red, which is better dated as a trade product than it is indigenously, is most abundant between 1050 and 1150 – the dates assigned to the type by Colton (1956). The tree-ring evidence shows that Tusayan Black-on-red certainly lasted until at least 1200. In the Tsegi Canyon area, the Dogoszhi variety of Tusayan Black-on-red lasted until 1300 (Sixth Southwestern Ceramic Conference 1964).

Tusayan Black-on-white

Reference. Colton 1955.

Occurrence by site. Indigenous – *13d (Room 36C), 15a, *15b, *15c, *15d, *15e, *15f, *15i, 15m, 111a, *111b, *111c, 111d, *111e, *111f, 111g, 111h. Trade – 7d, 8j, 9a—, *9c—, 10u, 13b(?), 14a, 66a, 67a, *92a(?) (Room 21), *98e.

Range and clusters of tree-ring dates. Indigenous – 977+ to 1289+; best between 1137b and 1285. Trade – 957+ to 1320; best between 1090 and about 1300.

Validity of tree-ring dating. Tusayan Black-on-white begins between about 1125 and 1150 and lasts until 1300, with its period of greatest abundance between 1250 and 1300.

Betatakin, Kayenta, Tusayan, and Wupatki black-on-whites are usually found together. Burgh (1959: 198) has ably demonstrated that because these pottery types are similar to one another, and because they occur in consistent association, there is a question as to whether valid identification of the individual types can be made, especially in sherd form.

Smith (1962: 1171) comments similarly on this subject, but he deals with a slightly different group of black-on-white pottery. Smith does not mention Wupatki Black-on-white nor does he include Polacca and Hoyapi black-on-whites in stating: "The characteristics of these five types are recognizable at Awatovi but not in consistently separable categories, with the result that here they would all appear to represent a single type . . ."

The four pottery types under discussion may be combined into a single "ceramic style" which fits Colton's (1953: 50, 75, 77) description of Kayenta Style.

I believe that Betatakin, Kayenta, Tusayan, and Wupatki black-on-whites constitute what may be termed "Kayenta-Anasazi–Late Pueblo III black-on-whites." And, because of their consistent association with each other and the difficulties of "type" identification, I believe they should be "dated" as a group and not as separate types.

It is difficult to say exactly when the "Kayenta-Anasazi–Late Pueblo III black-on-whites" made their appearance, but it was certainly between 1100 and 1200. They lasted until 1300 and were most abundant between 1250 and 1300.

Tusayan Corrugated

Reference. Colton 1955.

Occurrence by site. Indigenous – 13d (Room 36C), 13e(?), 15a, 15b, 15c, 15e, 15f, *15h, *15i, 15j, *15k, 15l, *15m, *17a, 76a, 77b, 111a, 111b, *111c, 111e, 111f, 118a. Trade – 7d, 8a, 8b, 8c, *8d, 8e, 8f, 8g, 8h, *8i, 8j, 8l, 8m, 8n, 8o, *8p, 9a—, *10d, 10e, 10i, 10k, *10n, 10p, *10q, 10s, 10u, 10v—, 10w, 11b—, 12a(?), 12b(?), *13a(?), 13b(?), *13c(?), 14b, 63b(?)—, 66a, 71a, 74e, 80a—, *98e, *109a.

Range and clusters of tree-ring dates. Indigenous – 977+ to 1390; best between about 1075 and 1285. Trade – 799+ to 1323+; best between 1000 and 1280.

Validity of tree-ring dating. The tree-ring evidence suggests a beginning date of 1000; however, Colton's (1955) beginning date of 950 is probably more correct. Tusayan Corrugated, which is better dated as a trade product than it is indigenously, lasts until at least 1275, and probably until 1300. It is most abundant between 1050 and 1150.

Tusayan Grayware

Reference. Colton 1955.

Occurrence by site. Trade – 10a, 10b, 10c, *10k, 10m—, *10r, *10aa, *114a.

Tusayan Polychrome

Reference. Colton 1956.

Occurrence by site. Indigenous – 15a, *15b, 15c, *15e, *15f, *15i, 15j, 15m, 111a, *111b, *111c, 111d (Room 6), *111f, 111g, 111h. Trade – 7d, 8a, 8b, 8k, 9c—, 12a(?), 14b, 53m, 53x, 64a, 66a, 71a, 98e.

Range and clusters of tree-ring dates. Indigenous – 977+ to 1289+; best between about 1250 and 1285. Trade – 914+ to 1282; best between about 1075 and about 1280.

Validity of tree-ring dating. The tree-ring evidence suggests dates of 1100 to 1300; however, the difficulty in distinguishing Tusayan from Citadel Polychrome in sherd form may account for the 1100 beginning date.

Because of the lack of excavated sites in the Kayenta branch that were occupied during the 1100 to 1200 period, Tusayan Polychrome seems to appear earlier in a trade rather than in an indigenous context.

Tuwiuca Black-on-orange

Reference. Colton 1956.

Occurrence by site. Trade – 14a.

Tuzigoot Black-on-gray

Reference. Colton and Hargrave 1937.

Occurrence by site. Indigenous – 64a.

Validity of tree-ring dating. The single date of 1185+ does not permit comment on the dating. Since Tuzigoot Black-on-gray does not appear in Colton (1958), one may raise the question of its validity as a type.

Tuzigoot Red

Reference. Colton 1958.

Occurrence by site. Indigenous – 64a.

Twin Trees Black-on-white

Reference. Abel 1955.

Occurrence by site. Indigenous – 90a@(?), 91a@(?)–. Trade – 121d.

Range and clusters of tree-ring dates. Indigenous and trade – 675+ to 898r; best(?) in the 800's.

Validity of tree-ring dating. Considering the poor tree-ring evidence, we can only say that Twin Trees Black-on-white appears during the 800's. The present information, which suggests a beginning date of about 600, does not support Abel's (1955) early beginning date of about 450.

Twin Trees Plain

Reference. Abel 1955.

Occurrence by site. Indigenous – 88cc (Pit Houses I and II). Trade – 121d.

Validity of tree-ring dating. Since the tree-ring dating is very weak, we can say only that this type is found in sites which date from the late 500's until about 900. Even though Abel (1955) dates Twin Trees Plain as about 450 to 850, the tree-ring evidence does not support the 450 beginning date. See also Chapin Black-on-white, Chapin Gray, and Twin Trees Black-on-white.

"Upper Gila Coil"

Occurrence by site. Trade – 5e.

Upper Gila Corrugated

Reference. Rinaldo and Bluhm 1956.

Occurrence by site. Trade – 2b.

Validity of tree-ring dating. This ceramic category is composed of several distinct corrugated types, including Reserve Plain, Reserve Incised, Reserve Punched, and Tularosa Patterned. As a group, these corrugated pottery types date from 950 to 1250 (Rinaldo and Bluhm 1956).

"Upper Gila Smudged"

Occurrence by site. Trade – 28a, 33a.

Verde Black-on-brown

Occurrence by site. Indigenous – 66a.

Validity of tree-ring dating. Colton (1958) does not mention this "type."

Verde Black-on-gray

Reference. Colton 1958.

Occurrence by site. Indigenous – *64a, *66a. Trade – 12b, 13b, 13d (Room 45A).

Range and clusters of tree-ring dates. Indigenous – 1023+ to 1185+; no apparent concentration of dates. Trade – 1135+ to 1187; best(?) between the 1140's and 1180's.

Validity of tree-ring dating. The tree-ring evidence, which is poor in both the indigenous and trade contexts, simply indicates that Verde Black-on-gray occurs during the time span of 1050 to about 1200. There are no tree-ring dates as late as Colton's (1958) end date of 1300.

Verde Black-on-gray often appears erroneously in the literature as Prescott Black-on-gray.

Verde Brown

Reference. Breternitz 1960a; Colton 1958.

Occurrence by site. Indigenous – 64a.

Verde Gray

Reference. Colton 1958, as Prescott Grayware.

Occurrence by site. Indigenous – *66a. Trade – 7d, 10m–, 10n, 13c, 13d (Room 45A).

Range and clusters of tree-ring dates. Indigenous and trade – 799+ to 1256; best between 1025 and about 1200.

Validity of tree-ring dating. Verde Gray is poorly dated. We can only say that it occurs at sites during the interval from 1025 to about 1200. There is no tree-ring material available that permits comment on Colton's (1958) end date of 1400.

Verde Polychrome

Reference. Colton and Hargrave 1937.

Occurrence by site. Indigenous – 66a.

Validity of tree-ring dating. Only one sherd of Verde Polychrome was found at Tuzigoot. The type is not described in Colton (1958).

Wallace Polychrome

Reference. Colton and Hargrave 1937; described as Kwakina Polychrome in Woodbury and Woodbury MS.

Occurrence by site. Trade – 21a, 28a.

Walnut Black-on-white

Reference. Colton 1955.

Occurrence by site. Indigenous – *7d, 8a, 8j, 8l, 8n, 8o, *9a–, *9c–, *10u, *12a, *12b, *13a, *13b, *13c, 13d, 14a(?), 14b(?), 17a, *76a, 77b, *118a. Trade – *64a, 66a, *98e, 111c–.

Range and clusters of tree-ring dates. Indigenous – 914+ to 1390; best between about 1085 and about 1250. Trade – 957+ to 1275; best between about 1050 and about 1200.

Validity of tree-ring dating. Walnut Black-on-white begins sometime between the eruption of Sunset Crater (about 1065) and 1100; it lasts until approximately 1250. This time span agrees in general with Colton's (1955) dates of about 1100 to 1250.

Colton believes this pottery was made just to the east of the Black Sand area – the area of ash and cinder deposits resulting from the eruption of Sunset Crater; thus, Walnut Black-on-white has been considered indigenous in the Sinagua sites listed. Walnut Black-on-white and other Little Colorado Whiteware pottery types were probably made from the clay deposits found in the Chinle formation along the Little Colorado River, to the east of the Black Sand area.

Walnut Corrugated

Reference. Colton and Hargrave 1937.

Occurrence by site. Indigenous – 7d. Trade – 77a.

"Wavy Indented Corrugated"

Occurrence by site. Indigenous – 105a.

See Exuberant Corrugated for possible dating inferences.

Whipple Black-on-white

See Reserve Black-on-white.

White Mound Black-on-white

Reference. Cibola White Ware Conference 1958; Hawley 1950.

Occurrence by site. Indigenous – 53a(?), 53v@, *76b (Kiva 2 and Roomblock subfloor), 98e–, *101b (Section 1, House 3). Trade – 14c–(House Q), 77m (Type II houses), 89a@, *104b, 104c (Storage Pit 3), 106a–.

Range and clusters of tree-ring dates. Indigenous – 720+ to 1275; best between about 750 and 910. Trade – 636+ to 1093c; best between about 675 and 775, or about 900(?).

Validity of tree-ring dating. The tree-ring evidence from both indigenous and trade contexts suggests 675 to 900 or more as the best probable dates for White Mound Black-on-white. It was probably most abundant between 750 and 800.

"White Mountain Area–Corrugated"

Occurrence by site. Trade – 53n.

Wide Ruin Black-on-white

Reference. Colton and Hargrave 1937.

Occurrence by site. Indigenous – 77b.

Validity of tree-ring dating. The Colton and Hargrave (1937) date of about 1275 is not substantiated by the tree-ring dates in the 1300's from Chakpahu. There is also some question as to whether Wide Ruin Black-on-white is a valid pottery type (Cibola White Ware Conference 1958).

Wingate Black-on-red

Reference. Carlson 1961.

Occurrence by site. Indigenous – 65a. Trade – 1d, 2a, 2d, 6c, 14b, 20a, 21a, 27a, 33a, 47a@, *48a@, 51a@, 51b(?), 53b@, 53c@, 53f@, 53g@, 53i@, 53k, 53l, 53m, 53n, *53s, *53u, 53w@, 53x, 53y, 58a, 99a, 115a, 116a.

Range and clusters of tree-ring dates. Indigenous – There is a single date of 1031+. Trade – 828 to 1447; best between about 1050 and 1200.

Validity of tree-ring dating. Wingate Black-on-red is dated almost solely on the basis of its occurrence as a trade product. I am in general agreement with Carlson's (1961) dates of 1047 to 1200. Apparently Wingate Black-on-red does not become abundant until about 75 years after its appearance. It is noteworthy that it appears in the Rio Grande area in at least five sites that have tree-ring dates between 1200 and 1350, and at one site with tree-ring dates in the mid-1400's.

A beginning date of 950 is frequently cited for this pottery type, but the tree-ring evidence, plus the data cited by Carlson (1961), indicate that this date is too early, at least for its appearance as a trade product.

A discussion of some of the regional varieties of Wingate Black-on-red may be found in the Second Southwestern Ceramics Seminar (1959).

Wingate Black-on-white

See Reserve Black-on-white.

Wingate Polychrome

Reference. In Carlson 1961, as a new taxonomic term for the combination of the two pottery types formerly called Houck Polychrome and Querino Polychrome.

Occurrence by site. Indigenous – 65a, 69a (lower level), 70a(?), 70b(?). Trade – 27a, 33a, 53k (Room 43), 76a, 80a–, 98e.

Range and clusters of tree-ring dates. Indigenous – 1031+ to about 1204; no concentration of dates. Trade – 957+ to 1275; best between 1074 plus and about 1200.

Validity of tree-ring dating. Carlson's (1961) dates of 1125 to 1200, with latitude at either end, appear to be the most logical dates for Wingate Polychrome at this time.

Wingfield Plain

Reference. Breternitz 1960b; Colton 1941.

Occurrence by site. Trade – 7d, 11a, 61a.

Range and clusters of tree-ring dates. Trade – 784+ to *1385*; no concentration of dates.

Validity of tree-ring dating. There are neither enough tree-ring dates nor archaeological controls available to date Wingfield Plain – the earliest and latest tree-ring dates are 600 years apart. Colton (1941) dates this type at about 1100, but subsequent archaeological work has shown that it appeared in the 700's(?) and lasted until about 1400.

Wingfield Plain is now described as a variety of Gila Plain (Breternitz 1960a, 1960b).

Winona Brown

Reference. Colton 1958.

Occurrence by site. Indigenous – *7d, *8b, *8d, *8e, *8f, *8g, *8h, *8i, *8j, *8k, *8l, *8m, *8n, *8o, *8p, *9a–, 9c–, 10d, 10e, 10l, 10r, 10u, 10v–, *12a, *12b, 13a, *13d, 13e(?), 118a.

Range and clusters of tree-ring dates. Indigenous – 813+ to 1279+; best between about 1075 and about 1200.

Validity of tree-ring dating. The tree-ring evidence indicates a dating range of about 1075 to about 1200, with the greatest abundance apparently from 1075 to 1125. Winona Brown, occurring only indigenously, is well dated.

Winona Brown is a post-Sunset Crater type; consequently, I am not in agreement with Colton's (1958) dates of about 1000 to 1150.

Winona Corrugated

Reference. Colton and Hargrave 1937.

Occurrence by site. Indigenous – 8c, *8o, 8p.

Range and clusters of tree-ring dates. Indigenous – 1062+ to 1121+; best from about 1080 to 1100.

Validity of tree-ring dating. See comments for Winona Smudged.

Winona Red

Reference. Colton and Hargrave 1937.

Occurrence by site. Indigenous – 9a–.

Validity of tree-ring dating. See comments for Winona Smudged.

Winona Red-on-buff

Reference. Colton and Hargrave 1937.

Occurrence by site. Indigenous – 8b, *8c, 8p, 9a(?)–.

Validity of tree-ring dating. This pottery type is considered with Coconino Red-on-buff for stronger dating. See comments for Coconino Red-on-buff.

Winona Smudged

Reference. Colton and Hargrave 1937.

Occurrence by site. Indigenous – 8b, 8c, 8h, 8j, 8k, 8l, 8o, 118a.

Range and clusters of tree-ring dates. Indigenous – 1058 to 1248; best between about 1080 and 1120.

Validity of tree-ring dating. According to Colton and Hargrave (1937), the Winona Corrugated, Winona Red, and Winona Smudged types were probably in use between 1050 and 1150. None are well dated, but they are associated, contemporaneous pottery types. The tree-ring evidence suggests that these three pottery types were made at least during the period from about 1080 to about 1120.

Winslow Polychrome

See Homolovi Polychrome.

Wiyo Black-on-white

Reference. Stubbs and Stallings 1953.

Occurrence by site. Indigenous – 1a, 1b, 1c, 2b, 5a, 5c, 5e, 6a, 6b, *36a, 42c, *45a, *46a, 57a, 58a, 58b, 58c, 58d, 116a. Trade – 3a, 4a (Plaza V), *5d, 53x–.

Range and clusters of tree-ring dates. Indigenous – 963+ to 1581+; best between 1300 and about 1400. Trade – 1008+ to 1437; best between 1299 and about 1425.

Validity of tree-ring dating. The published date of 1300 to 1400 (Smiley, Stubbs, and Bannister 1953: 58) remains the most plausible date for Wiyo Black-on-white.

Woodruff Red

Reference. Hawley 1950.

See Forestdale Red.

Woodruff Smudged

Reference. Haury 1940a; Hawley 1950.

Occurrence by site. Indigenous – 104a, 104b.

Validity of tree-ring dating. The tree-ring evidence permits only weak dating. Woodruff Smudged appears in sites that are occupied between the period of about 300 to about 700. Woodruff Smudged is a synonym for Forestdale Smudged.

Wupatki Black-on-white

Reference. Colton 1955.

Occurrence by site. Indigenous – *13d (Room 36C). Trade – 7d, 9a–, 13b(?), 14a, 66a.

Range and clusters of tree-ring dates. Indigenous and trade – 1023+ to 1320; best between about 1125 and about 1300.

Validity of tree-ring dating. Wupatki Black-on-white does not occur at any site that does not also have Tusayan Black-on-white. Stylistically, Wupatki Black-on-white is a variety of Tusayan Black-on-white. Although not as strongly dated, it should have approximately the same dates as Tusayan Black-on-white.

See comments for Tusayan Black-on-white.

Youngs Brown

Reference. Colton 1958.

Occurrence by site. Indigenous – 8d, 8f, *8h, 8j, 8k, 8m, 8n, 8o, 9a–, 13d, 118a.

Range and clusters of tree-ring dates. Indigenous – 1028+ to 1248; best between about 1075 and about 1150.

Validity of tree-ring dating. Youngs Brown, an intermediate form between Sunset Brown (Sunset Red) and Winona Brown (Colton 1958), is a post-Sunset Crater type beginning about 1075 and lasting until about 1150(?). It is most abundant between about 1090 and 1130.

Zoned Corrugated

Reference. Olson – 1959.

Occurrence by site. Indigenous – 79b.

Zuni Glazes

See Zuni Polychrome.

Zuni Polychrome

Reference. Chapman 1933–36; Kidder and Shepard 1936.

Occurrence by site. Trade – 5a, 67a, 69a (upper level).

Validity of tree-ring dating. Smiley, Stubbs, and Bannister (1953: 58) show a date of 1300 to recent times for Zuni Polychrome. The tree-ring evidence under consideration here only hints at a beginning date of about 1300.

SUMMARY

The dating validity of any pottery type depends upon its archaeological context and its association with the dated tree-ring specimens. It is important to note whether the pottery type is dated on the basis of its occurrence within the area of its supposed manufacture or whether it is considered to be intrusive, that is, trade material. There may be significant differences in the time period in which the pottery type persists as either a local product or as a tradeware. Again, it may be necessary to combine the associated dates for the pottery type from both the indigenous and trade situations to obtain a more adequate indication of its time span.

Widely traded pottery is more valuable for dating purposes, within certain obvious limits, than indigenous pottery. Decorated pottery is more valuable for dating than plainware. The addition of a painted decoration provides another criterion subject to change; hence, it is not only more useful for identification, but it is also more indicative of (we assume) shorter time segments than those usually shown by plainwares. Although Lino Gray, for example, is recorded from a considerable number of sites, the tree-ring information does not allow us to improve on the overall dating of this pottery type as it appears in the current literature. Lino Black-on-gray, however, which is simply Lino Gray with the addition of black-line decoration, is more accurately dated and consequently more useful as a dating tool.

Trade pottery is also generally well-identified as to type, particularly if it is decorated and, as Colton has frequently pointed out, decorated pottery is traded more widely than utility pottery.

The usefulness of the pottery type concept for dating purposes becomes apparent when we consider our inability to "date" pottery, whether locally made or intrusive, if it is given a descriptive name, such as "Corrugated, Grayware" or "Plainware." These categories are simply not specific enough to be useful for dating purposes.

The dating of each pottery type mentioned in this chapter must be judged on the basis of the individual merits of the tree-ring material and the archaeological association *for that particular pottery type.*

5. CONCLUSIONS

SOUTHWESTERN ARCHAEOLOGY is favored with a unique chronological tool for the interpretation of archaeological materials, namely dendrochronology or tree-ring dating. Approximately 5715 tree-ring specimens from about 342 sites have been used in the effort to "date" prehistoric Southwestern ceramics. (There would be over 10,000 tree-ring dates if individual dates were tabulated, and well over 500 for "sites" if individual architectural units were considered.) The time period covered begins roughly with the first evidence of fired pottery until approximately 1550 – the time of the Spanish arrival in the Southwest.

The specific provenience of the tree-ring specimens with "dates," their association with individual pottery types or ceramic categories, the validity of the dates in their archaeological association, and the pottery identifications have been summarized on the basis of the more detailed information available in Breternitz (1963). The pattern of tree-ring dates available for each site pertinent to the discussion of prehistoric Southwestern pottery (within the time period outlined) has appeared graphically in the Master Tree-Ring Date Chart (Table 3).

The interpretive possibilities suggested by the tree-ring dates have been discussed in Chapter 3. The examples selected for discussion have shown that accurate dating of Southwestern pottery types depends not only upon the quality and number of tree-ring dates and their association and archaeological context, but upon the validity of the identification of the pottery type and its archaeological context.

Discussion of the attempts to date "pottery types" and "ceramic styles" leads to one conclusion: the archaeological interpretation of tree-ring dates may be used to date Southwestern "pottery types," but it is not possible to date "ceramic styles" with the same degree of accuracy and validity. The concept of ceramic style represents a higher level of abstraction than that of the pottery type. The time periods involved in ceramic styles are longer and less rigidly delineated than those of pottery types. A perusal of the "illustrative types" used to define the pottery styles described by Wasley (1959) vividly show why tree-ring data cannot be used to accurately date this category of ceramic analysis, particularly after about A.D. 1000. Ceramic styles are defined on the basis of design elements, motifs, and patterns that crosscut pottery types; thus, the "in part" qualification is added to most of the pottery types used to define ceramic styles. This "in part" qualification makes it almost impossible to separate out the various styles that are included within the definition of these pottery types.

More accurate dating of ceramic styles than Wasley was able to offer can now be obtained, because of the availability of new information not previously at his disposal. For example, Wasley (1959: 262) estimates the date of the Sosi Style as about A.D. 800 to 1200, which hardly pinpoints the time period involved. Better dating of this style, and other pottery styles also, can be obtained only when each of the "illustrative types" within the style is "dated." This information can then be combined into a composite date for all the inclusive types. At this point there still remains the problem, which I defer to the definers of ceramic styles, of trying to separate the "in part" factor from pottery types that are included in any particular style.

Because of the difficulties of interpretation and determination of associations, I agree with Wasley (1959: 230, 233) that "horizon markers" are more useful in the Southwest than "horizon styles." In the later period of Southwestern prehistory a combination of "period" and "style" might be used for more accurate dating than the use of either criterion by itself, but the example of such a combination, the Kayenta-Anasazi – Late Pueblo III black-on-whites, is not conclusive. (See comments in Chapter 4 for Tusayan Black-on-white.)

In summary, the archaeological interpretation of tree-ring dates is most valid for dating *pottery types,* because they can be identified and classified as archaeological entities and, more important, they represent the most meaningful, consistent conceptual tool which can be used to identify Southwestern archaeological ceramic materials. It is not presently feasible to date *ceramic style* or *style of design* using tree-ring dates, because ceramic style involves a higher level of abstraction – a higher level of synthesis and interpretation – than that represented by the pottery type.

Chapter 4 is an inventory of 325 pottery types, varieties, and ceramic categories from all the Southwestern archaeological sites which have produced tree-ring dates prior to about 1550. Tabulation of the distribution of the pottery is done in terms of whether it is indigenous or trade. The qualification and quantification of the validity and association of the pottery are also indicated. The pottery type is then "dated" insofar as the information permits. This date obviously depends upon the factors of number and kind of occurrences of the pottery, the validity of the association with the tree-ring dates, and the archaeological provenience.

The preceding presentation and discussion of data indicates the class or classes of information most reliable for the interpretation of tree-ring dates in dating Southwestern ceramics. When speaking of the "validity" of the tree-ring dates themselves, we are concerned with (1) the "type" of date – whether a cutting date, bark date, or an incomplete specimen; (2) the archaeological associations and context of the dated specimen; (3) the repetition or number of actual dates available for use; and (4) the distribution in time, in terms of concentrations and clusters, of the tree-ring dates.

The "validity" of the pottery type for interpretation depends upon (1) the ability of the archaeologist to identify and classify the pottery to the satisfaction of his colleagues (perhaps a subjective, but nevertheless important aspect); (2) the distribution in time and space of the pottery type in indigenous and trade situations; (3) the repetition of the occurrence of the pottery type within any span of time and space; and (4) the archaeological context or provenience of the pottery. Specific information concerning both the tree-ring specimens and the pottery type permits more valid and accurate overall dating of any particular pottery type. This accuracy-validity is, in turn, partly dependent on certain categories of information – whether the pottery is a decorated or a utility type and whether it is found in an indigenous or a trade context.

Traded pottery types are, on the whole, well identified throughout the Southwest, more so in fact than the relative distributions of indigenous types in some areas. Because trade pottery is an exotic item, archaeologists are inclined to seek the advice and opinions of co-workers for identification, while at the same time, they tend to become "experts" on the indigenous pottery in their own areas of interest.

Some pottery types are better "dated" as tradewares than from within the area of home manufacture; this is probably a result of the accident of location and the availability of datable tree-ring specimens. I do not believe pottery types dated on the basis of their associations with tree-ring dates in a trade context are as well dated, or may be said to evidence the same degree of validity of dating, as types found in good indigenous archaeological contexts.

DISCUSSION

The validity of the overall interpretation of tree-ring dates and associated pottery types, as just discussed, brings up another important consideration – how is prehistoric Southwestern pottery distributed? We need some knowledge, particularly in the area of traded ceramics, of how pottery gets from one place to another, and what categories of pottery lend themselves to wide distribution in time and space.

Haury (1962: 123) states:

> Exchange of pottery is the most readily identifiable evidence of trade, and this we know took place on the village-farming community level between neighboring tribes. Again, not until late in prehistory, however – in the fourteenth century – do we see this reaching significant proportions, that is, when the volume became large enough to make commerce in pottery appear as an institutionalized activity.

Although the trading of Southwestern ceramics does increase in volume through time, particularly after 1200, I would not term the trade as "institutionalized," at least not in the same sense that the term is applicable to trade in Mesoamerica, for example. The acceleration of prehistoric Southwestern commerce in pottery vessels must have been an outgrowth of the increased mobility, dispersal, and contact which began about 1200, and reached its culmination in the 14th and early 15th centuries. The Southwest proper probably never benefited from a native trader class; trade was probably carried on between individuals on a face-to-face and hand-to-hand basis. The absence of actual institutionalized trade and full-time trading specialists is a primary contributing factor in our inability to date Southwestern ceramics more accurately, even with the aid of the "absolute" dating method of dendrochronology.

When pottery types are traded into an area, they repeatedly appear in association with later archaeological materials. Thus, in the later stages of Southwestern prehistory, we must look to the latest pottery type in *full association* in order to date the site, feature, room, pit house, or specific level. The phenomenon of traded ceramics appearing in archaeological contexts that are later than the actual period of manufacture of the specific pottery is more fully discussed in Breternitz (1963: 456–9).

Also, before 1200 it takes longer for trade pottery to reach outlying areas. "Early" pottery types tend to occur within a smaller geographic area than the "later" pottery types. Most of the decorated pottery types dated prior to 1000 remain within their "culture areas." The following example will illustrate the validity of this statement. Abajo Red-on-orange is recorded from sites with tree-ring dates *only* within the area designated as Anasazi. Later, Jeddito Black-on-yellow is found widely traded not only in its Anasazi home "culture area," but throughout the Southwest.

An associated feature of the post-1200 acceleration in the dispersal of traded pottery types is the increase in the number and type of local copies of widely traded pottery types, for example: the copies of Jeddito Black-on-yellow found at the Canyon Creek ruin, the copies of Four Mile and Kiet Siel polychromes found at the Point of Pines ruin, and the copies of Gila Polychrome found at Table Rock Pueblo and Casas Grandes.

The change in rates of dispersal through time in the southwestern United States does not agree with one of Edmundson's (1961: 84) basic tenets regarding Neolithic diffusion rates: "Provisionally, therefore, we can conclude that the real diffusion rate . . . is probably a constant." For the southwestern United States, there appears to be no constant rate of dispersal for traded ceramics between about 600 and 1450. If we were dealing with greater distances and perhaps longer time periods, the dispersal rate might tend to appear more constant; however, this is not the case. We also use a variety of pottery types as units of dated archaeological material that have their origins in various localities, not from a single point of origin, another important factor in Edmundson's proposition.

SUMMARY

The content of the preceding presentation of data and its interpretation may be summarized in a few brief statements:

1. Approximately 5715 tree-ring specimens from about 342 sites are available for interpretation of the prehistoric Southwestern period between the time of the introduction of pottery and the Spanish Entrada.

2. Correlation and discussion of the validity of the available tree-ring dates and the associated ceramics permits us to "date" Southwestern pottery types with varying degrees of accuracy.

3. Southwestern pottery is "dated" at the analytical level of "pottery types." "Ceramic style" represents a higher level of abstraction, which does not lend itself to as accurate dating using tree-ring data.

4. A general and progressive increase in the amount and range of traded pottery is noted, as well as a post-1200 increase in the local copying of traded pottery types.

5. Distribution of Southwestern pottery types was on the basis of person-to-person contact. This dispersal accelerated with the passage of time, but in the Southwest it never reached the degree of institutionalism seen in Mesoamerican trade. An associated feature was the emphasis on trade of small decorated vessels, as opposed to large utility or undecorated ceramic containers.

APPENDIX 1

SITE AND SITE-AREA INDEX

The numbers given for each site and site-area are those used in the text descriptions in Chapter 2, as shown on the location map (Figure 1), and listed sequentially in Appendix 2.

APPENDIX 2

NUMERICAL LISTING OF SITES AND SITE-AREAS

The sites and site-areas cited in the text and Appendix 1, and shown on Figure 1, are listed below in the order in which they appear in Chapter 2.

1. Arroyo Hondo Area
   - 1a. Chamisa Locita, LA 4
   - 1b. Los Alamos, LA 8
   - 1c. Arroyo Hondo, LA 76
   - 1d. Mocho, LA 191
   - 1e. Peña Negra, LA 235
2. Galisteo Creek Area
   - 2a. Lamy, LA 10
   - 2b. Lamy, LA 27
   - 2c. Galisteo, LA 309
   - 2d. Manzanares, LA 1104
3. San Cristobal
   - 3a. San Cristobal, LA 80
4. Pueblo Largo
   - 4a. Pueblo Largo, LA 183
5. Pecos Area
   - 5a. Pecos Pueblo, LA 625
   - 5b. Pecos Mission
   - 5c. Rowe (Guthe's Ruin), LA 108
   - 5d. Arrowhead Ruin, LA 251
   - 5e. Forked Lightning, LA 672
6. Santa Fe River Area
   - 6a. Pindi Pueblo, LA 1
   - 6b. Agua Fria, LA 2
   - 6c. Arroyo Negro, LA 114
7. Walnut Canyon Area
   - 7a. Walnut Canyon, NA 310
   - 7b. Walnut Canyon, NA 323
   - 7c. Walnut Canyon, NA 333
   - 7d. Walnut Canyon, NA 739
8. Winona Village and Ridge Ruin Areas
   - 8a. Piper's Crater Fort, NA 534
   - 8b. Winona Village, NA 2133A
   - 8c. Winona Village, NA 2133B
   - 8d. Winona Village, NA 2133C
   - 8e. Winona Village, NA 2133D
   - 8f. Winona Village, NA 2133G
   - 8g. Winona Village, NA 2134A
   - 8h. Winona Village, NA 2134E or E1
   - 8i. Winona Village, NA 2135C
   - 8j. Winona Village, NA 3644C
   - 8k. Winona Village, NA 3644J
   - 8l. Winona Village, NA 3644K
   - 8m. Winona Village, NA 3644P
   - 8n. Ridge Ruin, NA 1785
   - 8o. NA 3673R
   - 8p. Winona Village, NA 2134T
9. Elden Area
   - 9a. Elden Pueblo, NA 142
   - 9b. Elden Pit House, NA 1531
   - 9c. Turkey Hill Pueblo, NA 660
10. Deadmans Drainage Area
    - 10a. Baker Ranch, NA 2551
    - 10b. Baker Ranch, NA 2798
    - 10c. Baker Ranch, NA 2800
    - 10d. Jack Smith Alcove House, NA 408A
    - 10e. NA 192B
    - 10f. NA 1570A
    - 10g. NA 1920B
    - 10h. NA 1925B
    - 10i. Medicine Fort, NA 862
    - 10j. Medicine Cave, NA 863
    - 10k. NA 1238
    - 10l. NA 1244B
    - 10m. NA 1625B
    - 10n. NA 1625C
    - 10o. Medicine Pit House, NA 1680
    - 10p. NA 2001
    - 10q. NA 2002A
    - 10r. NA 2004B
    - 10s. NA 1121
    - 10t. Whistle House, NA 2004A
    - 10u. NA 2218
    - 10v. McCormack Spring, NA 5866
    - 10w. NA 3056
    - 10x. Jack Smith Alcove House, NA 1295A
    - 10y. NA 1571A
    - 10z. NA 1922A
    - 10aa. NA 1927A
11. Upper Rio de Flag Drainage Area
    - 11a. Coyote Range Pit House, NA 1959
    - 11b. NA 5903
12. Juniper Terrace
    - 12a. NA 1814C
    - 12b. NA 1814E
    - 12c. NA 1814, Burial 1
13. Wupatki Area
    - 13a. Citadel, NA 355
    - 13b. Nalakihu, NA 358
    - 13c. Lomaki, NA 379
    - 13d. Wupatki, NA 405
    - 13e. Heiser Spring, NA 1754A
14. Anderson Mesa Area
    - 14a. Kinnikinnick Pueblo, NA 1629
    - 14b. Pollock Site, NA 4317
    - 14c. Pershing Site, NA 7207
15. Tsegi Canyon Area
    - 15a. Swallows Nest, NA 2507
    - 15b. Betatakin, NA 2515
    - 15c. Kiet Siel, NA 2519
    - 15d. Lolomaki, NA 2530

15e. Bat Woman House, NA 2531
15f. Twin Caves, NA 2536
15g. NA 2542
15h. Ladder House, NA 2543
15i. NA 2606
15j. Lenaki, NA 2630
15k. RB 551, NA 3338
15l. Calamity Cave, NA 2637
15m. Turkey House, NA 2521
16. Hopi Villages
16a. Oraibi
16b. Shungopovi
16c. Shipaulovi
16d. Walpi
17. Tusayan Ruin
17a. Tusayan Ruin, Echo Cliffs 13:1
18. Vandal Cave
18a. Vandal Cave
19. Tocito Area
19a. Site at south end of Tocito, LA 7611
20. Three Rivers Area
20a. Three Rivers Ruin, LA 1231
21. Armstrong Ruin
21a. Armstrong Ruin, LA 1225
22. Tabira Mission
22a. Tabira Mission
23. Abo Mission
23a. Abo Mission
24. Quarai Mission
24a. Quarai Mission, LA 95
25. Acoma Mission
25a. Acoma Mission
26. Laguna Mission
26a. Laguna Mission
27. Rio Puerco Area
27a. Rio Puerco Ruin, LA 875
28. Cedro Ranger Station Area
28a. Cedro Ranger Station Ruin, LA 581
29. Star Lake Area
29a. Star Lake, LA 1063 and CM-139
30. Santa Ana Mission
30a. Santa Ana Mission
31. Cochiti Church
31a. Cochiti Church
32. Tunque Pueblo
32a. Tunque Pueblo, LA 240
33. Tecolote
33a. Tecolote, LA 296
34. Los Aguajes
34a. Los Aguajes, LA 5
35. Nambe Mission
35a. Nambe Mission
36. Cundiyo
36a. Cundiyo, LA 31
37. Santa Fe, New Mexico
37a. Guadalupe
37b. Cathedral
37c. Oldest House
37d. Palace of the Governors
37e. San Miguel
38. San Ildefonso
38a. San Ildefonso
39. San Juan–Santa Cruz Area
39a. San Juan Mission
39b. Santa Cruz Church
39c. La Vita Church
40. Trampas Church
40a. Trampas Church
41. Taos Area
41a. Talpa Chapel
41b. Ranchos de Taos Church
41c. Jeancon's Llano Site, LA 1892
41d. San Geronimo
42. Ojo Caliente Area
42a. Howiri, LA 71
42b. Hupobi, LA 380
42c. Posi, LA 632
43. Gobernador Area
43a. Muñoz Canyon, LA 1687
43b. Dos Cerritos, LA 2136
43c. Gobernador Canyon, LA 1868
43d. San Rafael, LA 1869
43e. San Rafael, LA 1872
43f. Pueblo Canyon, LA 1684
43g. La Jara, LA 2138
43h. Morris' Sites–Gobernador
43i. San Rafael, LA 1871
43j. Santo Niño, LA 2137
43k. Frances (Francais) Canyon, LA 2135
43l. LA 2298
43m. Gob-1, LA 2120
43n. Gob-12
43o. Gob-17
43p. Gob-25
43q. Gob-72
44. Cebolleta Church
44a. Cebolleta Church
45. Riana Ruin
45a. Riana Ruin, LA 920
46. Tsiping
46a. Tsiping, LA 301
47. Kin Ya-a
47a. Kin Ya-a
48. Kin Bineola
48a. Kin Bineola
49. Gallina Area
49a. Capulin, LA 641
49b. Kiva House, LA 653
49c. Chupadero, LA 654
49d. Cerrito Ruin
49e. Nogales Cliff House, Bg-3
49f. Cuchillo House, Bg-2
49g. Rattlesnake Point, Bg-21
49h. Rattlesnake Point, Bg-22
49i. Rattlesnake Point, Bg-23
49j. Llaves, Bg-30
49k. La Jara, Bg-50
49l. Evans Site, Bg-7
50. Chama River Area
50a. Abiquiu Mission
50b. Poshu, LA 274
50c. Santa Rosa de Lima
51. Chacra Mesa Area
51a. Pueblo Pintado
51b. Chacra Mesa, CM-100
52. Hawikuh
52a. Hawikuh
53. Chaco Canyon Area
53a. Judd's Pit House No. 2
53b. Peñasco Blanco
53c. Pueblo Bonito
53d. Una Vida
53e. Chetro Ketl
53f. Hungo Pavi
53g. Kin Klizhin
53h. Tzin Kletzin
53i. Wijiji
53j. Bc-50, Tseh Tso
53k. Pueblo del Arroyo
53l. Bc-51
53m. Bc-59

53n. Casa Chiquita
53o. Casa Rinconada
53p. Chetro Ketl, East Dump
53q. Half House
53r. Kin Chinde
53s. Kin Kletso
53t. Leyit Kin
53u. Tri-Wall Unit, Pueblo del Arroyo
53v. Shabik'eshchee Village
53w. Talus Rock Shelter
53x. Talus Unit No. 1
53y. Bc-192, Lizard House

54. Chihuahua H:11:1
 54a. Chihuahua H:11:1
55. Fort Grant Area
 55a. Fort Grant Pueblo
56. Te'ewi
 56a. Te'ewi, LA 252
57. Puye
 57a. Puye, LA 47
58. Bandelier National Monument Area
 58a. Frijolito, LA 78
 58b. Tyuonyi, LA 82
 58c. Tshirege, LA 170
 58d. Water Canyon Ruin, LA 545
 58e. Rainbow House, LA 217
 58f. Group M, Bandelier National Monument
 58g. Large Kiva, Bandelier National Monument
59. Jemez Area
 59a. Jemez Mission
 59b. Unshagi, LA 123
 59c. Kiatsekwa, LA 133
 59d. Vallecito Viejo or Policia, LA 136
 59e. Seshukwa, LA 303
 59f. Amoxiumqua, LA 481
60. Canyon Largo Area
 60a. NA 1740
 60b. NA 1741
 60c. Rincon Largo
 60d. H3, S13, C1
 60e. H5, S13, C2
 60f. H1, S19, C5
61. Gila Pueblo
 61a. Gila Pueblo
62. Chaco Yuma West
 62a. Chaco Yuma West
63. Tonto National Monument Area
 63a. Upper Tonto Ruin
 63b. Lower Tonto Ruin
64. Middle Verde River Area
 64a. Tuzigoot, NA 1261
65. Nutria Canyon Area
 65a. Village of the Great Kivas, Small Pueblo B
66. King's Ruin
 66a. King's Ruin, NA 1587
67. Kinishba Area
 67a. Kinishba
68. Pinedale Area
 68a. Pinedale, NA 1006
69. Showlow Area
 69a. Showlow (Whipple) Ruin, NA 1003
70. Klageto Area
 70a. Klageto, NA 1016
 70b. Klageto, NA 1017
 70c. Kinnazinde, NA 1018
71. Wide Ruin Area
 71a. Kin Tiel (Wide Ruin), NA 1015
72. Sierra Ancha Sites
 72a. Canyon Creek Ruin, Arizona C:2:8
 72b. Sierra Ancha, Arizona C:2:11
73. Sierra Ancha Sites
 73a. Sierra Ancha, Arizona C:1:38
74. Sierra Ancha Sites
 74a. Sierra Ancha, Arizona C:1:8
 74b. Sierra Ancha, Arizona C:1:14
 74c. Sierra Ancha, Arizona C:1:16
 74d. Sierra Ancha, Arizona C:1:21
 74e. Sierra Ancha, Arizona C:1:25
 74f. Sierra Ancha, Arizona C:1:30
 74g. Sierra Ancha, Arizona C:1:40
 74h. Sierra Ancha, Arizona C:1:44
 74i. Sierra Ancha, Arizona C:1:45
 74j. Sierra Ancha, Arizona C:1:46
75. Butler Wash Area
 75a. Butler Wash
76. Kin-Li-Chee Wash Area
 76a. Kin-Li-Chee (Rincon Red House), Arizona K:3:1
 76b. Cross Canyon Group, NA 8013
77. Jeddito Area
 77a. Kokopnyama, NA 1019
 77b. Chakpahu, NA 1039
 77c. Kawaika-a (Kawaikuh), NA 1001
 77d. Awatovi, NA 820
 77e. Pink Arrow
 77f. Site 4
 77g. Site 4A
 77h. Site 104
 77i. Site 106
 77j. Site 107
 77k. Site 111
 77l. Site 169
 77m. Jeddito Site 264
 77n. Naha Formation
78. Reserve Area
 78a. Turkey Foot Ridge
 78b. Twin Bridges Site
 78c. Wheatley Ridge Site
79. Point of Pines Area
 79a. Point of Pines Ruin, Arizona W:10:50
 79b. Point of Pines, Arizona W:10:51
80. Bloomfield Area
 80a. Solomon Ruin (Bloomfield Ruin and Chaco 8:7)
81. Bennett's Peak Area
 81a. Bennett's Peak Site, LA 8438
82. Pine River Area
 82a. Pine River
 82b. Cueva Grande
83. Alkali Ridge Area
 83a. Alkali Ridge, Site 13
84. Grand Gulch Area
 84a. Grand Gulch, Nelson's Site 74
 84b. Grand Gulch
85. Long Mesa Area
 85a. Long Mesa Ruin (Hill Canyon No. 1)
 85b. Hill Canyon Ruin No. 2

86. Falls Creek Area
  - 86a. Colorado B:9:1 (Ignacio 12:1)
  - 86b. Colorado B:9:2 (South Shelter and Ignacio 7:2)
  - 86c. Falls Creek, General
  - 86d. Ignacio 7:101, Talus Village
  - 86e. Ignacio 12:1
  - 86f. Ignacio 17A:6 (Colorado B:13:2)
  - 86g. Ignacio 16A:1
  - 86h. Cornelius Cave
  - 86i. North Shelter (Ignacio 7:2A)
  - 86j. Ignacio 7:23
  - 86k. Ignacio 7:30
  - 86l. Ignacio 7:31
  - 86m. Ignacio 7:36

87. Yampa Canyon Area
  - 87a. Marigold Cave

88. Mesa Verde National Park Area
  - 88a. Pit House C
  - 88b. Step House
  - 88c. Pit House No. 1
  - 88d. Pipe Shrine House
  - 88e. Slab Room under Pipe Shrine House
  - 88f. Bone Awl House
  - 88g. Mug House
  - 88h. Spruce Tree House
  - 88i. Balcony House
  - 88j. Cliff Palace
  - 88k. Hemenway House
  - 88l. Kodak House
  - 88m. Long House
  - 88n. Oak Tree House
  - 88o. Ruin No. 16
  - 88p. Spring House
  - 88q. Square Tower House
  - 88r. Buzzard House
  - 88s. New Fire House
  - 88t. Painted Kiva House
  - 88u. Pit Structure No. 1
  - 88v. Pit Structure No. 2
  - 88w. Far View House, Subfloor
  - 88x. Twin Trees Site, Deep Pit House
  - 88y. Slab House
  - 88z. Site 16
  - 88aa. Far View House
  - 88bb. ASS 1060
  - 88cc. Site 145

89. Stollsteimer Mesa Area
  - 89a. Piedra Ruin, Colorado B:15:1

90. Johnson Canyon Area
  - 90a. Johnson Canyon, Site 33

91. La Plata Area
  - 91a. La Plata, Site 25

92. Ackmen-Lowry Area
  - 92a. Lowry Ruin
  - 92b(1). Cahone Canyon, Site 1
  - 92b(2). Cahone Canyon, Site 2

93. Aztec Ruins National Monument Area
  - 93a. Aztec Ruin

94. Nine Mile Canyon Area
  - 94a. Sky House, Nine Mile 13
  - 94b. Nine Mile X
  - 94c. Upper Sky House, Nine Mile 28
  - 94d. Four Name House
  - 94e. Olger Ranch Ruin
  - 94f. Lookout House, Nine Mile 8

95. Kanab Area
  - 95a. Cave Du Pont

96. Prayer Rock District
  - 96a. Broken Flute Cave

97. Prayer Rock District
  - 97a. Obelisk Cave

98. Canyon de Chelly–Canyon del Muerto Area
  - 98a(1). Mummy Cave, Talus Specimens
  - 98a(2). Mummy Cave, Post-Basketmaker Cists and Rooms
  - 98a(3). Mummy Cave, Retaining Walls
  - 98a(4). Mummy Cave, Room in Talus
  - 98a(5). Mummy Cave, Timber from East End
  - 98a(6). Mummy Cave, Cave 1
  - 98a(7). Mummy Cave Tower
  - 98a(8). Mummy Cave, Provenience Unknown
  - 98b. Twin Cave
  - 98c. Sliding Ruin, Mindeleff No. 32
  - 98d. Mindeleff No. 15
  - 98e. White House, NA 2187

99. Mancos Canyon Area
  - 99a. Mancos Canyon, Site 1, LA 2390
  - 99b. Mancos Canyon, Site 4, LA 2387

100. Blanding Area
  - 100a. Five Kiva House

101. Allantown–White Mound Area
  - 101a. Allantown
  - 101b. White Mound Village

102. Lupton Area
  - 102a. Box Canyon
  - 102b. Arizona K:12:5
  - 102c. Arizona K:12:6

103. Red Rock Valley
  - 103a. Cave 1
  - 103b. Cave 2
  - 103c. Cave 6
  - 103d. Cave 7
  - 103e. Cave 8
  - 103f. Hospitibito Canyon
  - 103g. Prayer Rock Cove

104. Forestdale Valley
  - 104a. Bluff Ruin, Arizona P:16:20
  - 104b. Bear Ruin, Arizona P:16:1
  - 104c. Arizona P:16:2

105. Wingate Sites
  - 105a. Wingate 11:47
  - 105b. Wingate 11:49
  - 105c. Wingate 11:60

106. Mogollon Village
  - 106a. Mogollon Village, Mogollon 1:15

107. Starkweather Ruin
  - 107a. Starkweather Ruin

108. Natural Bridges National Monument Area
  - 108a. Natural Bridges Area

109. Three Turkey House
  - 109a. Three Turkey House, NA 1747 and NA 3467

110. Shumway Area
  - 110a. Shumway, Arizona P:12:6

111. Navajo Mountain Area
  - 111a. Little Granary House, NA 4083
  - 111b. Double-Walled Ruin, NA 4207
  - 111c. Red House, NA 2655

- 111d. Lost Mesa Ruin or Segazlin Ruin, NA 4075
- 111e. Cactus Rock Pueblo, NA 5815
- 111f. Lost Mesa, NA 7519A
- 111g. Lost Mesa, NA 7520B
- 111h. NA 7549

112. Vaqueros Canyon Sites
    - 112a–c. Vaqueros Canyon, Site 1 (LA 2120)
    - 112d–h. Vaqueros Canyon, Site 12 (LA 2122)
    - 112i. Vaqueros Canyon, Site 11 (LA 2121)
113. Big Bead Mesa
    - 113a. Big Bead Mesa
114. Red Butte Area
    - 114a. Red Butte, NA 5166C
115. Tohatchi Area
    - 115a. LA 2505
116. Tesuque Valley Area
    - 116a. Tesuque Valley Ruin, LA 742
117. Rio Pueblo Colorado Area
    - 117a. NA 3941A
118. Canyon Padre Area
    - 118a. Wilson Pueblo, NA 1139
119. Vernon Area
    - 119a. Table Rock Pueblo
120. Casas Grandes Area
121. Navajo Reservoir District
    - 121a. LA 4086
    - 121b. Sambrito Village, LA 4195
    - 121c. LA 4380
    - 121d. Serrano Site, LA 4408
122. Zia Pueblo
    - 122a. Zia Pueblo, LA 28

REFERENCES

Adams, R. N.

1951 Half House: A Pithouse in Chaco Canyon, New Mexico. *Papers of the Michigan Academy of Science, Arts, and Letters,* Vol. 35, 1949. Ann Arbor.

Abel, L. J.

1955 Pottery Types of the Southwest: Wares 5A, 10A, 10B, 12A, San Juan Red Ware, Mesa Verde Gray, and White Ware, San Juan White Ware. *Museum of Northern Arizona, Ceramic Series,* No. 3. Flagstaff.

Ambler, J. R., A. L. Lindsay, Jr., and M. A. Stein

1964 Survey and Excavations on Cummings Mesa, Arizona and Utah, 1960–1961. *Museum of Northern Arizona, Bulletin* 39, *Glen Canyon Series,* No. 5. Flagstaff.

Baldwin, G. C.

1934 The Prehistoric Pueblo of Kinishba. MS, master's thesis, University of Arizona, Tucson.

1935 Dates from Kinishba Pueblo. *Tree-Ring Bulletin,* Vol. 1, No. 4, p. 30. Flagstaff.

1939 Dates from King's Ruin. *Tree-Ring Bulletin,* Vol. 5, No. 3, pp. 23–4. Tucson.

Bannister, Bryant

1951 Tree-Ring Dates for the Gallina Area, New Mexico. *Tree-Ring Bulletin,* Vol. 17, No. 3, pp. 21–2. Tucson.

1959 Tree-Ring Dating of Archaeological Sites in the Chaco Canyon Region, New Mexico. Doctoral dissertation, University of Arizona. University Microfilms, Ann Arbor.

1960 Southwestern Dated Ruins. VII. *Tree-Ring Bulletin,* Vol. 23, Nos. 1–4, pp. 19–21. Tucson.

1962 The Interpretation of Tree-Ring Dates. *American Antiquity,* Vol. 27, No. 4, pp. 508–14. Salt Lake City.

1965 Tree-Ring Dating of the Archaeological Sites in the Chaco Canyon Region, New Mexico. *Southwestern Monuments Association, Technical Series,* Vol. 6, Pt. 2. Globe.

Bannister, Bryant, and T. L. Smiley

1955 Dendrochronology. In "Geochronology," edited by T. L. Smiley, pp. 177–95. *University of Arizona Bulletin Series,* Vol. 26, No. 2, *Physical Science Bulletin,* No. 2. Tucson.

Beals, R. L., G. W. Brainerd, and Watson Smith

1945 Archaeological Studies: A Report on the Archaeological Work of the Rainbow Bridge–Monument Valley Expedition in Northeast Arizona. *University of California Publications in American Archaeology and Ethnology,* Vol. 44, No. 1. Berkeley.

Bernheimer, C. L.

1930 Report of the Charles L. Bernheimer Expeditions, 1922–1930. MS, copies on file at Laboratory of Tree-Ring Research and Southwest Archeological Center, Tucson and Globe.

Bliss, W. L.

1960 Impact of Pipeline Archaeology on Indian Prehistory. *Plateau,* Vol. 33, No. 1, pp. 10–3. Flagstaff.

Bluhm, E. A.

1957 The Sawmill Site: A Reserve Phase Village, Pine Lawn Valley, Western New Mexico. *Fieldiana: Anthropology,* Vol. 47, No. 1. Chicago Natural History Museum, Chicago.

Brand, D. D., F. M. Hawley, F. C. Hibben and others.

1937 Tseh So, A Small House Ruin, Chaco Canyon, New Mexico (Preliminary Report). *University of New Mexico Bulletin, Anthropological Series,* Vol. 2, No. 2. Albuquerque.

Breternitz, D. A.

1957 1956 Excavations Near Flagstaff, Part I. *Plateau,* Vol. 30, No. 1, pp. 22–30. Flagstaff.

1960a Excavations at Three Sites in the Verde Valley, Arizona. *Museum of Northern Arizona, Bulletin* 34. Flagstaff.

1960b Orme Ranch Cave, NA 6656. *Plateau,* Vol. 33, No. 2, pp. 25–39. Flagstaff.

1962 Review of the Archaeology of the Flagstaff Region in the Light of Recent Tree-Ring Studies. MS, paper presented at the 27th Annual Meeting of the Society for American Archaeology, Tucson.

1963 The Archaeological Interpretation of Tree-Ring Specimens for Dating Southwestern Ceramic Styles. Doctoral dissertation, University of Arizona. University Microfilms, Ann Arbor.

Brew, J. O.

1946 Archaeology of Alkali Ridge, Southeastern Utah, with a Review of the Prehistory of the Mesa Verde Division of the San Juan and Some Observations on Archaeological Systematics. *Papers of the Peabody Museum, Harvard University,* Vol. 21. Cambridge.

BULLARD, W. R., JR. AND F. E. CASSIDY
1956 LA 2505. In *Pipeline Archaeology,* edited by Fred Wendorf, Nancy Fox, and O. L. Lewis, pp. 43–51. Laboratory of Anthropology and Museum of Northern Arizona, Santa Fe and Flagstaff.

BURGH, R. F.
1950 A Fremont Basket Maker House in Dinosaur National Monument. *Tree-Ring Bulletin,* Vol. 16, No. 3, pp. 19–20. Tucson.
1959 Ceramic Profiles in the Western Mound at Awatovi, Northeastern Arizona. *American Antiquity,* Vol. 25, No. 2, pp. 184–202. Salt Lake City.

CARLSON, R. L.
1961 White Mountain Red Ware: A Stylistic Tradition in the Prehistoric Pottery of East Central Arizona. Doctoral dissertation, University of Arizona. University Microfilms, Ann Arbor.
1963 Basketmaker III Sites near Durango, Colorado. *University of Colorado Studies, Series in Anthropology,* No. 8. Boulder.

CAYWOOD, L. R. AND E. H. SPICER
1935 Tuzigoot, The Excavation and Repair of a Ruin on the Verde River near Clarkdale, Arizona. *National Park Service, Field Division of Education.* Berkeley.

CHAPMAN, K. M.
1933–1936 *Pueblo Indian Pottery,* two volumes. C. Szwedzicki, Nice.

CHRISTENSEN, R. T.
1951 A Chronology for Nine Mile Canyon, Northeastern Utah. MS, on file at Laboratory of Tree-Ring Research, Tucson.

CIBOLA WHITE WARE CONFERENCE
1958 Museum of Northern Arizona. Flagstaff.

COLTON, H. S.
1939a Prehistoric Culture Units and Their Relationships in Northern Arizona. *Museum of Northern Arizona, Bulletin* 17. Flagstaff.
1939b The Date of Three Turkey House. *Tree-Ring Bulletin,* Vol. 5, No. 4, p. 26. Tucson.
1939c Three Turkey House. *Plateau,* Vol. 12, No. 2, pp. 26–31. Flagstaff.
1941 Winona and Ridge Ruin, Part II: Notes on the Technology and Taxonomy of the Pottery. *Museum of Northern Arizona, Bulletin* 19. Flagstaff.
1945 A Revision of the Date of the Eruption of Sunset Crater. *Southwestern Journal of Anthropology,* Vol. 1, No. 3, pp. 345–55. Albuquerque.
1946 The Sinagua: A Summary of the Archaeology of the Region of Flagstaff, Arizona. *Museum of Northern Arizona, Bulletin* 22. Flagstaff.
1953 Potsherds: An Introduction to the Study of Prehistoric Southwestern Ceramics and Their Use in Historical Reconstruction. *Museum of Northern Arizona, Bulletin* 25. Flagstaff.
1955 Checklist of Southwestern Pottery Types. *Museum of Northern Arizona, Ceramic Series,* No. 2. Flagstaff.
1956 Pottery Types of the Southwest: Wares 5A, 5B, 6A, 6B, 7A, 7B, 7C, San Juan Red Ware, Tsegi Orange Ware, Homolovi Orange Ware, Winslow Orange Ware, Awatovi Yellow Ware, Jeddito Yellow Ware, Sichomovi Red Ware. *Museum of Northern Arizona, Ceramic Series,* No. 3C. Flagstaff.
1960 *Black Sand: Prehistory in Northern Arizona.* University of New Mexico Press, Albuquerque.

COLTON, H. S. (EDITOR)
1958 Pottery Types of the Southwest: Wares 14, 15, 16, 17, 18. *Museum of Northern Arizona, Ceramic Series,* No. 3D. Flagstaff.

COLTON, H. S., AND L. L. HARGRAVE
1937 Handbook of Northern Arizona Pottery Wares. *Museum of Northern Arizona, Bulletin* 11. Flagstaff.

COSGROVE, C. B. AND H. S. COSGROVE
1925 Preliminary Survey of the El Paso Pueblo District (with section on "Pueblo on Senator Fall's Ranch, Three Rivers, New Mexico"). MS, on file at Centennial Museum, Texas Western College, El Paso.

CUMMINGS, BYRON
1940 *Kinishba: A Prehistoric Pueblo of the Great Pueblo Period.* Hohokam Museums Association and the University of Arizona, Tucson.

DAIFUKU, HIROSHI
1961 Jeddito 264: A Report on the Excavation of a Basket Maker III–Pueblo I Site in Northeastern Arizona, with a Review of Some Current Theories in Southwestern Archaeology. *Papers of the Peabody Museum, Harvard University,* Vol. 33, No. 1. Cambridge.

DANIELS, H. S. (COMPILER)
1940 *Durango Public Library Museum Project,* three volumes. Durango Public Library, Durango.

DEAN, J. S.
1962 Report of Tree-Ring Specimen Analysis for the Cross Canyon Group, NA 8013. MS, on file at Laboratory of Tree-Ring Research and Museum of Northern Arizona, Tucson and Flagstaff.
1964a Tree-ring dates from Betatakin Ruin, Navajo National Monument. Ms, on file at Laboratory of Tree-Ring Research, Tucson.
1964b Final Report: Kiet Siel Tree-Ring Dating Project. MS, on file at Laboratory of Tree-Ring Research, Tucson.

DITTERT, A. E. JR., J. J. HESTER, AND F. W. EDDY
1961 An Archaeological Survey of the Navajo Reservoir District, Northwestern New Mexico. *Monographs of the School of American Research and the Museum of New Mexico,* No. 23. Santa Fe.

DOUGLASS, A. E.
1935 Dating Pueblo Bonito and Other Ruins of the Southwest. *National Geographic Society, Contributed Technical Papers, Pueblo Bonito Series,* No. 1. Washington.
1936 The Central Pueblo Chronology. *Tree-Ring Bulletin,* Vol. 2, No. 4, pp. 29–34. Flagstaff.
1938 Southwestern Dated Ruins: V. *Tree-Ring Bulletin,* Vol. 5, No. 2, pp. 10–13. Tucson.
1944 Tabulation of Dates for Bluff Ruin, Forestdale, Arizona. *Tree-Ring Bulletin,* Vol. 11, No. 2, pp. 10–16. Tucson.
1947 Photographic Tree-Ring Chronologies and the Flagstaff Sequence. *Tree-Ring Bulletin,* Vol. 14, No. 2, pp. 10–16. Tucson.

DUTTON, B. P.
1938 Leyit Kin, A Small House Ruin, Chaco Canyon, New Mexico: Excavation Report. *Monographs of the School of American Research,* No. 7. Santa Fe.

EDMUNDSON, M. S.
1961 Neolithic Diffusion Rates. *Current Anthropology,* Vol. 2, No. 2, pp. 71–86. Chicago.

FERGUSON, C. W., JR.
1949 Additional Dates for Nine Mile Canyon, Northeastern Utah. *Tree-Ring Bulletin,* Vol. 16, No. 2, pp. 10–11. Tucson.

FEWKES, J. W.
1904 Two Summers' Work in Pueblo Ruins. *22nd Annual Report of the Bureau of American Ethnology,* Pt. 1, pp. 3–195. Washington.

FIFTH SOUTHWESTERN CERAMIC CONFERENCE
1963 Museum of Northern Arizona. Flagstaff.

FLORA, I. F.
1940 A Durango Home in 630 A.D. In *Sherds and Points,* edited by I. F. Flora and H. S. Daniels, Vol. 1, No. 4. Durango. [Originally published in the *Durango News,* November 8, 1940 issue. Durango.]

GETTY, H. T.
1935a New Dates from Mesa Verde. *Tree-Ring Bulletin,* Vol. 1, No. 3, pp. 21–3. Flagstaff.
1935b New Dates for Spruce Tree House, Mesa Verde. *Tree-Ring Bulletin,* Vol. 1, No. 4, pp. 28–9. Flagstaff.

GIFFORD, J. C.
1957 Archaeological Explorations in Caves of the Point of Pines Region. MS, master's thesis, University of Arizona, Tucson.

GILLIN, JOHN
1955 Archeological Investigations in Nine Mile Canyon, Utah: A Re-publication. *University of Utah Anthropological Papers,* No. 21. Salt Lake City.

GLADWIN, H. S.
1945 The Chaco Branch: Excavations at White Mound and in the Red Mesa Valley. *Medallion Papers,* No. 33. Gila Pueblo, Globe.
1957 *A History of the Ancient Southwest.* Bond Wheelwright, Portland.

GLADWIN, H. S., E. W. HAURY, E. B. SAYLES, AND NORA GLADWIN
1937 Excavations at Snaketown: I. Material Culture. *Medallion Papers,* No. 25. Gila Pueblo, Globe.

GLADWIN, WINIFRED AND H. S. GLADWIN
1930 Some Southwestern Pottery Types: Series I. *Medallion Papers,* No. 8. Gila Pueblo, Globe.

HACK, J. T.
1942 The Changing Physical Environment of the Hopi Indians of Arizona. *Papers of the Peabody Museum, Harvard University,* Vol. 35, No. 1. Cambridge.

HALL, E. T., JR.
1944 *Early Stockaded Settlements in the Governador New Mexico: A Marginal Anasazi Development from Basket Maker III to Pueblo I Times.* Columbia University Press, New York.
1951 Southwestern Dated Ruins. VI. *Tree-Ring Bulletin,* Vol. 17, No. 4, pp. 26–8. Tucson.

HARGRAVE, L. L.
1933 Wupatki National Monument: Collected Field Notes of the Museum of Northern Arizona. MS, on file at Museum of North-

ern Arizona and Southwest Archeological Center, Flagstaff and Globe.

1935 *Report on Archaeological Reconnaissance in the Rainbow Plateau Area of Northern Arizona and Southern Utah: Based Upon Fieldwork by the Rainbow Bridge–Monument Valley Expedition of 1933.* University of California Press, Berkeley.

HARLAN, T. P.

1962 A Sequence of Ruins in the Flagstaff Area Dated by Tree-Rings. MS, master's thesis, University of Arizona, Tucson.

HAURY, E. W.

1931 Kivas of the Tusayan Ruin, Grand Canyon, Arizona. *Medallion Papers,* No. 9. Gila Pueblo, Globe.

1934 The Canyon Creek Ruin and the Cliff Dwellings of the Sierra Ancha. *Medallion Papers,* No. 14. Gila Pueblo, Globe.

1935 Dates from Gila Pueblo. *Tree-Ring Bulletin,* Vol. 2, No. 1, pp. 3–4. Flagstaff.

1936a The Mogollon Culture of Southwestern New Mexico. *Medallion Papers,* No. 20. Gila Pueblo, Globe.

1936b Vandal Cave. *Kiva,* Vol. 1, No. 6. Tucson.

1938 Southwestern Dated Ruins: II. *Tree-Ring Bulletin,* Vol. 4, No. 3, pp. 3–4. Tucson.

1939 Report of the University of Arizona Archaeological Expedition into Northeastern Arizona, July 13 to August 26, 1927 [Vandal Cave Field Notes]. MS, on file in the Department of Anthropology, University of Arizona, Tucson.

1940a Excavations in the Forestdale Valley, East-Central Arizona. *University of Arizona Bulletin,* Vol. 21, No. 4, *Social Science Bulletin,* No. 12. Tucson.

1940b New Tree-Ring Dates from the Forestdale Valley, East-Central Arizona. *Tree-Ring Bulletin,* Vol. 7, No. 2, pp. 14–6. Tucson.

1945 The Excavation of Los Muertos and Neighboring Ruins in the Salt River Valley, Southern Arizona. *Papers of the Peabody Museum, Harvard University,* Vol. 24, No. 1. Cambridge.

1950 A Sequence of Great Kivas in the Forestdale Valley, Arizona. In *For the Dean,* edited by E. K. Reed and D. S. King, pp. 29–39. Hohokam Museums Association and Southwestern Monuments Association, Tucson and Santa Fe.

1958 Evidence at Point of Pines for a Prehistoric Migration from Northern Arizona. In "Migrations in New World Culture History," edited by R. H. Thompson, pp. 1–6. *University of Arizona Bulletin,* Vol. 29, No. 2, *Social Science Bulletin,* No. 27. Tucson.

1962 The Greater American Southwest. In "Courses Toward Urban Life," edited by R. J. Braidwood and G. R. Willey, pp. 106–31. *Viking Fund Publications in Anthropology,* No. 32. Wenner-Gren Foundation for Anthropological Research, New York.

HAURY, E. W. AND I. F. FLORA

1937 Basket-Maker III Dates from the Vicinity of Durango, Colorado. *Tree-Ring Bulletin,* Vol. 4, No. 1, pp. 7–8. Tucson.

HAURY, E. W. AND L. L. HARGRAVE

1931 Recently Dated Pueblo Ruins in Arizona. *Smithsonian Miscellaneous Collections,* Vol. 82, No. 11. Washington.

HAURY, E. W. AND E. B. SAYLES

1947 An Early Pit House Village of the Mogollon Culture, Forestdale Valley, Arizona. *University of Arizona Bulletin,* Vol. 18, No. 4, *Social Science Bulletin,* No. 16. Tucson.

HAWLEY, F. M.

1934 The Significance of the Dated Prehistory of Chetro Ketl, Chaco Cañon, New Mexico. *Monographs of the School of American Research,* No. 2. Santa Fe.

1950 Field Manual of Prehistoric Southwestern Pottery Types, revised edition. *University of New Mexico Bulletin, Anthropological Series,* Vol. 1, No. 4. Albuquerque.

HAYDEN, J. D.

1957 Excavations, 1940, at University Indian Ruin, Tucson, Arizona. *Southwestern Monuments Association, Technical Series,* Vol. 5. Globe.

HENDRON, J. W.

1940 Prehistory of El Rito de los Frijoles, Bandelier National Monument. *Southwestern Monuments Association, Technical Series,* No. 1. Coolidge.

HEROLD, JOYCE

1961 Prehistoric Settlement and Physical Environment in the Mesa Verde Area. *University of Utah, Anthropological Papers,* No. 53. Salt Lake City.

HESTER, J. J.

1962 Early Navajo Migrations and Acculturation in the Southwest. *Museum of New Mexico, Papers in Anthropology,* Number 6. Santa Fe.

1963 Excavations at the Serrano Site, LA 4408. In "Pueblo Period Sites in the Piedra River Section, Navajo Reservoir District," assembled by A. E. Dittert, Jr. and F. W. Eddy, pp. 44–79. *Museum of New Mexico, Papers in Anthropology,* No. 10. Santa Fe.

HEWETT, E. L.

1953 *Pajarito Plateau and its Ancient People,* revised by Bertha P. Dutton. University of New Mexico Press and School of American Research, Albuquerque and Santa Fe.

HIBBEN, F. C.

1937 Excavation of the Riana Ruin and Chama Valley Survey. *University of New Mexico Bulletin, Anthropological Series,* Vol. 2, No. 1. Albuquerque.

1939 The Gallina Culture of North Central New Mexico. MS, doctoral dissertation, Harvard University, Cambridge.

1948 The Gallina Architectural Forms. *American Antiquity,* Vol. 14, No. 1, pp. 32–6. Menasha.

1949 The Pottery of the Gallina Complex. *American Antiquity,* Vol. 14, No. 3, pp. 194–202. Menasha.

HOLDEN, JANE

1955 A Preliminary Report on Arrowhead Ruin. *El Palacio,* Vol. 62, No. 4, pp. 102–19. Santa Fe.

JUDD, N. M.

1924 Two Chaco Canyon Pit Houses. *Annual Report of the Smithsonian Institution for 1922,* pp. 399–413. Washington.

1954 The Material Culture of Pueblo Bonito. *Smithsonian Miscellaneous Collections,* Vol. 124. Washington.

1959a. The Braced-up Cliff at Pueblo Bonito. *Annual Report of the Smithsonian Institution for 1958,* pp. 501–11. Washington.

1959b. Pueblo del Arroyo, Chaco Canyon, New Mexico. *Smithsonian Miscellaneous Collections,* Vol. 138, No. 1. Washington.

KEUR, D. L.

1941 Big Bead Mesa: An Archaeological Study of Navaho Acculturation, 1745–1812. *Memoirs of the Society for American Archaeology,* No. 1. Menasha.

KIDDER, A. V.

1958 Pecos, New Mexico: Archaeological Notes. *Papers of the Robert S. Peabody Foundation for Archaeology,* Vol. 5. Andover.

KIDDER, A. V. AND C. A. AMSDEN

1931 The Pottery of Pecos, Vol. 1: The Dull-Paint Wares. *Papers of the Phillips Academy, Southwestern Expedition,* No. 5. Yale University Press, New Haven.

KIDDER, A. V. AND A. O. SHEPARD

1936 The Pottery of Pecos, Vol. 2: The Glaze Paint, Culinary, and other Wares. *Papers of the Phillips Academy, Southwestern Expedition,* No. 7. Yale University Press, New Haven.

KING, D. S.

1949 Nalakihu: Excavations at a Pueblo III Site on Wupatki National Monument, Arizona. *Museum of Northern Arizona, Bulletin* 23. Flagstaff.

KLUCKHOHN, CLYDE AND PAUL REITER (EDITORS)

1939 Preliminary Report on the 1937 Excavations, Bc 50-51, Chaco Canyon, New Mexico. *University of New Mexico Bulletin* 345, *Anthropological Series,* Vol. 3, No. 2. Albuquerque.

KNIPE, D. A.

1942 A Date from Chaco Yuma West, Southern Arizona. *Tree-Ring Bulletin,* Vol. 8, No. 3, p. 24. Tucson.

KUBLER, GEORGE

1940 *The Religious Architecture of New Mexico in the Colonial Period and Since the American Occupation.* The Taylor Museum, Colorado Springs.

LANCASTER, J. A. AND J. M. PINKLEY

1954 Excavation at Site 16 of Three Pueblo II Mesa-Top Ruins. In "Archeological Excavations in Mesa Verde National Park, Colorado, 1950," by J. A. Lancaster and others, pp. 23–86. *National Park Service, Archeological Research Series,* No. 2. Washington.

LANCASTER, J. A. AND D. W. WATSON

1943 Excavation of Mesa Verde Pit Houses. *American Antiquity,* Vol. 9, No. 2, pp. 190–8. Menasha.

1954 Excavation of Two Late Basketmaker III Pithouses. In "Archeological Excavations in Mesa Verde National Park, Colorado, 1950," by J. A. Lancaster and others, pp. 7–22. *National Park Service, Archeological Research Series,* No. 2. Washington.

LANGE, C. H.

1941 The Evans Site: A Contribution to the Archaeology of the Gallina Region, Northern New Mexico. MS, master's thesis, University of New Mexico, Albuquerque.

MC.GREGOR, J. C.

1934 Dates from Tsegi. *Tree-Ring Bulletin,* Vol. 1, No. 1, pp. 6–8. Flagstaff.

1936a Dating the Eruption of Sunset Crater, Arizona. *American Antiquity,* Vol. 2, No. 1, pp. 15–26. Menasha.

1936b Additional Dates from Tsegi. *Tree-Ring Bulletin,* Vol. 2, No. 4, p. 37. Flagstaff.

1936c Culture of Sites Which Were Occupied Shortly Before the Eruption of Sunset Crater. *Museum of Northern Arizona, Bulletin* 9. Flagstaff.

1936d Dates from Tsegi and Nalakihu. *Tree-Ring Bulletin,* Vol. 3, No. 2, pp. 15–6. Flagstaff.

1938a How Some Important Northern Arizona Pottery Types Were Dated. *Museum of Northern Arizona, Bulletin* 13. Flagstaff.

1938b Southwestern Dated Ruins: III. *Tree-Ring Bulletin,* Vol. 4, No. 4, p. 6. Tucson.

1941 Winona and Ridge Ruin: Part I, Architecture and Material Culture. *Museum of Northern Arizona, Bulletin* 18. Flagstaff.

1942a Dates from Wupatki Pueblo. *Tree-Ring Bulletin,* Vol. 8, No. 3, pp. 18–21. Tucson.

1942b Dates from Kinnikinnick Pueblo. *Tree-Ring Bulletin,* Vol. 8, No. 3. pp. 21–3. Tucson.

1951 *The Cohonina Culture of Northwestern Arizona.* University of Illinois Press, Urbana.

1956 The 1955 Pollock Site Excavation. *Plateau,* Vol. 28, No. 3, pp. 49–54. Flagstaff.

1958 The Pershing Site. *Plateau,* Vol. 31, No. 2, pp. 33–6. Flagstaff.

1960 Table Rock Pueblo, Arizona. *Fieldiana: Anthropology,* Vol. 51, No. 2. Chicago Natural History Museum, Chicago.

MARTIN, P. S.

1936 Lowry Ruin in Southwestern Colorado. *Field Museum of Natural History, Anthropological Series,* Vol. 23, No. 1. Chicago.

1939 Modified Basket Maker Sites, Ackmen-Lowry Area, Southwestern Colorado, 1938. *Field Museum of Natural History, Anthropological Series,* Vol. 23, No. 3. Chicago.

MARTIN, P. S. AND J. B. RINALDO

1947 The SU Site: Excavations at a Mogollon Village, Western New Mexico, Third Season 1946. *Field Museum of Natural History, Anthropological Series,* Vol. 32, No. 3. Chicago.

1950 Turkey Foot Ridge Site, A Mogollon Village, Pine Lawn Valley, Western New Mexico. *Fieldiana: Anthropology,* Vol. 38, No. 2. Chicago Natural History Museum, Chicago.

MARTIN, P. S., J. B. RINALDO, AND ERNST ANTEVS

1949 Cochise and Mogollon Sites, Pine Lawn Valley, Western New Mexico. *Fieldiana: Anthropology,* Vol. 38, No. 1. Chicago Natural History Museum, Chicago.

MARTIN, P. S., J. B. RINALDO, ELAINE BLUHM, H. C. CUTLER, AND ROGER GRANGE, JR.

1952 Mogollon Cultural Continuity and Change: The Stratigraphic Analysis of Tularosa and Cordova Caves. *Fieldiana: Anthropology,* Vol. 40. Chicago Natural History Museum, Chicago.

MARTIN, P. S. AND E. S. WILLIS

1940 Anasazi Painted Pottery in the Field Museum of Natural History. *Field Museum of Natural History, Anthropology Memoirs,* Vol. 5. Chicago.

MERA, H. P.

1938 Some Aspects of the Largo Cultural Phase, Northern New Mexico. *American Antiquity,* Vol. 3, No. 3, pp. 236–43. Menasha.

1939 Style Trends of Pueblo Pottery in the Rio Grande and Little Colorado Cultural Areas from the Sixteenth to the Nineteenth Century. *Memoirs of the Laboratory of Anthropology,* Vol. 3. Santa Fe.

1940 Population Changes in the Rio Grande Glaze-paint Area. *Laboratory of Anthropology, Archaeological Survey, Technical Series, Bulletin* No. 9. Santa Fe.

1943 An Outline of Ceramic Developments in Southern and Southeastern New Mexico. *Laboratory of Anthropology, Technical Series, Bulletin* No. 11. Santa Fe.

MILLER, C. F., JR.

1934 Report of Dates on the Allantown, Arizona, Ruins. *Tree-Ring Bulletin,* Vol. 1, No. 2, pp. 15–6. Flagstaff.

1935 Additional Dates from the Allantown, Arizona, Ruins. *Tree-Ring Bulletin,* Vol. 1, No. 4, p. 31. Flagstaff.

MILLER, J. L.

1942 Dates from Fort Grant Pueblo, Southern Arizona. *Tree-Ring Bulletin,* Vol. 8, No. 3, p. 24. Tucson.

MILLER, W. C., D. A. BRETERNITZ, AND R. C. EULER

MS Archaeological Investigations in Navajo Canyon and on White Mesa, Northeastern Arizona. In preparation.

MORRIS, E. H.

1917 The Ruins at Aztec. *El Palacio*, Vol. 4, No. 3, pp. 43–69. Santa Fe.

1919 The Aztec Ruin. *Anthropological Papers of the American Museum of Natural History*, Vol. 26, Part 1. New York.

1921 The House of the Great Kiva at the Aztec Ruin. *Anthropological Papers of the American Museum of Natural History*, Vol. 26, Part 2. New York.

1924 Burials in the Aztec Ruin: The Aztec Ruin Annex. *Anthropological Papers of the American Museum of Natural History*, Vol. 26, Parts 3–4. New York.

1928 Notes on Excavations in the Aztec Ruin. *Anthropological Papers of the American Museum of Natural History*, Vol. 26, Part 5. New York.

1936 Archaeological Background of Dates in Early Arizona Chronology. *Tree-Ring Bulletin*, Vol. 2, No. 4, pp. 34–6. Flagstaff.

1939 Archaeological Studies in the La Plata District, Southwestern Colorado and Northwestern New Mexico. *Carnegie Institution of Washington, Publication* 519. Washington.

1941 Prayer Sticks in Walls of Mummy Cave Tower, Canyon del Muerto. *American Antiquity*, Vol. 6, No. 3, pp. 227–30. Menasha.

1949 Basketmaker II Dwellings Near Durango, Colorado. *Tree-Ring Bulletin*, Vol. 15, No. 4, pp. 33–4. Tucson.

1952 Note on the Durango Dates. *Tree-Ring Bulletin*, Vol. 18, No. 4, p. 36. Tucson.

MORRIS, E. H. AND R. F. BURGH

1954 Basket Maker II Sites Near Durango, Colorado. *Carnegie Institution of Washington, Publication* 604. Washington.

MORRIS, E. A.

1957 Stratigraphic Evidence for a Cultural Continuum at the Point of Pines Ruin. MS, master's thesis, University of Arizona, Tucson.

1959a Basketmaker Caves in the Prayer Rock District, Northeastern Arizona. Doctoral dissertation, University of Arizona. University Microfilms, Ann Arbor.

1959b A Pueblo I Site Near Bennett's Peak, Northwestern New Mexico. *El Palacio*, Vol. 66, No. 5, pp. 169–75. Santa Fe.

MURPHEY, S. E.

1936 Description of Sherds found during Excavations of the Summer of 1935, Chaco Canyon, New Mexico. MS, on file at Southwest Archeological Center, Globe.

NELSON, N. C.

1914 Pueblo Ruins of the Galisteo Basin, New Mexico. *Anthropological Papers of the American Museum of Natural History*, Vol. 15, Part 1. New York.

NESBITT, P. H.

1938 Starkweather Ruin: A Mogollon-Pueblo Site in the Upper Gila Area of New Mexico and Affiliative Aspects of the Mogollon Culture. *Logan Museum Publications in Anthropology, Bulletin* No. 6. Beloit.

NICHOLS, R. F.

1962 Dates from the Site 1060 Pithouse, Mesa Verde National Park. *Tree-Ring Bulletin*, Vol. 24, Nos. 1–2, pp. 12–4. Tucson.

NORDENSKIOLD, GUSTAV

1893 *The Cliff Dwellers of the Mesa Verde, Southwestern Colorado: Their Pottery and Implements*. P. A. Norstedt and Söner, Stockholm.

O'BRYAN, DERIC

1950 Excavations in Mesa Verde National Park 1947–1948. *Medallion Papers*, No. 39. Gila Pueblo, Globe.

OLSON, A. P.

1959 An Evaluation of the Phase Concept in Southwestern Archaeology: As Applied to the Eleventh and Twelfth Century Occupations at Point of Pines, East Central Arizona. Doctoral dissertation, University of Arizona. University Microfilms, Ann Arbor.

PEARCE, W. M.

1937 A Study of Arrowhead Ruin. MS, master's thesis, Texas Technological College, Lubbock.

PETERSON, ALFRED

1935 Specimens from the Pueblo Area Collected by the First Beam Expedition 1923. *Tree-Ring Bulletin*, Vol. 1, No. 3, pp. 23–4. Flagstaff.

1937 Further Data on First Beam Expedition Specimens, 1923. *Tree-Ring Bulletin*, Vol. 3, No. 3, pp. 23–4. Flagstaff.

1939 Third Report on Hopi Specimens: Collections of Second Beam Expedition, 1928. *Tree-Ring Bulletin*, Vol. 6, No. 1, pp. 6–8. Tucson.

PHILLIPS, PHILIP

1958 Application of the Wheat-Gifford-Wasley Taxonomy to Eastern Ceramics. *American Antiquity*, Vol. 24, No. 2, pp. 117–25. Salt Lake City.

PHILLIPS, PHILIP AND J. C. GIFFORD

1959 *A Review of the Taxonomic Nomenclature Essential to Ceramic Analysis in Archaeology.* Harvard University, Cambridge.

PIERSON, L. M.

1949 The Prehistoric Population of Chaco Canyon, New Mexico: A Study in Methods and Techniques of Prehistoric Population Estimation. MS, master's thesis, University of New Mexico, Albuquerque.

1962 Excavations at the Lower Ruin and Annex, Tonto National Monument, 1952. In "Archeological Studies at Tonto National Monument, Arizona," edited by L. R. Caywood, pp. 33–69. *Southwestern Monuments Association, Technical Series,* Vol. 2. Globe.

POMEROY, J. A.

1962 A Study of Black-on-white Painted Pottery in the Tonto Basin, Arizona. MS, master's thesis, University of Arizona, Tucson.

REAGAN, A. B.

1919 The Ancient Ruins in Lower and Middle Pine River Valley, Colorado. *El Palacio,* Vol. 7, Nos. 9–12, pp. 171–6. Santa Fe.

REED, E. K.

1943 Excavations in Mancos Canyon. MS, on file at National Park Service, Southwest Region, Santa Fe.

1958 Excavations in Mancos Canyon, Colorado. *University of Utah, Anthropological Papers,* No. 35. Salt Lake City.

REITER, PAUL

1938 The Jemez Pueblo of Unshagi, New Mexico, with Notes on the Earlier Excavations at "Amoxiumqua" and Giusewa. *Monographs of the School of American Research,* Nos. 5–6. Albuquerque.

RINALDO, J. B.

1950 An Analysis of Culture Change in the Ackmen-Lowry Area. *Fieldiana: Anthropology,* Vol. 36, No. 5, pp. 93–106. Chicago Natural History Museum, Chicago.

RINALDO, J. B. AND E. A. BLUHM

1956 Late Mogollon Pottery Types of the Reserve Area. *Fieldiana: Anthropology,* Vol. 36, No. 7, pp. 149–87. Chicago Natural History Museum, Chicago.

RIXEY, RAYMOND

1948 Summary of Archaeological Materials from Stabilization Work at Walnut Canyon National Monument. MS, on file at Southwest Archeological Center, Globe.

1949 Archaeological Materials from Walnut Canyon National Monument. MS, on file at Southwest Archeological Center, Globe.

RIXEY, RAYMOND AND C. B. VOLL

1962 Archaeological Materials from Walnut Canyon Cliff Dwellings. *Plateau,* Vol. 34, No. 3, pp. 85–96. Flagstaff.

ROBERTS, F. H. H., JR.

1927 The Ceramic Sequence in Chaco Canyon and its Relationship to the Culture of the San Juan Basin. MS, doctoral dissertation, Harvard University, Cambridge.

1929 Shabik'eschee Village: A Late Basket Maker Site in the Chaco Canyon, New Mexico. *Bureau of American Ethnology, Bulletin* 92. Washington.

1930 Early Pueblo Ruins in the Piedra District, Southwestern Colorado. *Bureau of American Ethnology, Bulletin* 96. Washington.

1932 The Village of the Great Kivas on the Zuñi Reservation, New Mexico. *Bureau of American Ethnology, Bulletin* 111. Washington.

1939 Archeological Remains in the Whitewater District, Eastern Arizona: Part I. House Types. *Bureau of American Ethnology, Bulletin* 121. Washington.

1940 Archeological Remains in the Whitewater District, Eastern Arizona: Part II. Artifacts and Burials. *Bureau of American Ethnology, Bulletin* 126. Washington.

ROWE, CHANDLER

1947 The Wheatley Ridge Site. MS, master's thesis, University of Chicago, Chicago.

SAYLES, E. B.

1936 An Archaeological Survey of Chihuahua, Mexico. *Medallion Papers,* No. 22. Gila Pueblo, Globe.

SCHROEDER, A. H.

1940 A Stratigraphic Survey of Pre-Spanish Trash Mounds of the Salt River Valley, Arizona. MS, master's thesis, University of Arizona, Tucson.

SCHULMAN, EDMUND

1946 Dendrochronology at Mesa Verde National Park. *Tree-Ring Bulletin,* Vol. 12, No. 3, pp. 18–24. Tucson.

1948a Dendrochronology at Navajo National Monument. *Tree-Ring Bulletin,* Vol. 14, No. 3, pp. 18–24. Tucson.

1948b Dendrochronology in Northeastern Utah. *Tree-Ring Bulletin,* Vol. 15, Nos. 1–2, pp. 2–14. Tucson.

1949a An Extension of the Durango Chronology. *Tree-Ring Bulletin,* Vol. 16, No. 2, pp. 12–16. Tucson.

1949b Early Chronologies in the San Juan Basin. *Tree-Ring Bulletin,* Vol. 15, No. 4, pp. 24–32. Tucson.

1950a A Dated Beam from Dinosaur National Monument. *Tree-Ring Bulletin,* Vol. 16, No. 3, pp. 18–19. Tucson.

1950b Miscellaneous Ring Records. I. *Tree-Ring Bulletin,* Vol. 16, No. 3, p. 21. Tucson.

1951 Miscellaneous Ring Records. III. *Tree-Ring Bulletin,* Vol. 17, No. 4, pp. 28–9. Tucson.

1952 Extension of the San Juan Chronology to B.C. Times. *Tree-Ring Bulletin,* Vol. 18, No. 4, pp. 30–5. Tucson.

SECOND SOUTHWESTERN CERAMIC SEMINAR

1959 Museum of Northern Arizona. Flagstaff.

SENTER, F. H.

1938 Southwestern Dated Ruins: IV, Chaco Canyon, New Mexico. *Tree-Ring Bulletin,* Vol. 5, No. 1, pp. 6–7. Tucson.

SHINER, J. L.

1961a A Room at Gila Pueblo. *Kiva,* Vol. 27, No. 2, pp. 3–11. Tucson.

1961b Excavation of a Chaco-Type Kiva, Chaco Canyon, New Mexico. MS, on file at Southwest Archeological Center, Globe.

SIXTH SOUTHWESTERN CERAMIC CONFERENCE

1964 Museum of Northern Arizona. Flagstaff.

SMILEY, T. L.

1947 Dates from a Surface Pueblo at Mesa Verde. *Tree-Ring Bulletin,* Vol. 13, No. 4, pp. 30–2. Tucson.

1949a Pithouse Number 1, Mesa Verde National Park. *American Antiquity,* Vol. 14, No. 3, pp. 167–71. Menasha.

1949b Tree-Ring Dates from Point of Pines. *Tree-Ring Bulletin,* Vol. 15, No. 3, pp. 20–1. Tucson.

1950 Miscellaneous Ring Records. II. *Tree-Ring Bulletin,* Vol. 16, No. 3, pp. 22–3. Tucson.

1951 A Summary of Tree-Ring Dates from Some Southwestern Archaeological Sites. *University of Arizona Bulletin,* Vol. 22, No. 4, *Laboratory Bulletin of Tree-Ring Research,* No. 5. Tucson.

SMILEY, T. L., S. A. STUBBS, AND BRYANT BANNISTER

1953 A Foundation for the Dating of Some Late Archaeological Sites in the Rio Grande Area, New Mexico: Based on Studies in Tree-Ring Methods and Pottery Analyses. *University of Arizona Bulletin,* Vol. 24, No. 3, *Laboratory of Tree-Ring Research Bulletin,* No. 6. Tucson.

SMITH, WATSON

1952a Excavations in Big Hawk Valley, Wupatki National Monument, Arizona. *Museum of Northern Arizona, Bulletin* 24. Flagstaff.

1952b Kiva Mural Decorations at Awatovi and Kawaika-a, with a Survey of other Wall Paintings in the Pueblo Southwest. *Papers of the Peabody Museum, Harvard University,* Vol. 37. Cambridge.

1962 Schools, Pots, and Potters. *American Anthropologist,* Vol. 64, No. 6, pp. 1165–78. Menasha.

SPICER, E. H. AND L. R. CAYWOOD

1936 Two Pueblo Ruins in West Central Arizona. *University of Arizona Bulletin,* Vol. 7, No. 1, *Social Science Bulletin,* No. 10. Tucson.

STALLINGS, W. S., JR.

1933 A Tree-Ring Chronology for the Rio Grande Drainage in Northern New Mexico. *Proceedings of the National Academy of Sciences,* Vol. 19, No. 9, pp. 803–6. Washington.

1936 Dates from Five Kiva House, Utah. *Tree-Ring Bulletin,* Vol. 3, No. 2, pp. 13–14. Flagstaff.

1937 Southwestern Dated Ruins: I. *Tree-Ring Bulletin,* Vol. 4, No. 2, pp. 3–5. Tucson.

1941 A Basketmaker II Date from Cave Du Pont, Utah. *Tree-Ring Bulletin,* Vol. 8, No. 1, pp. 3–6. Tucson.

STANISLAWSKI, M. B.

1963 Wupatki Pueblo: A Study in Cultural Fusion and Change in Sinagua and Hopi Prehistory. MS, doctoral dissertation, University of Arizona, Tucson.

STEEN, C. R.

1962 Excavations at the Upper Ruin, Tonto National Monument, 1940. In "Archeological Studies at Tonto National Monument, Arizona," edited by L. R. Caywood, pp. 1–32. *Southwestern Monuments Association, Technical Series,* Vol. 2. Globe.

STUBBS, S. A. AND B. T. ELLIS
1955 Archaeological Investigations at the Chapel of San Miguel and the Site of La Castrense, Santa Fe, New Mexico. *Monographs of the School of American Research,* No. 20. Santa Fe.

STUBBS, S. A., B. T. ELLIS, AND A. E. DITTERT, JR.
1957 "Lost" Pecos Church. *El Palacio,* Vol. 64, Nos. 3–4, pp. 67–92. Santa Fe.

STUBBS, S. A. AND W. S. STALLINGS, JR.
1953 The Excavation of Pindi Pueblo, New Mexico. *Monographs of the School of American Research and the Laboratory of Anthropology,* No. 18. Santa Fe.

TAYLOR, W. W.
1958 Two Archaeological Studies in Northern Arizona. *Museum of Northern Arizona, Bulletin* 30. Flagstaff.

VIVIAN, GORDON
1959 The Hubbard Site and Other Tri-Wall Structures in New Mexico and Colorado. *National Park Service, Archeological Research Series,* No. 5. Washington.

VIVIAN, GORDON AND THOMAS MATHEWS
1965 Kin Kletso: A Pueblo III Community in Chaco Canyon, New Mexico. *Southwestern Monuments Association, Technical Series,* Vol. 6, Pt. 1. Globe.

VIVIAN, GORDON AND PAUL REITER
1960 The Great Kivas of Chaco Canyon and their Relationships. *Monographs of the School of American Research and the Museum of New Mexico,* No. 22. Santa Fe.

VIVIAN, G. R.
1960 The Navajo Archaeology of the Chacra Mesa, New Mexico. MS, master's thesis, University of New Mexico, Albuquerque.

WASLEY, W. W.
1959 Cultural Implications of Style Trends in Southwestern Prehistoric Pottery: Basket-Maker III to Pueblo II in West Central New Mexico. Doctoral dissertation, University of Arizona. University Microfilms, Ann Arbor.
1960a Salvage Archaeology on Highway 66 in Eastern Arizona. *American Antiquity,* Vol. 26, No. 1, pp. 30–42. Salt Lake City.
1960b Temporal Placement of Alma Neck Banded. In "Facts and Comments," *American Antiquity,* Vol. 25, No. 4, pp. 599–603. Salt Lake City.
1962 A Ceremonial Cave on Bonita Creek, Arizona. *American Antiquity,* Vol. 27, No. 3, pp. 380–94. Salt Lake City.

WATSON, D. W.
1947 Note on the Dating of Pipe Shrine House. *Tree-Ring Bulletin,* Vol. 13, No. 4, p. 32. Tucson.

WENDORF, FRED
1950 A Report on the Excavation of a Small Ruin Near Point of Pines, East Central Arizona. *University of Arizona Bulletin,* Vol. 21, No. 3, *Social Science Bulletin,* No. 19. Tucson.
1953a Archaeological Studies in the Petrified Forest National Monument. *Museum of Northern Arizona, Bulletin* 27. Flagstaff.
1953b Excavations at Te'ewi. In "Salvage Archaeology in the Chama Valley, New Mexico," assembled by Fred Wendorf, pp. 34–93. *Monographs of the School of American Research,* No. 17. Santa Fe.

WENDORF, FRED, NANCY FOX, AND O. L. LEWIS (EDITORS)
1956 *Pipeline Archaeology.* Laboratory of Anthropology and Museum of Northern Arizona, Santa Fe and Flagstaff.

WHEAT, J. B.
1955 Mogollon Culture Prior to A.D. 1000. *Memoirs of the Society for American Archaeology,* No. 10. Salt Lake City.

WHEAT, J. B., J. C. GIFFORD, AND W. W. WASLEY
1958 Ceramic Variety, Type Cluster, and Ceramic System in Southwestern Pottery Analysis. *American Antiquity,* Vol. 24, No. 1, pp. 34–47. Salt Lake City.

WILLEY, G. R. AND PHILIP PHILLIPS
1958 *Method and Theory in American Archaeology.* University of Chicago Press, Chicago.

WOODBURY, R. B. AND N. F. S. WOODBURY
MS Zuni Pottery Types. In preparation.

Zeitfracht Medien GmbH
Ferdinand-Jühlke-Straße 7
99095 Erfurt, Deutschland
produktsicherheit@kolibri360.de